ROYAL HISTORICAL SOCIETY

STUDIES IN HISTORY

New Series

LIBERALISM AND LOCAL GOVERNMENT IN EARLY VICTORIAN LONDON

LIBERALISM AND LOCAL GOVERNMENT
IN EARLY VICTORIAN LONDON

Benjamin Weinstein

THE ROYAL HISTORICAL SOCIETY
THE BOYDELL PRESS

First published 2011

A Royal Historical Society publication
Published by The Boydell Press
an imprint of Boydell & Brewer Ltd
PO Box 9, Woodbridge, Suffolk IP12 3DF, UK
and of Boydell & Brewer Inc.
668 Mt Hope Avenue, Rochester, NY 14620, USA
website: www.boydellandbrewer.com

ISBN 978–0–86193–312–9

ISSN 0269–2244

A CIP catalogue record for this book is available
from the British Library

The publisher has no responsibility for the continued existence or accuracy of
URLs for external or third-party internet websites referred to in this book, and
does not guarantee that any content on such websites is, or will remain,
accurate or appropriate.

Papers used by Boydell & Brewer Ltd are natural, recyclable products
made from wood grown in sustainable forests.

Printed and bound by CPI Group (UK) Ltd, Croydon, CR0 4YY

FOR SAM

Contents

Acknowledgements

I am deeply indebted to Peter Mandler, whose work has inspired in me an enduring fascination with Victorian political culture. Fourteen years after first reading *Aristocratic government in the age of reform* I can still vividly recall the immense thrill that Peter's analysis of Foxite cosmopolitan paternalism gave me in the summer of 1997. It was my great fortune that Peter came to Cambridge just as I began my research and agreed to be my supervisor from the beginning. Admired authors sometimes disappoint in the flesh, but this was emphatically not the case with Peter. Peter proved to be attentive, generous, astute, supportive and critical in just the right measure. Looking back on the early drafts of the chapters which were eventually revised to comprise this book, I am forcefully struck by Peter's patience and support. I can only hope that the following pages justify and reward that support sufficiently.

Boyd Hilton has provided me with invaluable advice, criticism and encouragement in the course of putting this book together. I am forever grateful to him for generously sharing his immense expertise and erudition. Jon Parry provided insightful guidance from a very early stage of my research and disabused me of many misconceptions about Victorian politics. One particular discussion on King's Parade, which he might not remember, but which I certainly do, on the relationship between English patriotism and the rhetoric of 'local self-government', has been crucial to this project. Larry Klein provided me with indispensible advice on the nature of eighteenth-century Whiggery and the particular importance of Addison to the Foxite self-identity. Iorwerth Prothero, who had a visiting fellowship at Selwyn College while I was a postgraduate student there, has been exceptionally generous in sharing his unrivalled expertise on the nature of early Victorian metropolitan radicalism. Without Iorwerth's input I simply would not have understood the social dynamics of 'shopocratic' liberalism. I owe him a tremendous debt of gratitude. I would also like to thank my fellow postgradu-ates Paul Corthorn, Michael Dolescal, Joe Bord and Jon Conlin for helping me to understand what 'political culture' actually means.

Miles Taylor is responsible for getting this project off the ground and for shaping it in its early stages. Without Miles's formative direction, this book would not exist. I am profoundly indebted to him for his belief that some-thing might be made out of my vague interest in urban paternalism. Hannah

Barker expertly shaped and polished the following pages into the finished product. I cannot think of a better or more encouraging editor than Hannah. I am also grateful to the Editorial Board of the Studies in History series, the anonymous readers of my manuscript, and most of all to Christine Linehan, who had the unenviable job of editing the manuscript of a detail-blind author such as myself. Christine's attention to detail has saved me from many embarrassing errors. I would also like to thank Arthur Burns for his early criticism, David Green for his very generous guidance in matters relating to poor law reform, Matthew Cragoe for his energetic defence of metropolitan relevancy (and for exposing me to 'curry Cragoe'), and David Cannadine for sharing his expertise on paternalism among urban landowners. Above all I would like to thank John Davis for his detailed and authoritative critique. Dr Davis's feedback has been perhaps the single most valuable source of criticism that any of my work has ever received.

I would like to acknowledge the encouragement and support given to me by my many colleagues over the years. I am greatly obliged to Jeremy Boulton, Fergus Campbell, Joan Allen, Holly Brewer, Michael Turner, Peter Wilson, Avram Taylor, Joe Coohill, Margot Finn, Matthew Thomson, Maxine Berg, Sarah Hodges, Trevor Burnard and Sarah Richardson. Central Michigan University has provided a fine environment in which to work and bring *Liberalism and local government* to fruition. I am grateful to everyone there for providing me with intellectual and personal support on a daily basis. I would also like to thank the staff and trustees of the following libraries and archives: the Bishopsgate Institute, the Bodleian Library, the British Library, the British Newspaper Library, Cambridge University Library, Durham University Archives and Special Collections, the Gwent Records Office, the Hackney Archives, the Minet Library, Lambeth Palace Library, the Lambton Park Archives, the University of London Library, the John Rylands University Library, the National Art Library, the National Co-operative Archive, the Public Record Office (Kew), University College London Special Collections, the University of Southampton Archives, Tyne and Wear Archive Services, and the Westminster Archives.

Liberalism and local government could not have been written without the unfailing love and support of my parents, Jan Weinstein and Katy Murphy, and my sister, Claire Weinstein. I will never be able to repay the debts that I owe to my family, and these acknowledgements cannot possibly convey my love for them and my gratitude for all that they have done for me. This book is dedicated to my wife, Samantha Ryan, to whom I owe all my happiness and inspiration. Sam has done, and sacrificed, more to sustain and improve this book, and its author, than any other person.

Benjamin Weinstein,
March 2011

Abbreviations

BHM	*Bulletin of the History of Medicine*
BIHR	*Bulletin of the Institute of Historical Research*
EHR	*English Historical Review*
HJ	*Historical Journal*
HWJ	*History Workshop Journal*
JBS	*Journal of British Studies*
LJ	*London Journal*
PH	*Parliamentary History*
P&P	*Past & Present*
TRHS	*Transactions of the Royal Historical Society*
VS	*Victorian Studies*

BL	British Library, London
Bodl. Lib.	Bodleian Library, Oxford
CRAS	Church Rate Abolition Society
GBH	General Board of Health
HLA	Health of London Association
HTA	Health of Towns Association
LWMA	London Working Men's Association
MAIDIC	Metropolitan Association for Improving the Dwellings of the Industrious Classes
MBW	Metropolitan Board of Works
MCA	Metropolitan Commission for Sewers
MSA	Metropolitan Sanitary Association
NPA	National Philanthropic Association
NPU	National Political Union
PP	Parliamentary Papers
RPA	Ratepayers' Protection Association
SRA	Southwark Reform Association

Introduction

This book considers the development of London's liberal political culture between the general election of 1832 and the establishment of the Metropolitan Board of Works in 1855. Such an undertaking is badly needed. While excellent work has been produced on London's Regency, mid-Victorian and late Victorian political culture, accounts of the early Victorian period are relatively scarce.[1] Moreover, much of what has been produced focuses quite narrowly on the sociology of early Victorian 'popular radicalism'. David Goodway's analysis of London Chartism and Geoffrey Crossick's study of politicised artisans in Kentish Town are representative of this approach, which seems to have grown out of D. J. Rowe's earlier engagements with London's early Victorian radical political culture.[2] Although William Thomas's *Philosophic radicals* pays greater attention to the impact of *ideas*, it is only incidentally *about* London, and in fact many of its various 'character studies' can be abstracted from the metropolitan context altogether. The same can be said of Miles Taylor's *Decline of British radicalism*, which contains

---

[1] The Regency period has been particularly well served. See J. A. Hone, *For the cause of truth: radicalism in London, 1796–1820*, Oxford 1980; J. Belchem, *Orator Hunt: Henry Hunt and English working-class radicalism*, Oxford 1988; I. McCalman, *Radical underworld: prophets, revolutionaries, and pornographers in London, 1795–1840*, Oxford 1993; J. Wiener, *Radicalism and freethought in nineteenth-century Britain: the life of Richard Carlile*, Westport, CN 1983; and I. Prothero, *Artisans and politics in the early nineteenth century: John Gast and his times*, London 1979. Prothero's monograph admittedly covers the late 1830s and early 1840s to good effect. For the best of mid- and late Victorian London see J. Davis, *Reforming London: the 'London government problem', 1855–1900*, Oxford 1988; D. Owen, *The government of Victorian London*, London 1982; and P. Thompson, *Socialists, Liberals, and Labour: the struggle for London, 1885–1914*, London 1967. The 'political' chapters of D. Feldman and G. Stedman Jones (eds), *Metropolis London: histories and representations since 1800*, London 1989, are likewise all concerned with late Victorian and Edwardian themes.
[2] David Goodway argues, for instance, that in London 'radicalism, political or industrial, was most closely correlated to the economic difficulties currently encountered by a given trade': *London Chartism, 1838–1848*, Cambridge 1982, 18. See also G. Crossick, *An artisan elite in Victorian society: Kentish London, 1840–1880*, London 1978; D. Large, 'London in the year of revolutions, 1848', in J. Stevenson (ed.), *London in the age of reform*, Oxford 1977, 177–211; D. J. Rowe, 'The London Working Men's Association and the "people's charter"', *P&P* xxxvi (1967), 169–74; 'The failure of London Chartism', *HJ* xi (1968), 472–87; and 'Class and political radicalism in London, 1831–2', *HJ* xiii (1970), 31–47; and I. Prothero, 'The London Working Men's Association and the "people's charter"', *P&P* xxxviii (1967), 169–74.

many insights into the metropolitan political culture, but which, given the book's scope, never lingers on London for long.[3]

Liberalism and local government proposes a fresh interpretation of London's early Victorian political culture. It does this by devoting particular attention to the relationship which existed within London between Russellite Whigs on the one hand, and vestry-based radicals on the other. In considering this relationship, this study argues that Whiggery – a political creed heretofore thought out of place and out of favour in large urban settings – was an especially potent force within early Victorian London. In the first place, Whiggery's metropolitan influence went a long way towards determining the character of metropolitan radicalism during this period. It can be argued, for instance, that the anti-statist and anti-aristocratic agenda promoted so successfully by *Reynolds*-style radicalism in the 1850s was resonant in London precisely because the Whig aristocracy, and the Russellite vision of an enlarged state in particular, remained such a prominent influence on metropolitan political culture during the '40s and '50s. Although metropolitan radicalism was by no means merely reactive to Whig policy, Whiggery did exert a powerful 'negative influence' on the construction of the early Victorian metropolitan radical identity. The decline of Toryism within the metropolitan boroughs after 1832, and Whiggery's simultaneous elevation into a creed of government, enhanced and ensured this influence. Each of these developments remobilised metropolitan radicals into a more direct confrontation with Whiggery in the metropolitan constituencies and this newly antagonistic relationship altered electoral strategies for Whigs and radicals alike. In this context, metropolitan radicals began to portray Whiggery as a creed of administrative centralisation while loudly promoting themselves as the defenders of English 'local self-government'.

However, despite these attacks, Whiggery remained a potent political force in the metropolitan boroughs. In addition to the widespread cultural permeation of the Russellite mission for social reform, Whiggery also exerted a surprisingly strong and immediate influence over London's electoral politics. In fact, by 1841, Whiggery's influence extended so far as to prompt *The Times* into describing London's largest and most plebeian borough, Tower Hamlets, as a 'Whig rotten borough'.[4] During the period covered in this book, 30 per cent (twelve out of forty) of all metropolitan MPs had strong ties to either the Melbourne or Russell ministries. Moreover, no fewer than five of these metropolitan members – Lord John Russell, Hugh

[3] W. Thomas, *The philosophic radicals: nine studies in theory and practice, 1817–1841*, Oxford 1979; M. Taylor, *The decline of British radicalism, 1847–1860*, Oxford 1995.
[4] *The Times*, 5 July 1841, 4.

Fortescue, Viscount Portman, Lord Robert Grosvenor and Charles Richard Fox – also belonged to the Grand Whig 'sacred circle of the great-grandmotherhood'. Russell, Grosvenor and Fox were each also sons of substantial metropolitan landowners, while Portman was a substantial metropolitan landowner himself. As this book argues, it was no mere coincidence that the metropolitan boroughs which contained both the greatest Whig landlords and the largest number of petty ratepayers were the same boroughs in which vestry radicals were most critical of Whiggery. This dynamic helps to explain the relative militancy of vestry radicalism in Marylebone and Westminster (which were, in fact, the only two boroughs with Hobhouse vestries) and the relative apathy of vestry radicalism in the 'Whig rotten borough' of Tower Hamlets.

In making the case for Whiggery's importance, this book hopes to problematise the view, articulated most forcefully by Donald Southgate, that 'a connection between the Whig aristocracy and a large popular electorate was not very common', and that Whiggery 'lacked vulgar appeal and mass support'.[5] While Peter Mandler has shown that many Whig grandees took 'vulgar appeal and mass support' very seriously, the reverse argument (i.e. that Whiggery benefited from 'mass support') has not been made.[6] Accounts of Russellite involvement in the pre-Metroplitan Board of Works struggle for metropolitan sanitation reform, meanwhile, have been presented almost exclusively in terms of high politics, and have consequently neglected the important role played by public opinion in the resolution of the struggle.[7] This book rounds off the decidedly 'high politics' picture drawn by Anthony Brundage, S. E. Finer and others by illustrating the ways in which Russellite Whigs found popular support for their sanitary agenda within the populous

---

5 D. Southgate, *The passing of the Whigs, 1832–1886*, London 1962, 96.
6 P. Mandler, *Aristocratic government in the age of reform: Whigs and liberals, 1830–1852*, Oxford 1990. Recent Whig revisionists have stopped short of this important point. For the 'Whig revision' see R. Brent, *Liberal Anglican politics: Whiggery, religion, and reform, 1830–1841*, Oxford 1987; T. A. Jenkins, *Gladstone, Whiggery, and the Liberal party, 1874–1886*, Oxford 1988; I. D. C Newbould, 'The Whigs, the Church, and education, 1839', *JBS* xxvi (1987), 332–46, and 'Whiggery and the dilemma of reform: liberals, radicals, and the Melbourne administration, 1835–9', *BIHR* liii (1980), 229–41; and J. P. Parry, 'Past and future in the later career of Lord John Russell', in T. C. W. Blanning and D. Cannadine (eds), *History and biography*, Cambridge 1996, 142–72.
7 See, particularly, S. E. Finer, *The life and times of Sir Edwin Chadwick*, London 1952; R. A. Lewis, *Edwin Chadwick and the public health movement, 1832–1854*, London 1952; C. Hamlin, *Public health and social justice in the age of Chadwick, 1800–1854*, Cambridge 1998; A. Brundage, *England's 'Prussian minister': Edwin Chadwick and the politics of government growth, 1832–1854*, University Park, PA 1988; and W. Lubenow, *The politics of government growth: early-Victorian attitudes toward state intervention, 1833–1848*, Newton Abbot 1971.

and open London boroughs. In particular it will argue that the Russellite social reform programme found a powerful support network amongst London's large professional community.

In the absence of Whiggery's metropolitan influence, London's radical culture would almost certainly have developed differently. As it happened, continual conflict between Whigs and radicals in the metropolitan constituencies kept both liberal subcultures fresh, and gave London a singularly contested and therefore vibrant and self-aware liberal political culture. Keeping this in mind, this book challenges the view that post-1832 metropolitan radicalism was in any way 'stagnant', or indeed 'impotent', as has been claimed.[8] It argues instead that opposition to a series of Whig engagements with the so-called 'London government problem' gave metropolitan radicals both an enemy to rally against (i.e. centralisation) and an issue to rally around (i.e. local self-government). As metropolitan radicals began to articulate coherent responses to Whig solutions to the 'London government problem', they began to develop into a unified and coherent group themselves. This book argues that, from the late 1830s, the cause of local self-government began to displace older narratives of 'constitutional purification' and 're-balance' within London, and in doing so drove metropolitan radicalism away from its earlier cosiness with Foxite Whiggery and towards a much more libertarian, anti-statist and anti-aristocratic liberalism.[9] While in some respects this move did not represent a major ideological break (metropolitan radicalism had always been critical of the leviathan state and its parasitic placemen), it none the less did have far-reaching repercussions for the construction of new radical identities.

Eventually, London's libertarian radicals would form an important core of supporters for Palmerstonian liberalism – an essentially capacious movement which contained Whiggish elements (Palmerston was, after all, an aristocratic Whig and a virtual reincarnation of Lord Melbourne) but which, in London, celebrated domestic retrenchment and patriotism as core 'liberal' values. From the mid-1830s these values had been increasingly incorporated

---

[8]   See, for instance, Rowe, 'London Chartism'. For a fuller discussion of this view see pp. 43–55 below.

[9]   Historians have recognised the importance of the movement for 'local self–government' in London, but most have misunderstood its nature and direction. For instance, F. D. Roberts claims that 'the northern radicals, proud of their growing cities and tenacious in their advocacy of laisses faire, took a much more hostile attitude to central government than did the London liberals, who were more philosophical and more mindful of the whole nation's welfare': The Victorian origins of the British welfare state, New Haven 1961, 79. In fact, mainstream metropolitan radicals (i.e. non-Benthamites) and liberals were almost certainly more outraged by and opposed to centralisation than their northern counterparts.

by the metropolitan vestry radical movement into a principled rejection of, and alternative to, what they identified as 'Whiggery'. In 1818 metropolitan radicalism was firmly attached to Burdettite Whiggishness; by 1855 it had largely shaken off Burdett's constitutionalist preoccupations and had embraced Palmerstonian liberalism. Although still Whiggish in many important respects, metropolitan radicalism had undergone a significant ideological, and indeed cultural, reorientation. In one sense, this book tells the story of how metropolitan radicalism accomplished this reorientation. The study therefore closes in 1855 with the establishment of the MBW – a resounding triumph for the libertarian principles of state retrenchment and local self-determination and a crushing defeat for Russellite Whiggery's bloated and, as some argued, corrupt centralism. Of course, 1855 was also the year of Palmerston's final ascension over Russell to the leadership of the 'Liberal' party. Metropolitan radicals were delighted by this changing of the guard, and many profited by it.

The move toward the Palmerstonian position should not, however, be understood as a liberal triumph over radicalism. Such an interpretation would overlook the extensive ideological interplay that characterised radical relationships to the newly emerging popular liberalism of the 1850s.[10] Although ultra-radicals were increasingly marginalised during the 1840s, and a metropolitan radical consensus began to consolidate around a moderate vestry-driven reform programme, mainstream metropolitan radicalism was by no means blindly subservient to its Palmerstonian allies. The relationship that the leading Palmerstonian Benjamin Hall maintained with the radicals of Marylebone provides a nice example of this dynamic.[11] While it is true that Hall's Metropolis Local Management Act could have done more to promote local democracy (many officers of the MBW were indirectly elected, for instance, and board membership was restricted by rather substantial property qualifications), the measure was none the less interpreted by metropolitan radicals as a firm victory not only for liberal notions of retrenchment and *laissez-faire*, but also for the idea of local self-government and self-determination. In London, as elsewhere, the radical movement collaborated with, but also subverted, liberalism and used its emergent language of retrenchment to service an agenda for greater individual freedom and political empowerment. Moreover, few ultra-radicals actually objected to the

---

10 For this interplay see T. Tholfsen, *Working-class radicalism in mid-Victorian England*, New York 1976; M. Finn, *After Chartism: class and nation in English radical politics, 1848–1874*, Cambridge 1993; and E. Biagini, *Liberty, retrenchment, and reform: popular liberalism in the age of Gladstone, 1860–1880*, Cambridge 1992.

11 The dynamics of this relationship are elaborated upon in chapter 5 below and in the conclusion.

entrepreneurial and retrenchment-minded agenda promoted in the vestries. G. M. Young once wrote that

> In many ways the change from early to late-Victorian England is symbolized in the names of two great cities: Manchester, solid, uniform, pacific, the native home of the great economic creed on which aristocratic England has always looked, and educated England was beginning to look [at the turn of the twentieth century], with some aversion and some contempt; Birmingham, experimental, adventurous, where old radicalism might in one decade flower into lavish Socialism, in another into pugnacious Imperialism.[12]

Tellingly, London did not figure in Young's vision of change. In explicit contrast to the so-called 'shock towns' of the north and midlands, London's political culture was characterised by Young in terms of continuity and even stagnation. Organic 'old radicalism', which was said to have 'blossomed' into new and advanced forms of radicalism in Birmingham, was in London characterised as a stubborn retardant to political innovation.

Over the years, Young's interpretation has found much support and suffered very little criticism. Asa Briggs's *Victorian cities*, for instance, whole-heartedly endorsed Young's view by casting Manchester as the 'symbol of a new age' and Birmingham as the birthplace of 'the civic gospel'. Like Young, Briggs conceived of the 1832 Reform Act as essentially London's final contribution to the national political life before the emergence of Fabian socialism in the 1880s.[13] This chronology has become a virtual orthodoxy of Victorian political historiography, and in the process it has left a 'politics-shaped' hole in the history of London, and a 'London-shaped hole' in the history of nineteenth-century politics.[14] One finds Francis Sheppard, for instance, claiming that 'from the early 1830s to the early 1880's, London's political influence was in eclipse ... it did not provide the main driving force behind many if the most important agitations ... if one ignores Sir Francis

---

[12] G. M. Young, *Portrait of an age: Victorian England*, London 1977, 128–9.

[13] A. Briggs, *Victorian cities*, Harmondsworth 1963, 327–43; Young, *Portrait of an age*, 166–7. While Paul Thompson criticises Briggs's view, he does so only with respect to the importance of the Fabians, and actually endorses Briggs's take on the unimportance of early and mid-Victorian London politics: *Socialists, Liberals, and Labour*, 294–5. For a more recent endorsement of this chronology see C. Waters, *British socialists and the politics of popular culture, 1884–1914*, Manchester 1990.

[14] Recently 'cultural' treatments such as L. Nead, *Victorian Babylon: people, streets, and images in nineteenth-century London*, London 2000, and D. Arnold (ed.), *Re-presenting the metropolis: architecture, urban experience and social life in London, 1800–1840*, London 2000, have flourished. For a useful survey of fairly recent work on Victorian London see John Davis, 'Modern London, 1850–1939', review article, *LJ* xx (1995), 56–90.

Burdett, who was more a survivor from the days of Wilkes than a portent of the future, London never had a great leader of its own, like Thomas Attwood or Joseph Chamberlain or Richard Cobden or John Bright'.[15] Patricia Garside has presented much the same story, within a slightly different time-frame, conceding that

> despite the hopes of a metropolitan radical movement, the focus of political attention began to shift to the provinces after 1815. Though the retreat of London radicalism should not be overemphasised, London failed to maintain its previously high level of political involvement and leadership ... in the half century between 1820–1870, London indeed appeared to be overshadowed by these provincial towns – economically, politically, administratively.[16]

Even H. J. Dyos, whose aim was always to illuminate why London mattered, could not escape the orthodox chronology of London's early and mid-Victorian unimportance. On metropolitan radical decline in the wake of 1832, he wrote that 'it was not until the 1880s that London was again capable of producing its own discontents in sufficient numbers to command any degree of national attention. It remained until then completely overshadowed by the provinces'.[17]

Of course, this picture of northern dynamism and metropolitan eclipse and stagnation should not be attributed entirely to Young's lingering influence. Labour and Chartist historians such as Simon Maccoby, John Foster and D. J. Rowe and, more recently, 'entrepreneurial' historians like G. R. Searle and Anthony Howe, have been equally responsible for reinforcing this interpretation.[18] According to these complementary analyses, London's relative unreceptiveness to both Chartism and the free trade movement (one the supposedly quintessential working-class movement of early Victorian Britain, and the other its equally quintessential middle-class counterpart) has

---

15 F. Sheppard, 'London and the nation in the nineteenth century', *TRHS* xxxv (1985), 56, 60.
16 P. L. Garside, 'London and the home counties', in F. M. L. Thompson (ed.), *Cambridge social history of Britain, 1750–1950*, I: *Regions and communities*, Cambridge 1990, 488, 490.
17 H. J. Dyos, 'Greater and greater London: metropolis and provinces in the nineteenth and twentieth centuries', in D. Cannadine and D. Reader (eds), *Exploring the urban past: essays in urban history by H. J. Dyos*, Cambridge 1982, 43.
18 S. Maccoby, *English radicalism, 1832–52*, London 1935; J. Foster, *Class struggle and the industrial revolution*, London 1974; Rowe 'London Chartism'; A. Howe, *The cotton masters, 1830–1860*, Oxford 1984; G. R. Searle, *Entrepreneurial politics in mid-Victorian Britain*, London 1993. See also D. Read, *The English provinces, 1760–1960: a study in influence*, London 1964, and A. Briggs, 'The local background of Chartism', in A. Briggs (ed.), *Chartist studies*, New York 1959.

contrasted metropolitan 'apathy' all too easily and neatly against provincial 'vigour' and, ultimately, relevance. Miles Taylor was undoubtedly right to bemoan the fact that the study of early and mid-Victorian radicalism has been 'subsumed by a wider social and economic history, to the point where many studies of mid-Victorian politics are now routinely based on the premise that British politics after 1848 were based on distinct middle and working-class strategies'.[19] London, which lacked the 'class' dynamics supposedly experienced by many so-called 'shock towns', has perhaps been the biggest loser under this socio-economically informed approach to Victorian politics. In the wake of more recent, avowedly politically informed interpretations of Victorian politics, London's role and relevance cries out for a reassessment.

Taking these recent historiographical developments into consideration, this book argues that historians who have characterised metropolitan politics as 'stagnant' have mistakenly interpreted metropolitan anti-aristocratic and anti-statist attitudes as proof of the continuance of 'old radicalism', when in fact these attitudes actually contributed to the development of the 'popular liberalism' or 'new radicalism' recently described by historians such as Margot Finn and Eugenio Biagini. In fact, this book argues that, by the 1840s, London was actually in the vanguard of 'popular liberalism' – a creed and movement which came to dominate the Victorian political landscape during the 1850s and beyond. When considered in this way, London's political culture assumes a far greater importance in the national Victorian political culture. At the same time, conflict between London's competing liberal subgroups produced a metropolitan political culture which, far from being stagnant or anachronistic, was both vibrant and dynamic.

The metropolitan *lacuna* created by socio-economic readings of early and mid-Victorian politics has both grown out of and reinforced the curious view that the 1832 Reform Act had a much more transformative effect on electoral politics in the north of England than on the political life of London. While it is undeniably true that the vast majority of new seats were given to the industrial districts of Yorkshire and Lancashire (meaning that, comparatively, northern industrial areas gained more from the act than London did), and that growing urban centres such as Manchester and Leeds were literally brought into parliamentary life, it is equally true that the 1832 act more than doubled the parliamentary representation of metropolitan London. Perhaps even more important, it can be argued that the 1832 act laid the foundations

---

[19] Taylor, *Decline of British radicalism*, 3. See also his 'Rethinking the Chartists: searching for synthesis in the historiography of Chartism', *HJ* xxxix (1996), 479–95.

for a complete revolution in metropolitan political culture by creating a cluster of metropolitan boroughs with wildly different interests. Like the great northern industrial cities, the fastest growing sections of the metropolis had been completely unrepresented under the unreformed system; and like these same industrial towns after the act, London's fastest-growing districts became thriving outposts of new political creeds and radicalisms. The parish of St Pancras, for instance, was itself larger than most provincial cities. When combined with the neighbouring parishes of St Marylebone and Paddington to form the parliamentary borough of Marylebone, St Pancras became part of one of the largest and wealthiest constituencies in the United Kingdom. Ironically, although 1832 was quite obviously a watershed moment in the history of metropolitan politics, it is precisely the point at which orthodox accounts of London's political life stop. Indeed, if the outcome of the 1832 act were to be judged according to how much has been written about the politics of localities after its passing, it would undoubtedly seem that London had been disfranchised rather than enfranchised.

Liberalism and local government re-evaluates London's early Victorian political culture by simultaneously critiquing the orthodox historiographical view of London's marginality to the construction of Victorian popular liberalism (a view which has been informed by serious misreadings and misrepresentations of London's Victorian social character), while also analysing, for the first time, the ways in which London's early Victorian local politics informed and were integrated with parliamentary politics in the metropolitan constituencies. Liberalism and local government begins with an examination of the ways in which both Whigs and constitutional radicals interacted with and understood the unreformed metropolis. Although Whigs and constitutional radicals often came into conflict in the unreformed metropolitan constituencies, they none the less tended to engage with the idea of 'London' in similar and complimentary ways. This investigation of pre-reform liberal attachments to London is followed, in chapter 2, by an analysis of the post-reform successes of parochialist ultra-radicals in Marylebone, Southwark, Westminster, Finsbury and Lambeth. As constitutional radicalism fell into disrepair (with the defections of Burdett to Toryism and Hobhouse to Whiggery) the ultra-radical movement became invigorated, and its metropolitan ascendancy was facilitated by two pieces of legislation: Hobhouse's Select Vestries Act of 1831 and the Poor Law Amendment Act of 1834. The first measure enabled ultra-radicals to organise themselves within the parish vestry, while the second gave them a Whig measure to rally against. Metropolitan radical opposition to Whiggery is explored in greater depth in chapter 3, as is the character and extent of the metropolitan support network for Russellite Whiggery. The polarisation of metropolitan liberalism, which took place primarily during the later 1830s and early 1840s, was prompted by cultural and social rifts as well as by political ones, and chapter 3 devotes a great deal of attention to the various cultural and social tensions which existed within the metropolitan middle class, and especially between London's hard-nosed commercial community (especially its shopkeepers, tradesmen and artisans) on the one hand, and its self-consciously 'gentlemanly' professional community on the other. In London, as elsewhere, ultra-radical opposition to Whiggery was articulated most forcefully through the cry for 'local self-government'. Whig policies which seemed to undermine local democracy, and enable state 'centralisation', came in for particularly trenchant criticism. Chapter 4 illustrates this through an examination of metropolitan debates over Whig policy on church rate reform and the tax system. Ultimately, both of these debates were cast by ultra-radicals as fights to reduce the reach of the state. Chapter 5, meanwhile, presents an analysis of the central issue in the metropolitan debate over 'centralisation': London government reform and the eventual creation of the Metropolitan Board of Works. Debates over the merits of a decentralised municipal administration dominated the 1854 Marylebone by-election, which is the subject of chapter 6, and the result of the election revealed as much about the hopeless position of Toryism in London as it did about the unpopularity of Russellite paternalism and the emerging strength of Palmerstonian liberalism. The study concludes with a discussion of the strength of 'Palmerstonian radicalism' in London in 1855.

1

Liberal Attachments to the Unreformed Metropolis

Prior to the 1832 parliamentary reform, the idea of 'London' was central to the ways in which both Whigs and constitutional radicals constructed their group identities. At the same time the idea of 'London' influenced the manner in which these liberal subgroups interacted with the metropolitan constituencies, and with one another. Interaction between Whigs and constitutional radicals was both vigorous and formative in the immediate pre-reform period. Francis Burdett's vacillation between the dinner table at Holland House, the debating table at Bentham's Queen Square salon, and the Speaker's table at the Crown and Anchor tavern is just one example of this interaction. Of course, any explanation of London's early Victorian political culture must also account for the ways in which these liberal subcultures interacted with London itself. This chapter therefore considers each group's unique pre-reform relationship to the metropolis in order to explain how such attachments ultimately influenced each group's approach to the 'London government problem' and to London's reformed political culture in general. Popular or constitutional radicals were, however, by no means the only ones with organic connections to London. Although Whigs and constitutional radicals interacted with and conceived of 'London' in discrete ways, each group also shared complementary assumptions about the proper construction of metropolitan political culture. In particular, both groups cherished London as a site of political heritage and as a stage for patrician political leadership.

London and the Whig identity, 1818–32

In July 1843 the *Edinburgh Review* published T. B. Macaulay's review of Aikin's *Life of Addison*. In keeping with the format favoured by the *Edinburgh Review*, Macaulay's essay said very little about Aikin's work and very much about Addison's.[1] Not surprisingly, given Addison's place in the Whig

---

[1] Walter Bagehot described the typical *Edinburgh Review* article as 'the review-like essay

cosmology, Macaulay's assessment was unreservedly admiring. In Macaulay's view Addison deserved to be 'considered not only as the greatest of the English essayists, but also as forerunner of the great English novelists'.[2] The essay supported this claim by illustrating the precociously novelistic qualities of the *Spectator* series, and by praising what Macaulay believed to be Addison's two greatest characters: Mr Spectator, considered by Macaulay to be Addison's greatest 'serious' character, and the *Freeholder*'s Foxhunter, considered by Macaulay to be Addison's greatest satirical character. But while Macaulay's *Review* essay purported to judge Addison's work on purely literary grounds, much of its real interest lay in politics. In particular, Macaulay's decision to contrast Mr Spectator with the Foxhunter seems to reveal much more about Macaulay's hopes for contemporary Whiggery than it does about Addison's literary talents. Whereas the essay recognises in Mr Spectator a 'faultless' articulation of the Whig ideal, it holds up the Foxhunter as Mr Spectator's 'perfect' Tory foil. Macaulay's description of Mr Spectator emphasises the character's sophistication and urbanity *vis-à-vis* the parochial narrow-mindedness of the Foxhunter. 'The Spectator', Macaulay writes,

> is a gentleman who, after passing a studious youth at the university, has traveled on classic ground, and has bestowed much attention on curious points of antiquity. *He has, on his return, fixed his residence in London, and has observed all the forms of life which are to be found in that great city, has daily listened to the wits of Will's, has smoked with the philosophers of the Grecian, and has mingled with the parsons at Child's, and with the politicians at St. James. In the morning he often listens to the hum of the Exchange; in the evening, his face is constantly to be seen in the pit of Drury Lane theatre.*[3]

The Tory Foxhunter, on the other hand, is described by Macaulay as 'ignorant, stupid, and violent ... the original of Squire Western'.[4] Little wonder, then, that Macaulay elsewhere described Addison as a member of 'our caste'.[5]

Although 'advanced Whigs', Foxites, and Russellites were not 'Addisonian' in any strict sense, they nevertheless greatly admired Addison's metropolitan prejudices and often invoked Addison's vision of Whiggery's fundamentally metropolitan orientation. It is worth noting, for instance, that C. J. Fox – the metropolitan Whig *par excellence* – was often presented to his

---

and the essay-like review'. See J. Shattock, *Politics and reviewers: the Edinburgh and the Quarterly in the early Victorian age*, London 1989, 109–10.

[2] T. B. Macaulay, 'Life and writings of Addison', in E. Bloom and L. Bloom (eds), *Addison and Steele: the critical heritage*, London 1980, 420.

[3] Ibid. 419.

[4] Ibid. 426–7.

[5] J. Hamburger, *Macaulay and the Whig tradition*, Chicago 1976, 251 n. 76.

supporters as the heir to the Addisonian legacy.[6] For a later generation of Whigs, who defined their own identity in opposition to the narrow-minded, parochial and political economy-obsessed Peelite gentry and 'bobby Lords', Addison's various attempts to define Whiggery by its metropolitan sophistication and urbanity, and against the self-interested and narrow-minded parochialism of the Tory squierarchy, struck a particularly resonant chord.[7] Lord John Russell's critique of Toryism's popularity among 'the unlettered squires, with heads muddled by their own ale' is just one illustration, among many, of how this attitude was articulated.[8] Whig criticism of Liverpool's domestic policy in the 1820s, meanwhile, was underpinned by the related belief that liberal Toryism proceeded from a one-eyed, 'mean' and self interested parochialism.[9] During the 1810s and '20s Russell, Morpeth, Lord Robert Grosvenor, Normanby and others, ever conscious of Toryism's rustic appeal, lived their own lives according to the 'Whig life-cycle' set down by Addison in the Spectator series. A classical education was followed by the Grand Tour, which in turn was itself followed by a life of sustained metropolitan social engagement. Although Russell's shyness seems to have prevented him from fully enjoying metropolitan club life and fashion, many of his closest political allies were completely at home within London's high society.[10] Normanby and Grosvenor cut particularly fashionable and urbane figures, and even the comparatively serious Morpeth claimed to have practi-

6   For Addison's influence on Holland House see also L. Sanders, *The Holland House circle*, London 1909, esp. p. 91. For a typical Foxite appropriation of Addison's ideas see R. Bisset, *The Spectator: a new edition in eight volumes; with illustrative notes, to which are prefixed the lives of the authors*, London 1794, i, esp. pp. iii–v.
7   The original Foxite jibe at Pittite 'bobby Lords and squires' was made by Lord Holland in 1826: L. Mitchell, *Holland House*, London 1980, 174. Creevey's opinion that the Pittite mind was 'a mean and little structure, much below the requisite for times like these – active, intriguing, and most powerful, but all in detail, quite incapable of accompanying the elevated views of Fox', is representative of the Whig view of Tory narrow-mindedness: Thomas Creevey to Raikes Currie, 1 May 1804, in *Creevey papers*, ed. H. Maxwell, London 1909, i. 26.
8   J. Russell, *An essay on the history of the English government and constitution*, London 1823, 219–20.
9   William Russell (Lord Tavistock) to J. C. Hobhouse, n.d. [31 Mar. 1830?], Baron Broughton papers, BL, MS Add. 36466; John Russell (6th duke of Bedford) to Charles Grey (2nd Earl Grey), 5, 11 Apr. 1822, 2nd Earl Grey papers, Durham University, Archives and Special Collections, GRE/B6/17, fos 78–9.
10   As John Parry has pointed out, Russell considered London Society to be 'always wrong'. At the same time, Russell's preference for the 'more popular and rational kind of society' provided by the company of writers, scientists, and other intellectuals was best realised in metropolitan salons such as Holland House: 'Past and future', 153.

cally lived at Brookes's during the 1820s.[11] However, in addition to honouring the Addisonian commitment to metropolitan high society, club life and conviviality, these latter-day Foxites also engaged surprisingly fully with issues of actual political importance to London. This deeper engagement, and particularly the Russellite desire to combat London's social problems by extending central government into everyday metropolitan affairs, reinforced and extended the Addisonian engagement with London to new levels of intimacy.

In addition to informing Foxite and Russellite self-understandings, the Addisonian dictate for sustained metropolitan engagement also advertised Whiggery's cultural distinctiveness to potential supporters who might otherwise have struggled to distinguish between similarly anti-democratic aristocratic factions. Conflation of Whiggery and Toryism was particularly pronounced in London, where a broad populist hostility toward the 'idle' and 'corrupt' aristocracy meant that the two parties were often characterised as two faces of a single 'aristocratic interest'. The claim of the St Pancras radical Thomas Murphy that metropolitan radicals had 'always looked upon the two factions of Whig and Tory as one, having a common interest in the maintenance of despotic and aristocratic principles, to the prejudice of the industrious classes and unrepresented millions', was fairly representative of this view.[12] In this context, the Whig devotion to London became an important advertisement for Whiggery's progressive party principles and policies. While further distinguishing Whiggery from its more reactionary aristocratic counterpart, engagement with metropolitan life was therefore deployed as a means of winning the support of reformers without making concessions to 'the absurd doctrines of ultra-radicalism'. The old Foxite John Russell, 6th duke of Bedford, advertised his party as a group of moderate, cosmopolitan progressives for precisely this reason.[13]

Of course, not all Whigs fully embraced their party's metropolitan preju-

[11] George Howard (Lord Morpeth) to Elizabeth Vassal-Fox (Lady Holland), 31 Oct. 1835, Holland House papers, BL, MS Add. 51583, fo. 88. See also D. D. Olien, *Morpeth: a Victorian public career*, Washington, DC 1983, 19, Normanby was a particularly metropolitan character, and correspondingly dissatisfied with life on his Yorkshire estates. See Hon. W. F. Cowper to Lady Holland, 22 Dec. 1841, Holland House papers, MS Add. 51559, fos 126–7.

[12] T. Murphy, *A letter to the radicals of the United Kindom, describing the position of the radicals of Marylebone*, London 1838, 6. For further articulations of this view see Anon., *To the electors of Westminster*, London 1819, 2; *The London Dispatch; and People's Political Reformer*, 16 Oct. 1836, 36; and Anon, *Another lay minstrel, dedicated to Sir Francis Burdett*, London 1810, 22.

[13] Bedford to Grey, 25 Feb. 1821, 2nd Earl Grey papers, GRE/B6/17, fos 75, 75a.

dices. The so-called 'Young Whigs', many of whom became politically influential during the 1820s, were particularly unsympathetic to metropolitan high life and all that went with it.[14] As they became increasingly mindful of their religious, familial and estate responsibilities, Althorp, Milton and Tavistock abandoned London altogether to embrace rural pursuits. Yet, while the Young Whigs rejected engagement with London in favour of rural solitude and estate management, London still remained an integral part of the Whig identity. In fact, most orthodox Whigs considered the retreat of the Young Whigs to be either misguided or ridiculous. Lady Sarah Lyttelton's verdict on Althorp's love of country living is illustrative: 'Oh, Bob', she wrote to Lord Robert Spencer, 'what a pity!'[15] Three factors ensured London's enduring influence on Whiggery. In the first place, extensive Whig metropolitan landownership had by the 1820s been partially translated into a paternalist feeling of guardianship over metropolitan political culture. Outside of the crown, the three largest landowners in unreformed Westminster (namely, the duke of Bedford, Richard Grosvenor, 2nd marquis of Westminster, and Henry Richard Vassal-Fox, 3rd Baron Holland) were particularly prominent and active Whigs. Secondly, the continued importance of political salons such as Holland House, Devonshire House and Brooks's ensured that Whiggery's institutional and spiritual headquarters remained metropolitan. Thirdly, the lingering influence of Foxite ideals committed a handful of Whiggery's grandest and most able young members to Fox's uniquely metropolitan mission and prejudices. In the wake of the Reform Act, these various attachments buoyed Whiggery's commitment to the metropolitan constituencies.

Whig metropolitan landlordship

If, as Cobbett claimed, London was an unruly organic growth, parts of the metropolitan fabric were still meticulously planned and magnificently realised. Coherent planning was particularly evident in the West End, which during the first half of the nineteenth century witnessed the development of many of London's largest and most profitable estates. The Bedford and Westminster estates underwent particularly dramatic development during this period. The building agreements for Belgravia, Pimlico, Tyburnia and northern Bloomsbury, for instance, were each reached in 1825.[16] A mere

---

14 For the 'Young Whig' preference for estate life see D. Spring, *The English landed estate in the nineteenth century: it's administration*, Baltimore 1963.
15 H. Wynham, *Correspondence of Sarah Spencer, Lady Lyttelton*, London 1912, 56.
16 D. Olson, *The growth of Victorian London*, London 1976, 13.

thirty years later, Tyburnia had been transformed into a 'city of palaces'; Belgravia, the development of which had flourished under Cubitt's direction, had been settled by what a Royal Commission called the 'richest population in the world'; and Pimlico, though less aristocratic, also bore the unifying mark of Cubitt's mind. Holland Park, meanwhile, also developed apace.

Parcels of land lying to the north of Oxford Street, such as the Portman and Portland estates, also continued in their own development and produced great and still fashionable neighbourhoods. Although Cavendish Square and Portman Square (the centrepieces of the Portland and Portman estates respectively) had each been completed towards the end of the eighteenth century, both retained and indeed solidified their aristocratic characters well into the mid-nineteenth century, when they became the 'new hives for the migrating swarm'.[17] Further to the east, the Russells continued their well-managed development of Bloomsbury. Like the Portman and Portland estates, Bloomsbury stretched northwards to the New Road bypass, and threw up a series of well-related squares, rows and places on its way. The years between 1820 and 1829 alone witnessed the completion of Tavistock Square, Woburn Place, Woburn Square, Torrington Place and most of Gordon Square, although Gordon Street, Endsleigh Street and Endsleigh Place remained unfinished until 1858. As early as 1823 commentators began to remark on the many London streets and squares named either Russell, Tavistock or Bedford. One went so far as to claim that Lord John Russell could walk virtually from St Pancras Church to Covent Garden without ever having to view a street name to which he was not related.[18]

Significantly, almost all these Regency and early Victorian metropolitan developments were carried out on Whig estates. The 2nd marquis of Westminster, for instance, was responsible for the great aristocratic neighbourhoods of Belgravia and Mayfair; Viscount Portman and Lord Fitzroy were two of the largest landlords in rapidly developing Marylebone; Lord Holland's estate underwent perhaps the fastest growth of any West London district in the 1820s and '30s; and the 6th and 7th dukes of Bedford were responsible for the largest developments in north London. During the 1820s and '30s these Whig families began to reap massive financial rewards from their metropolitan holdings. However, financial incentive was by no means the only engine of Whig estate development. Whig grandees often felt sharp paternal obligations to improve metropolitan life. The 6th duke of Bedford's condemnation of the flimsy, third-rate building on Lord Somers's adjacent estate, for

---

[17] J. F. Murray, *Physiology of London life*, London 1844.
[18] See S. Percy and R. Percy, *The Percy history and interesting memorial on the rise, progress, and present state of all the capitals of Europe*, London 1823, ii. 343.

instance, was motivated by much more than concern for property values. In particular, the duke felt quite strongly that by allowing leaseholders to erect slum housing, Somers had neglected important paternal obligations towards his tenants. Bedford himself took great care in overseeing the development of his own socially mixed estate, and made sure that artisanal districts such as Woburn Walk were well built.[19] In Belgravia and Pimlico the Grosvenor family displayed a similar attitude. According to Henry Trelawny Boodle, agent for the Grosvenor estate, the 2nd marquis of Westminster carried out his developments not for personal or financial gain, but

> chiefly … on public grounds … because he desires better houses, and he is a great lover of architecture and likes a handsome town, and he would sacrifice enormously to carry that out on his estate. By far the most important element, in his mind, is the present improvement of London quite irrespective of what his children or grandchildren may succeed to.[20]

As this example suggests, the step from mere landownership to a more over-arching paternalist interest in the state of metropolitan society was often a quick one for Whig landlords. Moreover, there is compelling evidence that, during the first half of the nineteenth century, Whig grandees took a corresponding interest in the tone and character of metropolitan political culture – an interest which was sometimes translated into electoral meddling.[21] In early June 1818, for instance, James Perry, then the editor of the Whig *Morning Chronicle* and secretary of Brooks's Fox Club, was accused by radicals of assisting the duke of Bedford in identifying vulnerable Bloomsbury tenants who might be coerced into pledging support for Samuel Romilly, the Westminster Foxite candidate. In consultation with Barber Beaumont and Bedford's steward, Perry was said to have 'listed out the names of some leasees whose term was nearly ended and who were consequently in a state of dependence for a renewal of their leases, and to them they both went, and

---

[19] For the development of Bedford's Bloomsbury estate see H. Hobhouse, *Thomas Cubitt: master builder*, London 1971, 58–82.

[20] Quoted in D. Olson, *Town planning in London: the eighteenth and nineteenth centuries*, New Haven 1964, 23. M. J. Hazelton-Swales has argued that the Grosvenors presided over their metropolitan estates as 'aristocratic paternalists' and 'improving landlords': 'The Grosvenors and the development of Belgravia and Pimlico in the nineteenth century', unpubl. Phd diss. London 1981, 412–15.

[21] See, for instance, Bedford's letter to Grey in which he 'rejoices' at Whitbread's return for 'my holdings': Bedford to Grey, 19 Oct. 1807, 2nd Earl Grey papers, GRE/B6/17, fo. 28. S. C. Whitbread's 1820 Middlesex campaign was also enthusiastically supported by the duke and other Whig grandees: S. Whitbread to Grey, 5 May, 1820, GRE/B57/10, fos 1–2.

obtained their signatures'. According to Francis Place, 'this trick was also played on the estates of other Noble Whig Grandees' – most notably that of the 2nd marquis of Westminster.[22] In a later diary entry relating to the same incident, Place went into particulars, claiming that '[tenants] Richards and Allen, both of Tavistock street, signed it [the requisition] on being urged in the way above named – both were negotiating for new leases'.[23] Almost twenty-five years later Lord Robert Grosvenor confidently asserted his brother's right to influence the votes of his tenants. By 1865 the Grosvenors were considered to have one 'nomination' seat in Middlesex.[24] Tories as well as radicals fumed over the deployment of inappropriate Whig influence. The Tory Drummond Wolffe, for instance, once claimed that metropolitan lease-holders were 'the vassels of Whig Dukes who rule us through a lot of solici-tors'.[25]

As this meddling suggests, to be a Whig candidate in certain metropolitan boroughs was to be something of a proprietary, or even in some cases a nominee, candidate. In his posthumously published memoirs Romilly admitted that Lord Holland and the duke of Bedford had been 'very sealous and active' on his behalf during the 1818 Westminster election, and that Holland in particular did a great deal of electioneering among the crowd. A subscription was also levied by Holland and, in a move reminiscent of Fox's 1784 Westminster campaign, Whig hostesses like Lady Lansdowne and Lady Jersey were put out to canvass.[26] In the wake of Romilly's suicide, the young Lord John Russell and S. C. Whitbread, each of whom had close personal connections to the 6th duke, were mooted as possible replacements but ultimately passed over. When George Lamb was finally selected as the Whig candidate, Bedford led Whig subscriptions, giving Holland (who often took on important responsibilities in managing Whig metropolitan electoral campaigns) permission to draw on him for any sum needed.[27] Fourteen years

---

[22] Francis Place papers, BL, MS Add. 27841, fo. 17.

[23] Ibid. fo. 124.

[24] See, Lord Robert Grosvenor to William Gladstone, 8, 10 July, 1841, William Ewart Gladstone papers, BL, MS Add. 44358, fos 56, 61. See J. L. Sanford and M. Townsend, *The great governing families of England*, London 1865, i. 123.

[25] R. Quinault, 'Lord Randolph Churchill and Tory democracy, 1880–1885', *HJ* xxii (1979), 148.

[26] See S. Romilly, *Memoirs of the life of Sir Samuel Romilly, written by himself with a selection from his correspondence*, London 1840, iii. 356, 359.

[27] See, for instance, George Tierney to Grey, 21 Dec. 1818, 2nd Earl Grey papers, GRE/B55, fo. 257.

later, when Lord Palmerston considered standing for election in Lambeth, Holland offered advice and campaigning assistance.[28]

In the wake of the 1832 Reform Act other Whig metropolitan landowners took even more drastic and immediate approaches to influencing the outcome of parliamentary elections in their respective boroughs. In Marylebone, Edward Berkeley Portman himself stood in the constituency's first parliamentary election.[29] Prior to 1832 Portman had represented Dorset, where he was also a large landowner, and where he had enjoyed an almost complete absence of political opposition. With the creation of the new metropolitan boroughs, Portman immediately quit Dorset to take a more active political interest in his much more valuable metropolitan holdings. Portman's local standing was both a blessing and a curse. Although his social prominence and universally acknowledged 'personal integrity' quickly made him a very popular candidate, borough ultra-radicals found it easy to criticise Portman's overly aristocratic manner, which, they claimed, prevented him from 'mixing freely and confidently with the electors'.[30] Moreover, in the run-up to the election, Portman's opponents made frequent mention of his substantial constituency landholdings as a potential source of electoral corruption and as an 'illegitimate influence' over the free suffrages of the borough's new electorate.[31] Radical disquiet over Portman's borough interest eventually prompted him to promise publicly that he 'should not himself use any influence whatever over the votes of any man'.[32] Despite this, radical candidates made numerous objections to the 'bribery' and 'intimidation' used by Portman and his Whig cronies to secure Whig returns.[33] The ultra-radical Thomas Murphy, who polled a mere 900 votes to Portman's 4,500, went so far as to claim that he would have been returned 'if they [the electors] could have given their votes free from corrupt influence … in this election, corruption had been used to defeat me, and to ensure the triumph of the ministerial

---

28 Henry Richard Vassal-Fox (3rd Baron Holland) to Henry John Temple (3rd Viscount Palmerston), 20 July, 6 Oct. 1832, 3rd Viscount Palmerston (Broadlands) papers, University of Southampton Archives, GC/HO/84, GC/HO/86/1. Ultimately, Palmerston chose to contest Hampshire, which Holland confessed to find a much more 'natural' constituency for him.

29 Unlike Bedford and Holland, Portman was neither a counsinhood figure, a Foxite nor even a particularly urban character. In fact, Portman married into a staunchly Pittite family (Henry Lascelles, 2nd earl of Harewood was his father-in-law) and spent most of his time on his estates in Devon. In politics, however, Portman consistently supported Whig and liberal governments. For Portman's 'Lansdowne set' devotion to the principles of retrenchment see his *Substance of a speech to the electors of the borough of Marylebone*, London 1832.

30 *The Times*, 4 Oct. 1832, 3.

31 Murphy, *Letter to the radicals of the United Kingdom*, 4; *Morning Herald*, 11 Dec. 1832, 3.

32 *Morning Chronicle*, 10 Dec. 1832, 3.

33 Portman ran in tandem with the Whig solicitor-general Sir William Horne. For Horne's campaign see chapter 2 below.

candidates'.[34] In his lengthy condemnation of the election proceedings, Murphy linked Portman's extensive borough proprietorship with Whig bribery and intimidation, and in doing so exposed both the degree to which landownership and politics overlapped and the lengths to which Whigs would go to win important metropolitan constituencies.

Whig salon culture and club life

Metropolitan salon culture and club life were each central to the construction of the Whig identity. Without venues such as Devonshire House, which provided an important institutional headquarters for Foxite Whiggery until the late 1820s, or Stafford House, which became the supreme physical articulation of Whiggery's grand metropolitan pretensions during the 1840s, Macaulay would never have been justified in contrasting Whig urbanity to Tory parochialism. Of course, Tories had their own metropolitan salons and political houses. Holderness House, Apsley House and Fife House, for instance, were in many respects Tory foils to Devonshire House, Burlington House and Holland House. Moreover, many Tory aristocratic town houses vied with the great Whig town houses for grandeur, although, as F. M. L. Thompson has noted, 'in the short term [i.e. before the twentieth century] the Whigs won this race'.[35] Although London town houses were used by both parties as sites of political debate and policy-making, Tory meetings were held much less frequently and attended by much smaller groups. This was partly due to the fact that the Tory leadership felt obligated to consult with 'country gentlemen' who were rarely in London. Even with Young Whigs increasingly at their country seats, the Whig leadership held much more frequent and well-attended town house meetings.[36] Of London's many great Whig houses and salons Holland House stands out as, if not the 'grandest', than certainly the most important. Throughout the early nineteenth century, it fulfilled a double role, as epicentre of both political Whiggery and of English cosmopolitanism, though not necessarily of metropolitan 'high society'. Greville, for one, described Holland House as 'not only the most brilliant, but the only great house of reception and constant society in England', and he also noted that it was the first port of call for important

[34] *Morning Chronicle*, 12 Dec. 1832, 3; *Morning Herald*, 13 Dec. 1832, 3.
[35] F. M. L. Thompson, 'Moving frontiers and the fortunes of the aristocratic town house, 1830–1930', *LJ* xx (1995–6), 69. See also C. S. Sykes, *Private palaces: life in the great London houses*, London 1985, 251, and M. H. Port, 'West End palaces: the aristocratic town house in London, 1730–1830', *LJ* xx (1995–6), 38–9.
[36] A. Aspinall, 'English party organisation in the early nineteenth century', *EHR* xli (1926), 393–5.

liberal-minded European visitors.[37] Although Holland House was part of a network of aristocratic great houses of reception, it stood apart from this network in a number of ways. In the first place, Holland House was a much more thoroughly politicised context than Stafford House, for instance, or the Tory Holderness House, both of which valued lavish balls over political debate and party strategising. Even Devonshire House, which remained an important site of Whig strategising throughout the 1810s and '20s, never matched Holland House's complete devotion to politics. Whereas Devonshire's political events were interspersed with non-political social events and parties, every Holland House dinner was a political event. Holland House stood out even further when Devonshire House lapsed into 'years of torpidity' from the late 1820s.[38] At Holland House, politics and society were uniquely inseparable. In the wake of Fox's death, therefore, Tierney reported that a number of Whigs refused to vote unless they were 'asked to dine at Holland House at least ten days before the meeting'.[39] As this suggests, Holland House was crucial to party cohesion during the lean years. When party spirit was flagging, Holland House dinners offered rejuvenation and inspiration. 'A few Holland House dinners', Tierney hopefully announced in 1817, 'may perhaps put some life into us.'[40]

Greville's description of Holland House as 'the *only* great house of … *constant* society' suggests yet another way in which it stood out. Whereas all other aristocratic town houses were abandoned out of season, Holland House remained occupied, and active, all the year round. Lord Holland himself disliked country life and pursuits, and only felt truly at ease in London.[41] Similarly, the Holland House 'circle' of regular guests was perhaps the supreme embodiment of Whig cosmopolitanism and urbanity. Macaulay and his fellow Holland House regulars (or 'inmates' as he called them) revered both the Addisonian and Foxite approaches to Whiggery. In their enlightenment manner, the Holland House circle valued the metropolis as a site of modernity, and consistently attempted to contrast their own progressive values against the type of world view produced by 'country' living.[42] Whereas

---

37 C. C. F. Greville, *Greville's England: selections from the diaries of Charles Grevill, 1818–1860*, ed. C. Hibbert, London 1981, 182, 203.

38 See John Lambton (1st earl of Durham) to 2nd Earl Grey, 23 May 1820, 2nd Earl Grey papers, GRE/V/B4, fo. 13, and Sykes, *Private palaces*, 269.

39 Tierney to Holland, 6 June, 1807, Holland House papers.

40 Tierney to Grey, 5 Dec. 1817, 2nd Earl Grey Papers, GRE/B55, fo. 243. See also Tierney's lament in 1814: 'to all those who are anxious to keep up the show of party … the shutting up of Holland House will be a sad grievance': Tierney to Grey, 26 Sept. 1814, GRE/B55, fo. 187.

41 For a particularly good illustration of this attitude see Mitchell, *Holland House*, 173.

42 For an illustration of this tendency see Lord Morpeth to Lady Holland, 6 Aug. 1843, Holland House papers, MS Add. 51583, fo. 97.

most other political salons were 'metropolitan' only by virtue of being physically situated within London, Holland House exhibited an almost transcendental commitment to the idea of 'London' and to metropolitan values more generally. Indeed, the conflation of Whiggery as a political creed with Whiggery as a set of cosmopolitan and urbane values was embodied nowhere so completely as at Holland House.

Insofar as Foxite Whiggery had an institutional headquarters, Holland House was it. As Leslie Mitchell put it, 'everything that happened at Holland House happened under the shadow of Charles James Fox ... Fox's career guaranteed the Hollands's place in politics and was the rock on which Holland House itself was built'.[43] Yet, if Holland House was the brightest 'social light of England' and the most prominent embodiment of Whiggery's Foxite attachment to London, it was certainly not the only metropolitan venue where Whig cosmopolitanism and Foxite politics intersected. Brooks's Club could lay an almost equal claim to represent the Foxite legacy. Like Holland House, Brooks's was a symbol of Whig metropolitan institutional investment without Tory equal. White's, the traditional Tory rival, had by the 1830s become essentially apolitical, only to be superseded in the wake of the Reform Act by the Carlton Club. Whereas White's had become less political in the wake of the Napoleonic wars, Brooks's had become more so. As Thomas Raikes put it, the Carlton Club was established 'to have a counterbalancing meeting to Brooks's, which is now purely a Whig reunion; White's which was formerly devoted to the other side, being now of no colour, and being frequented indiscriminately by all'.[44] Although the Carlton Club certainly did provide the Tories with their own metropolitan venue, the new club lacked Brooks's organicism – it had to be suddenly hatched as a fully developed rival to Brooks's Whiggery and was a completely new *type* of club – artificial in its 'business only' attitude whereas Brooks's existed to mix business with pleasure. The same can be said of the Reform Club, which was founded specifically to provide a liberal rival to the Carlton. By the 1850s the Reform Club had become a firmly Palmerstonian liberal club.[45] Throughout

---

[43] Mitchell, *Holland House*, 39, 60.

[44] Quoted in N. Gash, *Politics in the age of Peel: a study in the technique of parliamentary representation, 1830–1850*, New York 1953, 398. Anthony Lejuene tells us that in comparison to Brooks's, 'White's was never so intensely political a club': *White's: the first three hundred years*, London 1993, 3. One should note, for instance, that Whig grandees like Carlisle and Devonshire belonged to both clubs (White's for its pleasant atmosphere, Brooks's for its politics).

[45] See L. Fagan, *The Reform Club, 1836–1886: its founders and architect*, London 1887, 82–91.

the 1810s and '20s Brooks's was an important social centre for the Whig party. Large pre-session dinners supplemented the more intimate (and exclusive) Holland House gatherings, and provided the party with an extra source of cohesion.[46] At times, Brooks's was also used as a venue for more important events, such as Tierney's nomination as party leader in 1818.[47] After the Whigs came to power, Clarendon quipped that one might as well go to Brooks's as to a meeting of the Cabinet – there was no difference.[48] Like Holland House, Brooks's combined social functions with political ones in a way that ultimately bound Whiggery to a metropolitan lifestyle. This was at least partly accomplished through the club's watchfulness over Fox's legacy. Brooks's was in many ways a shrine to Fox's memory.

London and the Foxite legacy

The Whig equation of party organisation with club and salon life reinforced Whiggery's reputation as an urbane and metropolitan phenomenon. It is no coincidence that the metropolitan landlords Holland and Bedford were the most dedicated guardians of the Foxite legacy. If Holland House and Brooks's were important symbols of Whiggery's metropolitan commitment and orientation, they also fulfilled the complementary role of preserving and passing down the Foxite legacy to a new generation of Whigs. Fox's social character had been formed in the metropolitan salons and amongst great Londoners such as Dr Johnson, and metropolitan social excess remained a significant component of the Foxite attachment to London. Thomas Creevey's description of Fox's 'old devotees' as 'having all the air of shattered debauchees, of passing gaming, drinking, and sleepless nights', suggests the attraction.[49] However, in the years following his conversion to Whiggery, Fox's interest in London began to extend far beyond the worlds of fashion and fun. By 1780 he had been returned for Westminster, the borough which he would represent until his death in 1806 and the context within which Foxite Whiggery would

---

46 For descriptions of these dinners see *Morning Chronicle*, 11 June 1813, and 4 Feb. 1819.

47 William Frizwilliam (4th Earl Fitzwilliam) to Grey, 18 July 1818, 2nd Earl Grey papers, GRE/B14/11, fo. 34; Tierney to Grey, 21 Aug. 1818, GRE/B55, fo. 254. Aspinall has noted that a handful of prominent Whigs felt alienated by the nomination process. Henry Brougham, for instance, resented being 'dictated to by a cabal, meeting in London when every one is in the country except for their few selves': Henry Brougham (Lord Lambton) to Sir Robert Wilson, 19 July 1818, quoted in Aspinall, 'English party organisation', 392.

48 P. Ziegler, 'Brooks's and the Reform Club', in P. Ziegler and D. Seward (eds), *Brooks's: a social history*, London 1991, 45.

49 Creevey to Raikes Currie, 11 May 1803, *Creevey papers*.

ultimately discover its identity. It was there that Fox first began to present himself as a 'man of the people', and it was quite clearly within Westminster that Fox chose to locate his rather limited vision of 'the people' (which included gentlemen, tradesmen, professionals, artisans and shopkeepers – precisely his support base in Westminster – but certainly not labourers and the mass of London's poor). Hence, Fox's double identity as 'man of the People' and 'man of the Westminster electorate'.[50] Fox described Westminster as his 'refuge and protection', his 'citadel', and in turn Fox became 'the Westminster watchman', the guardian of Westminster's civic virtue and the promoter of its liberty.[51] In fact, Fox became so intimately identified with London that at times support for him barely extended beyond the metropolitan area.[52] It was no mere coincidence that Fox's henchman George Byng sat for Middlesex with only one brief interruption (he was one of the so-called 'Fox martyrs' in 1784) for roughly half a century. Moreover, Fox's fondness for, and mastery of, oration rendered Westminster his ideal political context. He was as much at home proposing a toast at the Crown and Anchor or delivering an impromptu speech at the New Palace Yard, as he was hatching party plans at Brooks's or making eloquent remonstrations to the House of Commons. In Westminster, as nowhere else, Fox found continual engagement and conversation, and hence continual vigilance over liberty. To put it another way: for Fox, as for Addison before him, metropolitan life was Whiggish insofar as it offer unparalleled opportunities for popular engagement through enlightened and paternal leadership.

Fox's influence over metropolitan politics hardly lessened after his death. The 6th duke of Bedford, for one, kept Fox's metropolitan engagement at the heart of his own political mission.[53] It is true, as Jon Parry has pointed out, that

the Fox who [Lord John] Russell venerated was not the young debauched rake, but the more mature cultured patriotic martyr. Reading Russell's account of him ... we see him as the affectionate, benevolent gentleman at home in St.

---

[50] See J. Dinwiddy, 'Charles James Fox and the people', *History* lv (1970), 342; P. Corfield, E. Green and C. Harvey, 'Westminster man: Charles James Fox and his electorate, 1780–1806', *PH* xx (2001), 162, 184.
[51] Corfield, Green and Harvey, 'Westminster man', 167, 182–4.
[52] P. Kelly, 'Radicalism and public opinion in the general election of 1784', *BIHR* xlv (1972), 75.
[53] Bedford to Grey, 23 May 1807, 2nd Earl Grey papers, GRE/B6/17, fo. 19. In fact, Bedford remained faithful to the Foxite mission long after his old freind Grey had abandoned it: Bedford to Grey, 16 Apr., 11 Sept. 1827, GRE/B6/17, fos 91, 100.

Anne's Hill in Surrey, far from the corruption of the city and the tainted political arena.

However, Fox's metropolitan legacy none the less inspired Russell to (almost) stand for Westminster in 1819.[54] Moreover, the Westminster electoral successes enjoyed by Samuel Romilly, George Lamb, J. C. Hobhouse and even Francis Burdett had more than a little to do with Fox's lingering influence. Indeed, throughout the period 1818–32, Whigs repeatedly invoked Fox's memory when contesting metropolitan constituencies. George Byng used his credentials as a *bona fide* 'Foxite martyr' to retain representation of Middlesex throughout the period. In Westminster Romilly and Lamb each used Fox's memory to gain support and popularity. During the 1819 election, for instance, Lady Caroline Lamb helped her brother-in-law by taking on the famous role first performed by the duchess of Devonshire in 1784, thus drawing firm parallels between George Lamb and C. J. Fox.[55] When Lord John Russell's attempts at nomination for Westminster failed in 1819, Fox's old enemy Francis Place happily declared that 'it is now no use to talk of old Foxey, who was always insincere, always a friend of the people, when out of office, always willing to sacrifice them to get into place'.[56] But Place's judgement was ill made, for the 'radical' candidate himself (John Cam Hobhouse) was one of Fox's greatest admirers – a trait which, if kept relatively secret in 1818, would be dramatically exposed in years to come. Indeed, when Hobhouse first offered himself to the Westminster electors, he revealed to Place that 'he should endeavour to tread in the steps of that illustrious man the late Charles James Fox'.[57] Nor did Hobhouse's eventual departure from Westminster in 1833 sever the Foxite connection with metropolitan electoral politics. Eight years later, when Lord Holland's eldest son, C. R. Fox, finally entered politics as a candidate for Tower Hamlets, he professed to standing on exactly the same principles that had motivated his father and uncle before him.[58] When he was returned to parliament Lady Holland

---

54 See Parry, 'Past and future', 155.
55 D. Miles, *Francis Place, 1771–1853: the life of a remarkable radical*, Brighton 1988, 130.
56 Place papers, MS Add. 27842, fo. 42; Broughton papers, MS Add. 56540, diary entry for 17 Nov. 1818.
57 Place's memorandum of 1818 election, written 1 June 1826, Place papers, MS Add. 27843, fo. 391. On the Westminster hustings in 1919 Hobhouse declared 'my principles have been those of the Whigs of 1798 in contradistinction to the Whigs of 1819': *An authentic narrative of the events of the Westminster election which commenced on Saturday, February 13 and closed on Wednesday, March 3 1819*, London 1819, 282. Further references to Fox appear on pp. 119, 238 and 246.
58 *The Times*, 10 June 1841, 6.

attributed this success to his unique genealogy and the unique political training that he had received within the walls of Holland House. 'His name, his father's son', she claimed, 'gave the impetus to their [the electors'] zeal. They remembered how warmly their cause had been advocated by him, who lived but to promote peace and amity among mankind.'[59]

For most of the nineteenth century the Foxite legacy was also kept alive in London's political salons and social clubs. Brooks's Fox Club, in particular, ensured that Fox's memory was honoured in a suitably metropolitan and cosmopolitan context. From the later 1830s, by which time the Fox cult had come under the direction of Lord John Russell, Brooks's had become something of a church, with Fox as its deity.[60] In 1843 the Fox Club established its headquarters in Brooks's great room, and memorabilia from Fox's life (such as an old gambling table which had been altered to accommodate his corpulence) assumed the status of relics and 'sacred objects'.[61] Fittingly, in addition to the customary toasts to Fox, Earl Grey and Lord Holland, a fourth toast 'to the memory of Lord John Russell' was added in 1878 and is repeated at each Fox dinner to this day.

Westminster and the constitutional radical movement, 1818–32

Historians have tended to agree that, during the immediate pre-reform period, London was the focal point for the constitutional radical movement. The national (and international) prominence of metropolitan radical figures such as John Cartwright, John Horne Tooke, Thomas Hardy, Richard Carlile, Francis Place, Francis Burdett and others ensured London's importance. Yet, for all the attention that has been given to the radical preeminence of the unreformed metropolis, very little effort has been made to decode the ways in which constitutional radicals engaged with the idea of 'London'.[62] It may be suggested that, if Foxite and Russellite Whigs attached

---

[59] Lady Holland to Henry Holland (4th baron Holland), 2 July 1841, in E. Vassall, *Elizabeth, Lady Holland to her son, 1821–1845*, ed. G. S. H. Fox-Strangeways, 6th earl of Ilchester, London 1946, 193.

[60] See F. Sitwell, 'The Fox Club', in Ziegler and Seward, *Brooks's*, 112–18. Although the Fox Club really took off in the 1830s, Fox dinners and commemorations were common during the immediate post-war period. Fox club dinners were held at hotels throughout London on the anniversary of his birth. For descriptions see *Morning Chronicle*, 26 Jan. 1818, 29 Jan. 1820, 29 Jan. 1821, 25 Feb. 1822.

[61] R. Neville, *London clubs: their histories and treasures*, London 1911, 106.

[62] See, for instance, D. Cannadine's criticism of J. A. Hone's *For the cause of truth*: 'the book cannot really be described as London history at all ... there is very little analysis, no

themselves to London out of a combination of paternal duty (i.e. landowner-ship), devotion to Foxite principles, and the need to articulate the most fundamental differences between themselves and their Tory rivals, metropol-itan constitutional radicals often engaged with London in surprisingly similar ways. Westminster Committee radicals and representatives were particularly prone to 'Whiggish' engagements with London, and many shared the Whig propensity to treat London as a stage for national leadership, a site of, and for, cosmopolitanism, and a context of (in this case radical) heritage. Throughout the late eighteenth century, radicals had admired London as the ideal context for grand, theatrical, paternalist and independent radicalism. Although some of the more extreme elements within metropolitan radi-calism began to dissent from this view during the 1820s, many radicals continued to value these metropolitan qualities above all others. In partic-ular, 'aristocratic radicals' such as Sir Francis Burdett tended to value London as a stage for national leadership and as a living link to an eighteenth-century radical heritage. London's unique social structure enabled aristocratic radi-cals to perpetuate distinctly eighteenth-century radical discourses and modes of presentation. While many of these persisted well into the 1850s and beyond, they were increasingly challenged and ultimately replaced during the early 1830s by more democratic engagements.

The 'Old Society': independence, paternalism and radicalism in unreformed Westminster

During the immediate pre-reform period, Westminster's social structure exhibited many traits of what Harold Perkin has called the 'Old Society': 'a finely graded hierarchy of great subtlety and discrimination', held together by a 'mesh of personal loyalties' rather than by broad class-based ones, and by the related principles of property, patronage and aristocratic paternalism.[63] Moreover, it has been suggested that the artisanal dynamic within London's social structure was strengthened in the years following 1815, and that during this period London became nothing less than the 'Athens of the artisan'. From 1818 to 1832 small trades predominated in the metropolis, with tailors, shoemakers and carpenters accounting for roughly 35 per cent of London's

map of London, no sense of the metropolitan environment, nor of how it influenced radical activity'; *Pleasures of the past*, London 1990, 162.
[63] Harold Perkin has described late Georgian and early Victorian London as 'the focal centre of the personal system of social relationships': *The origins of modern English society*, London 1969, 24, 52.

male working population in 1831. Innkeepers, shopkeepers, printers and other small traders comprised a further 15 per cent.[64] Moreover, Westminster's pre-industrial social structure was reflected in the organisation of its politics. While the borough's 'scot-and-lot' electorate was dominated by independent craftsmen, shopkeepers and artisans, its political leadership was dominated by aristocratic paternalists and other like-minded social elites.[65] The Westminster career of Sir Francis Burdett provides perhaps the best illustration of the relationship between Westminster's radical leadership and radical rank-and-file. Burdett himself was said to be 'unmistakably patrician – his tall, thin figure, his sharp, proud features, and careful attention to dress looked out of place among more homely reformers'.[66] This patrician bearing was reflected in Burdett's social and political priorities. Burdett's political success in Westminster was often attributed to his strict independence from popular dictation, his enlightened paternalism and his 'Country' insistence on the political leadership of men of property. Many members of the Westminster Reform Committee shared Burdett's elitist outlook. Even Francis Place admitted to its appeal. As he wrote to Hobhouse in 1830:

> The truth is that the [Westminster] vulgarity will not choose men from among themselves; they never do so when left perfectly free to choose. In all such cases they invariably choose men of property, in whom they expect to find the requisite appropriate talent, honesty, and business-like habits, and they make fewer mistakes than other men are apt to do. The reason for this is they have fewer sinister interests to induce them to do wrong; their choice is influenced by the desire to do good to themselves, and it so happens that their good must always be the public good.

Place simultaneously claimed that his fellow members of the Westminster Reform Committee were too poor and 'unshowy' to stand for Westminster and confessed to feeling nothing but 'contempt' for the sort of 'vulgar popularity' exploited by ultra-radicals like Henry 'Orator' Hunt.[67] Instead, he celebrated 'popularity produced by an enlightened sense of justice displayed in

---

[64] See E. P. Thompson, *The making of the English working-class*, London 1980, 253–7; D. Green, *From artisans to paupers: economic change and poverty in London, 1790–1870*, Aldershot 1995, 19; and L. Schwarz, *London in the age of industrialisation: entrepreneurs, labour force and living conditions, 1700–1850*, Cambridge 1992.

[65] J. M. Main, 'Radical Westminster, 1807–1820', *Historical Studies: Australia and New Zealand* xii (1966), 186.

[66] T. H. Duncombe, *The life and correspondence of T. S. Duncombe, late MP for Finsbury*, London 1868, i. 79.

[67] Place papers, MS Add. 27809, fo. 29.

the conduct of public men'.[68] The 1818 Westminster pollbook suggests that Place's views were shared by the overwhelming majority of Westminster's enfranchised shopocracy and artisanate.[69]

The 'Old Society' foundations of metropolitan radicalism meant that Westminster artisans and shopkeepers remained particularly receptive to eighteenth-century 'Country' and 'historicist' political discourses. Place's explanation to Hobhouse of the Westminster rank-and-file dependence on elite leadership was classically 'neo-Haringtonian' or 'Country' in a number of respects. Country discourses stressed the importance of personal qualities such as independence, virtue and disinterestedness. In particular, they described the duty of independent landowners to restore supposedly ancient liberties by fighting political corruption and by displaying the kind of disinterested civic virtue that landed wealth supposedly imparted to them.[70] Westminster's two pre-1832 radical MPs both lived up to this ideal, and often advertised the advantages that their disinterestedness and independence gave them over their 'party' rivals.[71] As one handbill advertising Burdett's 1818 Westminster candidature noted: 'here is what the faction [the Whigs] hates more than you hate corruption – here is Independence – here is SIR FRANCIS BURDETT THE REFORMER [sic]'.[72] J. R. Dinwiddy has noted Burdett's aversion to pledges, and has further observed that 'although pledges and instructions had been hallmarks of Wilkite radicalism, Burdett looked back to an older brand of "patriotism" which had been identified with independence'.[73]

This emphasis on independence and incorruptibility remained central to Westminster radicalism right through the Reform Bill debate, when *The Spectator* publicly lamented the fact that 'Sir Francis Burdett and Sir John Cam Hobhouse have been returned by considerable majorities; notwithstanding their absolute refusal before, during, and subsequent to the election, to give a decided opinion [i.e. a pledge] on any one of those interesting and

---

68 Ibid. MS Add. 35150, fos 135–7.
69 See Main, 'Radical Westminser', 201.
70 J. G. A. Pocock, *The Machiavellian moment: Florentine political thought and the Atlantic republican tradition*, Princeton 1975; H. T. Dickinson, *Liberty and property: political ideology in eighteenth-century Britain*, London 1977; P. Harling, *The waning of Old Corruption: the politics of economical reform in Britain, 1779–1846*, Oxford 1996.
71 Caroline Hodlin argues that Burdett pursued a consistently 'Country' agenda throughout his career: 'The political career of Sir Francis Burdett', unpubl. DPhil. diss. Oxford 1989, 18–19.
72 Handbill advertising Burdett and Kinnaird, Place papers, MS Add. 27841, fo. 133.
73 J. R. Dinwiddy, 'Sir Francis Burdett and Burdettite radicalism', in J. R. Dinwiddy, *Radicalism and reform in Britain, 1780–1850*, London 1992, 117.

important subjects which they will be called upon to discuss in the reformed parliament.'[74] But the metropolitan radical invocation of independence from the electorate was not confined to Westminster. In Southwark, William Brougham attacked pledging with gusto, saying that

> I hold, and always have held, that the system of pledging is utterly indefensible. It is degrading no less to the candidate than to the constituent ... it is degrading to the candidate, because, by giving it, he admits, if an untried man, that private worth is no guarantee of public virtue – if a tried man, that his past shall be no test of his future conduct.[75]

Brougham's 'manly' and romantic defence of the sacredness of 'conscientious' and enlightened representation was rewarded with a landslide victory in the first reformed election. Even Sir Samuel Whalley, who by 1833 could rightly be described as 'a nominee in the hands of ... certain Democrats of a very questionable political character, in the parish of St. Marylebone', refused to make pledges and promised only to act according to his own conscience.[76]

Burdett's own conception of 'independence' was double-edged. On the one hand, it emphasised the importance of independence from party – which is to say the independence of conscience. On the other hand, as illustrated by his refusal to make pledges, Burdett stressed the importance of independence from popular demand. In his mind both conditions were essential to the realisation of true public spiritedness.[77] Beyond its preoccupation with 'independence', Burdett's patriotism also looked back with nostalgia and romance to the supposed purity of past eras. Burdett bemoaned the loss of 'old England', which he described in 1830 as 'now half destroyed by railroad enclosures and canals', and he looked to rebuild the ancient Saxon constitution.[78] Within the metropolitan boroughs Burdett eventually came to be known as 'Old England's Pride, Her Star and Guide' and 'a fine old English Gentleman, one of the olden time'.[79]

Given the continuing receptiveness of London's electorate to these eighteenth-century radical discourses and modes of presentation, metropolitan constituencies appealed greatly to elite romantics like Burdett,

---

[74] *The Spectator*, 15 Dec. 1832, 1183.
[75] Ibid. 1 Dec. 1832, 1131.
[76] J. W. Brooke, *The democrats of Marylebone*, London 1839, 142.
[77] P. Spence, *The birth of romantic radicalism: war, popular politics and English reformism, 1800–1815*, Aldershot 1996, 24–5.
[78] Francis Burdett to J. Hobhouse, 21 Sept. 1830, Broughton papers, MS Add. 47222, fo. 259.
[79] Anon., *Another lay*, 75; J. Doyle, *A fine old gentleman, one of the olden time*, London 1837.

Hobhouse and Kinnaird, each of whom excelled in deploying the 'Country' rhetoric of political corruption and constitutional imbalance. Moreover, each of these figures recognised the leadership opportunities that engagement with metropolitan radicalism might bring, and each relished such opportunities for personal promotion.[80] The metropolitan radical leadership was dominated by heroic and inspiring figures – flamboyant orators who were often 'martyred' on behalf of 'the cause' and who often rose to national prominence in consequence of such martyrdom. Indeed, the demands placed upon metropolitan radical leaders were every bit as theatrical as they were practical or political. Burdett's arrest and imprisonment in 1810 is a perfect example of what was expected from the Westminster radical leadership, and of the rewards that could be reaped if theatricality and romance were deployed skilfully and convincingly.[81] From the very beginning of his tenure in Westminster, Burdett was presented to the electors in nothing less than heroic terms. Upon his return in 1807 he was honoured with a highly ceremonious (almost imperial) and immensely popular 'chairing'. Burdett's 'chair' was actually an elaborate carriage, mounted, we are told,

> on four wheels, superbly ornamented ... and on the posterior part of the platform was a pedestal, on which was placed a gothic chair for the hero of the day. He sat with his head uncovered, and his wounded limb rested on a purple cushion [Burdett had been injured in a duel with a rival candidate], while the other was sustained on a sort of imperial foot stool, under which the monster, Corruption, was seen in an agonising attitude.[82]

This picture of Burdett being exulted as the great and noble (and even injured) hero, elevated to almost royal status by his constituents, gives a good idea of why romantic and high-bred radicals like him might have favoured metropolitan constituencies.

In 1818 Major Cartwright's candidacy was rejected by the Westminster Committee specifically because they thought that he lacked the theatricality and flamboyance needed to capture the popular imagination. Place, for one,

---

[80] Peter Spence has argued that romantic radicals placed great importance on the personal qualities of their leadership figures, and that romantic radicalism's biggest failing lay in its leadership's inability to live up to the moral qualities expected of them: *Birth of romantic radicalism*, 169–78.

[81] It was widely reported in the radical press that, as the bailiffs broke into Burdett's Picadilly townhouse to arrest him, Burdett sat reading passages from the Magna Carta to his young son: M. W. Patterson, *Sir Francis Burdett and his times, 1770–1844*, London 1931, i. 469–71.

[82] F. Burdett, *Memoirs of the life of Francis Burdett*, London 1810, 39.

found him unacceptable on a number of fronts, including his 'old age, poor health, weak voice and dullness of verbosity as an orator'.[83] Yet, this did not stop Major Cartwright's supporters from presenting him as a romantic hero. Cobbett, for instance, appealed to the fact that he was 'an English Gentleman born and bred, of fortune independent and character PERFECTLY SPOTLESS'. He also played up Cartwright's status as a veteran of many struggles against 'tyranny', from the dark and dangerous days of the radical cause. Here was Cartwright cast as the romantic hero.[84] If, as Place claimed, the 'vulgarity' regularly refused to choose members of their own rank to represent them, the Westminster Committee was every bit as guilty of deferring to their social betters. The committee tended to support foppish, larger than life, romantic heroes. As E. P. Thompson has noted, this prejudice effectively 'confined the choice of candidates to men of means, no one on Place's committee would have conceived of putting one of their own number as candidate'.[85]

This social prejudice can be partially explained by the fact that in the decades leading up to reform, Westminster was generally held to be the nation's premier radical constituency. As one 'Address to the electors of Westminster' put it: 'the example of Westminster is everywhere held up to admiration – in many Cities and Boroughs, – in England and in Scotland, the People are anxiously endeavouring to follow your example'.[86] Just as Westminster was the nation's premier radical constituency, so Westminster's leading radicals were expected to be leaders of the national movement. Even Burdett's ultra-radical critics conceded that 'it is very notorious, that the reformers looked up to Sir Francis Burdett as the man who was to be the great advocate of their cause in parliament'.[87] Burdett's double role as 'Westminster's pride and England's hope' ensured that his radicalism was necessarily somewhat abstracted from the metropolitan context, and his engagement with Westminster in particular was often either superficial or naively undifferentiated. Like Fox before him, Burdett seems to have conceived of Westminster as a microcosm of the wider political nation and as a stage for leadership, rather than as a constituency with its own unique problems and issues. This often put strain on Burdett's relationships with locally-minded radicals, and with Francis Place in particular.

---

[83] Miles, *Francis Place*, 120.
[84] Copy of a speech read by Cobbett at the anniversary dinner of the triumph of Westminster, 23 May 1818, Place papers, MS Add. 27841, fo. 77.
[85] Thompson, *Making of the English working-class*, 468.
[86] Place papers, MS Add. 27841, fo. 133.
[87] *Cobbett's Weekly Political Register*, xxxii.741, 13 Sept. 1817

By 1818 Burdett's position as leader of the popular radical movement had been further reinforced by his continual engagement with Westminster's heritage of radical leadership. Just as a handful of Whigs remained committed to Westminster out of homage to Fox's legacy there, so radicals often envisioned themselves as heirs to Westminster's radical, or at least populist, heritage. Burdett cleverly positioned himself as an heir to John Wilkes, and indeed many of his supporters conceived of Burdett as the latest incarnation of the 'Lord of Misrule'. Burdett became, as John Belchem has noted, 'a veritable successor to Wilkes', that quintessential London radical whose war cry 'Wilkes and Liberty' became the template for so much popular sloganeering within the metropolis.[88] By 1806, owing chiefly to his high-profile advocacy of prison reform, Burdett's name had supplanted Wilkes's in the well known cry. 'Burdett and Liberty' resounded in the metropolis in 1810, for instance during Burdett's great chairing.

Ironically, however, Burdett was perhaps even more convincing as an heir of Fox than as the successor to Wilkes. Burdett regarded Fox as 'the wonder of the age, whose mind is so superior to the age in which he lives, whose abilities and integrity will adorn the page of History when his opponents will have shrunk into everlasting oblivion', and his faith in Fox was rewarded at Holland House, where he had become a very welcome guest. In fact, Burdett remained close to the Foxite Whig leadership throughout the unreformed period. During his early career in Middlesex, he remained very close to Fox and Byng, and indeed at one point in the late 1810s Burdett came to be considered by Francis Jeffrey as the figure most capable of revitalising Foxite Whiggery. Burdett's ties to Whiggery peaked around 1821, when Lord John Russell began to count Burdett among the core group of the party's most influential and useful members.[89] Later, at the height of the reform crisis, Burdett co-operated closely with Grey, and was even offered a peerage for his service. Although Burdett refused the offer, he promised to 'contribute in every way in my power to the support of your [Grey's] administration'.[90] At the same time, it must be said that Burdett preserved his cherished 'independence' by never fully committing to the Whig political agenda and by often

---

[88] J. Belchem, 'Henry Hunt and the evolution of the mass platform', *EHR* xciii (1978), 741; G. Rude, *Wilkes and liberty: a social study, 1763–1774*, Oxford 1962, 26–7.

[89] See *Copy of the poll for the election of two knights of the shire to serve in parliament for the county of Middlesex*, London 1803; *Report of the proceedings during the late contested election for the county of Middlesex*, London 1803; *A full report of the speeches of Sir Francis Burdett at the late election*, London 1804, 63–70; Place papers, MS Add. 27837, fo. 111; Mitchell, *Holland House*, 75; Lord John Russell to Lady Holland, Sept. 1821, Holland House papers, MS Add. 51679, fo. 30; and Thomas, *Philosophic radicals*, 56, 58.

[90] Burdett to Grey, Aug., 6 Sept. 1831, 2nd Earl Grey papers, GRE/B8/11, fos 6–8, 10.

criticising it in harsh terms. When disillusioned with his Whig allies, for instance, Burdett referred to Whiggism as 'that barbarous word'.[91] None the less, in Westminster, and in London generally, Burdett prospered from his close links to the Foxite legacy. He justified his refined rabble-rousing by appealing to and invoking the Wilkite heritage. Radicals like Burdett and Hobhouse flourished when invoking Westminster's heritage of grand, theatrical, disinterested and paternalist radical leadership.

As Burdett's importance to the Foxite legacy suggests, the unreformed Westminster radical leadership was quite 'Whiggish'. From the early 1820s the Westminster Reform Committee began to display its own Whiggish priorities and personnel as ultra-radical committee members such as William Adams and Samuel Brooks were displaced by the much more respectable likes of Joseph Hume, Scrope Davis, Henry Bickersteth, Thomas DeVear, J. C. Hobhouse and Sir Thomas Throckmorton. This new generation of committee-men was held together by society connections and by common membership of elite 'radical' dining clubs such as the Rota and the Hampden.[92] Bickersteth, for instance, claimed that his fellow Rota members would teach the lower orders 'how to avoid mixing up absurd and dangerous notions as in their cry for reform', and Hobhouse himself was always more comfortable working with Whigs than with radicals.[93] The Whiggish mentality of the new leadership, meanwhile, was demonstrated not least through the committee's universal desire to have Burdett's 1818 candidacy for Westminster linked with Romilly's.[94] Although they occasionally fought the Whig electoral threat in Westminster, Rump-affiliated radicals more often co-operated with latter-day 'Foxite' elites such as Douglas Kinnaird. Like these erstwhile Foxites, Westminster committee members tended to value London as a stage and as a site of political leadership. Moreover, the overwhelming majority tended to understand London in essentially eighteenth-century terms and viewed the metropolis as the ideal context for independent politics. By 1832 London radicals could still thrive without having to give pledges. Aristocratic and paternalist radicals enjoyed operating within a political culture in which they did not need to be completely

[91] See Burdett to Henry Holland, 29 Dec. 1818, Holland House papers, MS Add. 51569, fo. 15.
[92] For the Rota Club see M. Joyce, *My friend H: John Cam Hobhouse, Baron Broughton of Broughton de Gyfford*, London 1948, 122–3.
[93] Henry Bickersteth to Hobhouse, 5 May 1818, Broughton papers, MS Add. 36456, fo. 25.
[94] Joseph Hume to Francis Place, 3 June 1818, and Sturch to Burdett and Kinnaird Committee, 15 June 1818, Place papers, MS Add. 27841, fos 152, 238; Wilson to Hobhouse, 27 June 1818, Broughton papers, MS Add. 36457, fos 61–2.

accountable to their constituents. With the Rump behind them, Westminster radical MPs were uniquely unaccountable to the constituency's electorate. Yet, while relatively free from the demands of public opinion, Westminster MPs still had to answer to their political masters on the Westminster Committee. During the 1818 election, Brougham likened that committee to a Westmorland boroughmonger who sent eleven nominees to parliament.[95]

From 1818 Westminster Committee dictation and collusion with Whiggery outraged and alienated a substantial section of Westminster radicals, and ultimately precipitated a deep split in Westminster's radical ranks. At around this time a group of ultra-radicals, which had recently coalesced around Henry Hunt, became particularly outspoken in opposition to the Rump's supposed imposition of its own reform agenda upon the Westminster radical rank-and-file. Throughout the 1818 election, Hunt railed against the Westminster Committee's elitist character as well as against its aristocratic dictation of the reform agenda.[96] Hunt's opposition to the Rump hinged on an objection to the committee's whole world view, including the way in which it evaded engagement with metropolitan pluralism and grass roots radicalism. His own conception of London as a context of pluralism, populism and multiplicity was inherent in this criticism.[97] With the support of John Gale Jones and William Cobbett, Hunt used the issue of radical public meetings to highlight the Westminster Committee's elitism and artificially monochrome engagement with 'London'. All three ultra-radicals were particularly critical of the methods by which the committee managed and manipulated supposedly 'open meetings' of radical electors at the Crown and Anchor Tavern, so that dissent and criticism of Westminster's radical MPs was effectively stifled. Moreover, by the late 1820s this view was widely

---

95 *Morning Chronicle*, 17 June 1818. Place papers, MS Add. 27842, fos 43–54, 57–9, also illustrate the influence that the leading Westminster Committee men had in deciding who would represent the borough's radical movement in parliament. In this case John Cam Hobhouse was chosen by a handful of powerful figures to contest Romilly's recently vacated seat. The best work on the influence of the Westminster Committee remains unpublished. See, particularly, A. M. S. Prochaska, 'Westminster radicalism, 1807–1832', unpubl. DPhil. diss. Oxford 1974, and W. E. Saxton, 'The political importance of the "Westminster committee" of the early nineteenth century, with special reference to the years 1807–1822', unpubl. PhD diss. Edinburgh 1967.

96 Belchem, *Orator Hunt*, 78–84.

97 *The triumphal entry of Henry Hunt, esq. into London*, London 1818, for instance, illustrates Hunt's own eagerness to engage with London's organicism and 'plural' popular culture. Hunt's address to his supporters explicitly contrasts this eagerness to the staged and managed nature of Burdett's public engagemetns. See esp. p. 5.

shared by Westminster radicals. Of the managed nature of the Westminster Committee's Crown and Anchor meetings, one radical satirist wrote that

> we should employ our learned brains
> and spare no diligence and pains
> in drawing resolutions fit
> well crammed with wisdom and with wit
> for us to pass when at the Crown
> and Anchor we pull Placemen down
> we'll make such resolutions as
> we like; for they are sure to pass:
> but whatsoever we propose
> for them to swallow down it goes;
> however large, they make no question,
> nor care about its hard digestion;
> as if the stomachs, where they take
> such food, were of the ostrich make.[98]

The jibe was undoubtedly aimed at the Rota Club's 'eminent literary men'. Essentially, ultra-radicals charged the committee with running the Crown and Anchor Tavern as a private 'feasting' club masquerading as a public arena for public participation in the process of choosing candidates and debating issues. *Cobbett's Political Register*, for instance, regularly poured venom over what he termed Burdett's 'snug little dinners', while John Gale Jones claimed that these events had degenerated into 'mere tavern meetings, where none but the honorary members and favoured visitors … are allowed to take any part in the discussions … where a strange and motley mixture hashed up and compounded of apostate Whigs and equivocal Reformers attend to promote their own personal views and Electioneering purposes'.[99]

It is interesting that Place's own journal entries relating to the management of Westminster radical public meetings attest to the validity of these accusations.[100] This procedure gave many radicals the impression that Westminster public meetings were staged events, and appealed to aristocratic and theatrical radicals like Burdett for obvious reasons. It also saved paternalist radicals from the humiliation not just of receiving political instructions, but of ever having to be accountable to their supporters. By 1832 some important organs of the radical political press found themselves agreeing with this

---

[98] Anon., *Sir frantic, the reformer; or, the humors of the Crown and Anchor*, London 1809, 34–5, in Place papers, MS Add. 27850, fos 215–16

[99] See *Cobbett's Political Register*, 3 Oct. 1818, esp. col. 101; *Westminster election: a correct report of the meeting, 1 June 1818*, London 1818, 10–11. See also *Cobbett's Political Register*, 17 Oct. 1817.

[100] Place papers, MS Add. 27850, fo. 58.

ultra-radical critique. The *Examiner*, once affiliated to the Westminster Committee, could by this time lament that 'Westminster has, for the time past, afforded but a sorry specimen of popular representation. Sir Francis Burdett has dwindled into a mere aristocrat – a man of his order; and Sir John Cam Hobhouse, after various rallies and relapses, has dropped into place, and become a man of his party.'[101] The *Morning Herald*, meanwhile, admonished Westminster's two 'worthy baronets' for long acting 'as if they were Lords of a nomination borough' rather than representatives of a populous City.[102]

In 1832 *The Spectator* sensed change in the air:

> Never was any Roman mob more severely lectured by a haughty patrician, than the electors of Westminster have been, by the very men who owe all their importance to popular support ... the electors, however, have kissed the rod; and after a feeble attempt to bar them out, the authority of their masters is re-established, <u>for the present</u>.[103]

Indeed the 'present' did not last long. The type of unaccountable and patrician leadership provided by Burdett and Hobhouse began to suffer drastically diminishing returns from the early 1830s. In a political culture increasingly informed by the democratisation and rationalisation of both local and national government, radical engagement with London became both more responsive and organic, not to mention romantic, and began to celebrate metropolitan plurality, variegation and heterogeneity. Whereas Whigs continued to conceive of 'London' as an abstraction and embodiment of their cosmopolitanism and heritage, metropolitan radicals increasingly began to reject the idea of 'London' altogether and to embrace what they felt to be the essential experience of metropolitan life: localism. Francis Place's well-known description of London as a conurbation which 'has no local or particular interest as a town, not even as to politics ... its several boroughs in this respect are like so many very populous places at a distance from one another, and the inhabitants of any one of them know nothing, or next to nothing, of the proceedings in any other', is illustrative of this view.[104] Moreover early Victorian radical opinion-shapers agreed with Place. The *Spectator*, for instance, declared in 1849 that London was a mere 'constellation or cluster of cities, each having its separate district and conditions of existence – physical, moral, and political'.[105]

---

101 *The Examiner*, 25 Nov. 1832, 753.
102 *Morning Herald*, 12 Dec. 1832, 2.
103 *The Spectator*, 15 Dec. 1832, 1183.
104 This is quoted in G. Wallas, *Life of Francis Place, 1771–1854*, London 1918, 383–4.
105 This is quoted in K. Young and P. Garside (eds), *Metropolitan London: politics and urban change, 1837–1981*, London 1982, 20.

From the late 1820s this ready recognition of metropolitan 'disconnected-ness' and plurality became central to radical approaches to political reform. Place himself became interested in metropolitan local government reform, for instance, because as an issue it engaged most truthfully with the reality of London's civic character. From 1822 he began to work closely with the vestry reformers of St Martin's-in-the-Fields to overturn that parish's select vestry. In 1827 an unfavourable judicial ruling on the St Martin's agitation inspired similar vestry reform movement throughout London, and Place's input once again became instrumental to many of these.[106] By 1829 Place had become the motivating force behind Hobhouse's attempt to liberalise metropolitan local government. Place's high-profile involvement in London's newly energised vestry reform movement brought to the Westminster Committee a greater understanding and more subtle appreciation of London's character and identity. Perhaps more important, the embrace of localism in turn threw the contrast between Whigs and radicals in London into much greater relief and pushed radicalism into a far more direct electoral confrontation with Whiggery in the metropolitan constituencies.

---

[106] For some details of these agitations, and Robert Fenn's role in particular, see *The Times*, 4 Apr. 1828, 3; 5 Apr. 1828, 3; 7 Apr. 1838, 3; 8 Apr. 1828, 2.

2

The 'Radicalisation' of Metropolitan Political Culture, 1832–1841

In late November 1831 Charles Grey dismissed fears that parliamentary reform would precipitate social revolution. In particular, Grey did not share the concern, voiced by many Tory opponents of reform, that London's increased representation would result in a flood of plebeian ultra-radicals into parliament. Although he acknowledged that the proposed Whig reform bill would extend the metropolitan franchise quite far down the social ladder (owing to higher metropolitan property prices), Grey had been reassured by Lord Durham and by Lord Althorp that the £20 householder, rather than the £10 householder, would predominate in the metropolitan electorate.[1] Grey consequently anticipated the return of 'respectable' middle-class men. In Tower Hamlets and Finsbury, Grey claimed, 'the returns will probably be commercial, in Marylebone probably of persons connected with the law, or of those who are supported by the better description of persons resident in that opulent and extensive quarter'.[2] Grey's predictions were sensible and, as it turned out, fairly accurate. At the first reformed election, Tower Hamlets returned William Clay, a successful merchant and chairman of two metropolitan water companies; Marylebone, meanwhile, chose as its representative Sir William Horne, a prominent barrister and longtime resident of that 'opulent and extensive quarter'. Finsbury defied Grey's vision by returning the wealthy barrister Robert Grant and, because Charles Babbage and Thomas Wakley split the radical vote, a Tory military man. Although Finsbury had

---

[1] *Hansard* 3rd ser. vi.602, 25 Aug. 1832. *The Spectator* agreed with this assessment, noting that, of a sample of 12,443 rated houses in Marylebone, only 964 were rated at under £10. The great majority (5,010) were rated between £20 and £50, and 2,077 were rated between £10 and £20: *The Spectator*, 8 Dec. 1832, 1159. See also M. Brock, *The Great Reform Act*, London 1973, 164–7.

[2] Grey to Sir Herbert Taylor, quoted in R.W. Davis, 'The Whigs and the idea of electoral deference: some further thoughts on the Great Reform Act', *Durham University Journal* lxvii (1974–5), 83.

fallen to a Whig lawyer and a Tory patrician, Lambeth stayed true to its commercial and industrial character by returning as its first MP Benjamin Hawes, a soap manufacturer who, according to Richard Monckton Milnes, embodied perfectly 'the respectable and intelligent bourgeois'.[3]

Such respectable returns exposed the groundlessness of Tory foreboding. But Whigs had further reasons to be pleased. For in addition to rebuffing predictions of social levelling, the first reformed election reaffirmed the essential 'Whiggishness' of metropolitan political culture. Many of London's new MPs harboured attachments to Grey's (admittedly mixed) Whig government. William Horne, for instance, had been solicitor-general since 1830, and in November 1832 he had been raised to the post of attorney-general. During his tenure as solicitor-general, Horne had become close to Brougham, and the Whig Lord Chancellor was untiring in his exertions on behalf of Horne's career.[4] Horne pushed a predictably strict party line in parliament and was often criticised by Marylebone radicals for a perceived over-reliance on the influence of his aristocratic Whig friends.[5] Largely on account of these social and political connections Marylebone radicals came to recognise Horne as a 'Whig of the old school'.[6] Horne's Whig running mate in Marylebone, E. B. Portman, enjoyed similarly close relations with the ministry, and at the borough election Marylebone radicals accused him of providing unquestioning support for a government which had 'insulted the people'.[7] However, this 'unquestioning support' did not prevent Portman from polling more votes than any other candidate in the metropolitan constituencies, including Joseph Hume in Middlesex, in 1832.

Marylebone's relatively wealthy electorate might have been expected to return a pair of Whigs in 1832. Somewhat surprisingly, however, that 'opulent and extensive quarter' was by no means alone in its appreciation of Whiggish candidates. In Tower Hamlets, which in 1832 was the poorest and most solidly plebeian metropolitan borough, Stephen Lushington was returned at the head of the poll.[8] Lushington, like Horne, was a Whig legal placeman who had formed strong links to Brougham during their shared defence of Queen Caroline and their mutual devotion to the Society for the

---

3 Southgate, *The passing of the Whigs*, 160n.
4 In 1834 Brougham also got Horne appointed to the bench in the court of the exchequer. For the details of his manoeuvering, and his loyalty to Horne, see H. Brougham, *The life and times of Henry Lord Brougham*, London 1871, iii. 341–54.
5 *Morning Herald*, 12, 13 Dec. 1832, 3.
6 Murphy, *Letter to the radicals of the United Kingdom*, 7.
7 *The Times*, 13 Dec. 1832, 3.
8 The old Foxite Lincoln Stanhope managed to poll nearly 3,000 votes and came a relatively close third in this contest.

Diffusion of Useful Knowledge.[9] During the 1820s Lushington had also worked within the Whig opposition to abolish West Indian slavery and to repeal the civil disabilities of the Jews. These causes brought Lushington into a close working relationship with a number of leading Whigs, including Lord John Russell. Indeed, throughout his 1832 campaign for Tower Hamlets, Lushington made frequent public professions of being 'closely politically allied to Ld. Melbourne and Ld. John'.[10] In Finsbury, Robert Grant struck a very similar figure. Like Lushington, Grant had worked closely with Russell on Jewish emancipation and had been rewarded with appointments to both the board of control (1830) and the privy council (1831). During the 1832 election, Grant flaunted his desire to work even more closely with the government. When asked to justify his candidacy, Grant made no mention of serving Finsbury's interests. Instead, he simply advertised the fact that he 'was identified with the present Administration, and it was upon that ground that he solicited the support of the electors'.[11] Shortly after the election Grant was appointed judge advocate-general, making him the third metropolitan MP to become a high-ranking Whig legal placeman. Together with the Southwark representative William Brougham, brother of the ambitious Lord Chancellor, Grant, Horne and Lushington were quickly labelled by the radical press as 'the place holding and place coveting members for the metropolis'.[12]

Somewhat surprisingly, Benjamin Hawes, who in 1832 became Lambeth's first MP, was not included by the radical press in this group of place-holders and seekers.Yet Hawes was every bit as eager to work with (and for) the government, and in 1832 he sought out his own place energetically. 'I cannot better describe my political principles', he claimed in 1832, 'than by stating that they are in strict accordance with the policy pursued by his majesty's present government.'[13] Although not commented upon by the radical press, Hawes's constant manoeuvering for personal promotion and place did not go

9 Grey noted Brougham's efforts to promote Lushington, and Brougham's anger when another candidate was promoted over him: Grey to Creevey, 13 Dec. 1827, *Creevey papers*, ii. 140

10 S. M. Waddams, *Law, politics, and the Church of England: the career of Stephen Lushington, 1782–1873*, Cambridge 1992, 78.

11 *The Times*, 7 Dec. 1832, 3. Burdett cursed Grant's decision to cosy up to the Whigs, writing in September 1830 that 'the Grants and Palmerstons will join the devil – after all our rage are the best men going': Burdett to Hobhouse, Sept. 1830, Broughton papers, MS Add. 47222, fos 260–1.

12 *The Spectator*, 4 May 1833, 401.

13 B. Hawes, 'Address to the electors of Lambeth', in G. Hill (ed.), *The electoral history of Lambeth since its enfranchisement in 1832 with portraits and memoirs of its representatives during 46 years*, London 1879, 17.

unnoticed by the Lambeth electorate. According to one constituency hand-bill Hawes's 'strict accordance' to government policy 'must have to bias his mind to future confederacy with his Friends and Patrons ... B. Hawes is there-fore disqualified for the representation of the Boro' of Lambeth'.[14] The older constituencies of Westminster and Middlesex, meanwhile, returned Whigs of their own – for by 1832 Hobhouse had officially fallen back into league with the Whigs and the old Foxite George Byng had once again been returned for the metropolitan county.[15] This meant that in 1832 every metropolitan constituency returned at least one Whig, the majority of whom either held government office or government place.[16] In the wake of these metropolitan victories, Lord Tavistock could not help but gloat that 'I cannot say how much pleasure these triumphs have given me ... what an answer to conserva-tive foreboding has been furnished by the metropolitan districts.'[17]

In London, as elsewhere, 1832 marked something of a high-water-mark for Whig electoral strength. By the middle months of 1833, attitudes within London towards the suitability of government-affiliated representatives had undergone a considerable alteration. The 1833 Westminster by-election ended in defeat for Hobhouse, largely on account of his 'official connexions', and in March of the same year the Whig C. A Murray (who enjoyed the public support of Lord Milton, Lord Russell, Lord Ebrington and Lord Morpeth) was embarrassed in Marylebone – drawing a mere 791 votes to Samuel Whalley's 2,869 in the by-election held in the wake of Portman's resignation. The radical *Spectator* drew a prescient conclusion from Murray's defeat. 'It appears', the paper gleefully wrote, 'that the circumstance of being a ministerialist is no longer a passport in the metropolis to a seat in the House of Commons.'[18] Whig electoral fortunes remained robust in certain metropol-itan boroughs after 1832, but as radicals began to organise themselves into reform committees and parochial bodies and to populate the organs of parochial administration, the positions occupied by these Whigs became increasingly vulnerable.

---

[14] *Union of magisterial and Parliamentary duties incompatible with the true interests of the boro' of Lambeth,* in Charles Tennyson D'Eyncourt papers, Minet Library, Lambeth Archives, London, IV/3/2d. See also Thomas, *Philosophic radicals,* 332.

[15] On the eve of reform, the *Examiner* wrote that Hobhouse 'would have had himself believed staunch radical by the electors, and aristocratic Whig by the Whigs': *Examiner,* 16 Dec. 1832, 802.

[16] Even Greenwich, which in many ways stood outside early Victorian London, returned James Whitley Deans Dundas – a loyal Whig throughout his political career – at the top of the poll.

[17] Lord Tavistock to Hobhouse, 12 Dec. 1832, Broughton papers, MS Add. 47223, fo. 62.

[18] *The Spectator,* 23 Mar. 1833, 257.

This chapter provides an analysis of the ways in which London's political culture was progressively radicalised between 1833 and 1841. It does so by charting the emergence of a new metropolitan culture of ultra-radicalism in the wake of the 1832 parliamentary reform, and by considering the effects that the emergence of this new culture had on metropolitan parliamentary politics. Although the Great Reform Act ultimately enabled this process of change by giving political voice to previously voiceless radical communities in Finsbury, Lambeth, Marylebone and Tower Hamlets, the radicalisation of London's political culture became most pronounced during the mid-1830s as Hobhouse's Select Vestries Act began to revolutionise the culture of metropolitan local government, and with the emergence of a pan-metropolitan radical opposition to the Poor Law Amendment Act in 1834.

In this political climate, ultra-radical advocates of 'local self-government' began to supplant London's Whiggish old guard. In fact, from the mid-1830s, opposition to Whiggery became even more fundamental to metropolitan radical culture than opposition to Toryism. The decline of Toryism within the metropolitan boroughs after 1832, and Whiggery's simultaneous elevation into a creed of government, enhanced and ensured this dynamic. At the same time metropolitan radical aggression towards Whiggery was a direct consequence of the radical 'localist' agenda increasingly promoted from within London's reformed vestries. By engineering alliances between middle-class liberals, lower order ultra-radicals and romantic elites, the 'vestry radical' agenda for further government retrenchment and a greater measure of local ratepayer self-determination managed to do what almost every other pre-reform metropolitan radical movement had failed to achieve.

Parochial reform and the radicalisation of metropolitan electoral politics, 1833–7

Hobhouse's fall from grace in Westminster is illustrative of the ways in which metropolitan attitudes towards the Whig government, and indeed towards Whiggery as a political creed, began to sour in the immediate post-reform period. As secretary for war and then as chief secretary to the lord lieutenant of Ireland in Grey's post-reform government Hobhouse endured a constant stream of criticism from Westminster radicals. According to his critics, these ministerial jobs ensured that Hobhouse would never be more than a mere 'silent ornament of the Treasury bench'.[19] At the same time, Hobhouse's sudden refusal to pledge support for universal suffrage, annual parliaments or

---

[19] *Morning Advertiser*, 21 Nov. 1832, 2.

the ballot, and his role in implementing the government's unpopular Irish policy, further alienated him from Westminster's radical electorate and presented Francis Place with the excuse that he had long been seeking to remove Westminster Committee support for Hobhouse.[20] According to Place, Hobhouse was both talented and well meaning, but also irredeemably lazy and under-achieving.[21] Such shortcomings were, to Place's mind, confirmation of Hobhouse's essentially Whiggish personality. At the height of the reform crisis, Place confided to Burdett his opinion that 'Lord Brougham talks about his part in the subject like a fashionable woman, not a brave man in troublesome times … Lord Grey and his colleagues are not … equal to the charge they have undertaken.'[22] With the collapse of his radical support network, Hobhouse became ever more dependent on his Whig friends and colleagues, and indeed by late 1832 the Whig *Morning Chronicle* had begun to defend Hobhouse for refusing to be 'a mere tool in the hands of Mr. Place'.[23] Disraeli famously, and savagely, ascribed Hobhouse's *rapprochement* with Whiggery to opportunism and place-hunting, writing in an open letter to Hobhouse that his

> metamorphosis into a Whig and a cabinet Minister has always appeared to me even less marvellous than your transformation into a wit and leader … that a politician may at different periods of his life, and under very different aspects of public affairs, conscientiously entertain varying opinions upon the same measure, is a principle which no member of the present House of Commons is entitled to question. I would not deny you, Sir, the benefit of the charity of society; but when every change of opinion in a man's career is inevitably attended by a corresponding and advantageous change in his position, his motives are not merely open to question – his conduct is liable to conviction.[24]

Amid such accusations and acrimony, Hobhouse himself called for the May 1833 by-election that would ultimately seal his fate in Westminster. Hobhouse's precise reasons for calling the election were complicated. At the

---

[20] Despite claims to the contrary within Westminster, Hobhouse's personal influence on Irish policy was moderate and conciliatory. See Hobhouse to Grey, 19 Apr. 1833, Broughton papers, MS Add. 36466, fo. 441.

[21] Place to Joseph Parkes, 17 July 1834, Place papers, MS Add. 35149, fo. 310.

[22] Place to Burdett, 19 Oct. 1832, ibid. fo. 101.

[23] *Morning Chronicle*, 20 Nov. 1832. It is interesting that Hobhouse himself accused Place of demanding the pledges for precisely this reason: Place papers, MS Add. 27844, fos 34–41, 59–60; MS Add. 35149, fo. 329.

[24] B. Disraeli, *Whigs and Whiggism*, London 1913, 294, 296.

heart of his decision, however, lay a conflict between his responsibilities as a government minister and his responsibilities as a metropolitan representative. In early May Hobhouse resigned from the government over its failure to abolish the window tax, perhaps the most hated of all the assessed taxes levied in the metropolis, and one to which Hobhouse had long been personally opposed. Although Hobhouse publicly supported abolition of the tax, as a minister he felt compelled to abstain from voting on Althorp's decision to renew it. As Hobhouse explained his dilemma to Grey:

> I cannot vote for Lord Althorp's resolution this evening without violating my voluntary engagements with my constituents and I cannot consent to hold office whilst repairing my support to the administration on a question decisive of their stability. Under these circumstances, I beg leave to retire from the Chief Secretaryship of Ireland, assuring your Lordship at the same time of my sincere regret at being thus compelled, by a sense of public duty as well as of private service to separate myself from those to whom both personally and politically I am, and I trust ever shall be, most warmly attached.[25]

After stepping down and thus forcing a by-election, Hobhouse was heavily criticised by his radical opponent George DeLacy Evans for not voting against the measure.[26] In a three-way contest, and without the support of the Westminster Committee, Hobhouse was soundly defeated, losing in seven of the borough's ten parishes. Considering the personal sacrifice that Hobhouse had made for the continued support of his radical constituents, Tavistock was outraged by 'the base and ungrateful and disgusting opposition to [Hobhouse] in Westminster', but most observers felt that Hobhouse got what he deserved.[27] *The Spectator*, for instance, took an unsympathetic view, arguing that Hobhouse's defeat had more to do with his prior attachment to the Whig government than with his apparently decreasing commitment to reform. 'The result of this contest', claimed the paper, 'and the circumstances which led to it, inculcate a useful moral ... avoid official connexions.'[28] The

---

[25] Hobhouse to Grey, 30 Apr. 1833, 2nd Earl Grey papers, GRE/B8/4.

[26] *Morning Chronicle* 8 May 1833, 2. The radical D. W. Harvey, who went on to represent Southwark and became an influential metropolitan radical from 1834, made a similar criticism of Hobhouse's failure to vote against the taxes: ibid. 4 May 1833, 1.

[27] Tavistock to Hobhouse, Broughton papers, MS Add. 47223, fo. 60. Regarding the 'base and ungrateful opposition' suffered by Hobhouse, Greville records that Hobhouse was even pelted with mud at one large open meeting of electors: *The Greville memoirs, 1814–1860*, ed. L. Strachey and R. Fulford, London 1938, iii. 371, entry for 16 May 1833.

[28] *The Spectator*, 11 May 1833, 424.

Morning Advertiser agreed, congratulating Westminster for choosing a candidate unencumbered by ministerial obligations.[29]

Ironically, just as Hobhouse was being expelled from Westminster as a failed ministerialist, one of his earlier legislative achievements began to precipitate a radicalisation and democratisation of the wider metropolitan political culture. In the course of 1833 Hobhouse's Select Vestries Act, which had become law in October 1831, finally began to bear fruit.[30] The act aimed to liberalise and regularise London's piecemeal and anachronistic arrangements for local government by chipping away at the 'close' vestry system, which kept parochial administration in the hands of the privileged few, and which had prevailed in many metropolitan parishes since the early eighteenth century. It did this by giving a wider constituency of ratepayers the opportunity to elect vestry representatives and to hold these representatives accountable for the management (or mismanagement) of the parish rates. Although the legislation stopped short of 'reopening' vestries to all ratepayers, it nevertheless satisfied the demands of metropolitan reformers by establishing an inclusive vestry franchise and by introducing into this franchise innovations such as vote by secret ballot.[31] Under the terms of Hobhouse's act, each ratepayer in a reformed parish, whether male or female, was entitled to one vote for the election of vestrymen, who served terms of three years, one-third retiring annually, and who worked under the scrutiny of a board of five auditors. Whereas any ratepayer, regardless of however lowly assessed, was entitled to vote for vestrymen, only men in occupation of premises rated at £40 or over were entitled to sit as vestrymen.

During the bill's passage through parliament, opposition from those interested in the continuation of the 'close' system had been stiff. Sturges Bourne

---

[29] *Morning Advertiser*, 10 May 1833, 2.

[30] 1&2 Will. IV c. 60 *An act for the better regulation of vestries and for the appointment of auditors of accounts in certain parishes of England and Wales.*

[31] Whereas open vestries were considered to be more democratic, and therefore preferable, by provincial ultra-radicals, metropolitan parish reformers tended to value the efficiency of an administrative body: S. Webb, *The English local government franchise from the revolution to the Municipal Corporations Act: the parish and county*, London 1924, 272. London's rapid growth during the early Victorian period ensured the existence of a handful of open vestries. Although some of these (Lambeth and Clapham, for instance) were reorganised under the terms of the Sturges Bourne Acts, others (such as Camberwell and Wandsworth) remained 'open' until 1855: J. Roebuck, *Urban development in nineteenth-century London: Lambeth, Battersea, and Wandsworth, 1838–1855*, London 1979, 8–15; H. J. Dyos, *Victorian suburb: a study of the growth of Camberwell*, Leicester 1961, 138–41. Of course, not all open vestries were radical, although in London this tended to be the case. St George-the-Martyr, Southwark, and St Leonard's, Shoreditch, were also notoriously radical and practically open to all rated parishioners.

himself sat on the 1830 parliamentary select committee appointed to examine the issue of vestry reform, and pushed repeatedly for anti-democratic controls such as plural and absentee voting, both of which featured in the 1818 Select Vestry Act bearing Sturges Bourne's name. Hobhouse complained that his natural allies on the select committee (Hume and O'Connell) rarely attended meetings, which left him outnumbered and over-powered by his Tory opponents.[32] Place, however, was generally unsympathetic to Hobhouse's complaints of isolation, and worried that Hobhouse's inability to apply and assert himself might ultimately undermine this important reform. Indeed, although the legislation carried Hobhouse's name, Francis Place was the true motivating force. In addition to instructing Hobhouse on the desirable (i.e. radical) ends of reform, Place motivated Hobhouse by reminding him that both his reputation and his borough career were on the line.[33] In fact, it is likely that Place's loss of faith in Hobhouse as a radical representative was crystallised by his many frustrations over Hobhouse's ineffectual championing of vestry reform. Place felt, for instance, that Hobhouse had been too easily 'overpowered and subdued by Sturges Bourne' and that he did not 'push his examination of witnesses to the extent he ought to have done'. It is revealing that Hobhouse all but admitted that finding a suitable solution was beyond his powers.[34] Hobhouse's radical constituents were equally demanding, and it is clear that he sometimes felt underappreciated. Recalling the events of 3 December 1830, for instance, Hobhouse sulkily described a deputation from the metropolitan parishes respecting his bill, 'the essential clause of which displeases them, so all my labour has been in vain. This is the fate of most men who try to reconcile contending interests. Thankless Metropolis! My bones shall not rest in either of your cemeteries!'[35]

The act that ultimately emerged was radical and yet also conciliatory

---

[32] See Broughton papers, MS Add. 35148, fo. 49, and Hobhouse diary, MS Add. 56554, entry for 14 June 1830. Hobhouse complained , for instance, that 'Mr. Ross, who had all the select vestries in London to back him, did everything to thwart me in every way, and he has contrived to load the evidence with nonsense and irrelevant matter.' Hobhouse was equally critical of Sturges Bourne. Despite overwhelmingly negative testimony from a number of respondents, the select committee praised the terms of the Sturges Bourne Acts: *Reports of the select committee appointed to inquire into the general operation and effect of the laws and usages under which select and other vestries are constituted in England and Wales*, PP (1830), iv. 89–90, 111–12.
[33] See Broughton papers, MS Add. 36465, fo. 94, and Place papers, MS Add. 35154, fo. 125.
[34] Hobhouse to Place, 16 Apr. 1830, Place papers, MS Add. 35154, fo. 124; MS Add. 35146, fo. 102.
[35] J. C. Hobhouse *Recollections of a long life*, New York 1910, iv. 75.

towards critics of vestry reform. By the terms of the act, the personnel of the old 'close' vestries were replaced gradually. In St Marylebone, an initial election took place in late May 1832, by means of which forty of the 120 select vestrymen were replaced by radicals. The same happened in May 1833, giving the radicals a two to one majority, and then again in 1834, giving the radicals almost complete control of the vestry.[36] More important, in order to overcome opposition from both Tories and provincial radicals, Hobhouse's measure was made provisional rather than mandatory. To adopt the act, at least one-fifth of a parish's ratepayers, or a minimum of fifty, needed to requisition their vestry's churchwardens to hold a poll open to all ratepayers. If two-thirds of the votes cast at this poll were cast in favour of reform, and if the total number of votes cast equalled at least half the number of ratepayers in the parish, the vestry would be reformed. The five parishes which did go on to adopt the act did so by enormous majorities.[37] Although only five metropolitan parishes managed to adopt Hobhouse's act, the measure none the less represented an enormous innovation in metropolitan local governance, and ultimately had a significant impact on the wider metropolitan political culture. By liberalising a handful of London's largest select vestries, three of which contained more than 50,000 ratepayers, Hobhouse's Select Vestries Act provided institutional space for the development and organisation of new radical groups and inspired local government reform movements in many of those parishes which failed, for whatever reason, to adopt Hobhouse's reform in the first instance. By May 1834 practically the entire St Marylebone vestry shared the same set of radical political principles and the same desire to communicate these principles to the borough's parliamentary representatives. Predictably, the social dynamics of the reformed vestries were also quickly transformed. In 1815 fully 40 per cent of St George, Hanover Square, vestrymen were titled aristocrats. By 1845 this figure had been halved and the departed aristocrats had been replaced almost exclusively by middle-class commercialists.[38]

The radicalised Hobhouse vestries were almost immediately put to use by these new vestrymen not just as organs for setting local rates, but as stepping stones to larger political reforms. By the middle months of 1833 a group of Marylebone radicals (members of the so-called 'Barlow Street committee')

---

[36] See F. Sheppard, *Local government in Saint Marylebone, 1688–1835*, London 1958, 301–3.
[37] See *True Sun*, 19, 27 Mar.; 3, 4, 17, 18 Apr. 1832. See also vestry minutes of St James, Westminster, Westminster Archives, entry for 1 May 1832.
[38] See St George, Hanover Square, vestry minutes, Westminster Archives, vols c778 and c784.

had successfully converted their newly radicalised vestry into an organ through which the borough's radical parliamentary politics could be organised. Among the leading members of the Barlow Street committee were Thomas Potter, John Savage, William Kensett, William Wilson and William Hovendon. 'These men', noted a journalist who had infiltrated the Barlow Street meetings, 'had as much in view a political as a parochial object, indeed, the majority of the leaders of the ultra reform party, were and are more notorious for their violence in politics, than celebrated for their services, in the management of parochial affairs.'[39]

In 1833 the Barlow Street committee took the opportunity presented by Portman's resignation to promote a parliamentary candidate of its own. Their choice was Sir Samuel S. B. Whalley, a romantic figure of mysterious background and advanced views. Whalley's electoral success in 1833 provided the St Marylebone vestry radicals with a powerful platform for their political reform agenda, and heralded a complete break from the Country or Whiggish notions of representative 'independence' so cherished by Burdett and other patrician 'radicals' in the unreformed metropolitan boroughs. According to the journalist James Williamson Brooke, admittedly a severe critic of the reformed St Marylebone vestry, Whalley was from the very beginning of his political career a 'nominee in the hands of certain democrats of a very questionable political character, in the parish of St. Marylebone'.[40] The astute Westminster Committee campaign manager Thomas DeVear agreed with this assessment, claiming in a letter of 1834 to Hobhouse that

> nothing can be said of ultimate success [for Whig candidates in Marylebone] unless we were sure of Whalley's friends, who are the shopkeepers and clerks and many of them very honest men – Potter, Wilson, Mills, Green, etc., etc.. *Potter prefers delegation to representation and it is believed is accustomed to dictate to Whalley his daily proceedings.* He has also the folly to propose the representation to himself at some future period.[41]

Whalley's regular attendance of St Marylebone vestry meetings, where his parliamentary advocacy of the Barlow Street committee's reform agenda could be reviewed and informed, contrasted starkly with the Whig William Horne's absence and comparative neglect of local interests.[42] By 1837 Whalley enjoyed the support of all the Marylebone radicals, but continued to

---

39 Brooke, *Democrats of Marylebone*, 31.
40 Ibid. 143.
41 Thomas DeVear to Hobhouse, [Jan?] 1834, Francis Burdett–Coutts papers, Bodleian Library, Oxford, MS.Eng.hist.b.200, fo. 190b.
42 *The Vestryman and Metropolitan Parochial Gazette*, 28 June 1834; *True Sun*, 25 June 1834.

owe his position to the patronage of the Barlow Street committee.[43] Benjamin Hall, who became Marylebone's principle representative in 1838 when Whalley was unseated, found himself in a similar position. At his introduction to the borough in 1837, Hall appointed William Hovendon chairman of his election committee and in later years worked closely with Hovendon on matters of policy as well.[44]

By 1835 Marylebone's radical vestry political culture had begun to influence the character of the wider metropolitan radical movement. Stirred into action by the exceptionally unpopular New Poor Law of 1834, a handful of vestry reformers in Westminster, Southwark and Lambeth began to emulate Marylebone.[45] In Westminster, the parliamentary candidate George DeLacy Evans began to court the support of the borough's vestry reformers in 1834, and made his opposition to the Poor Law Amendment Act an overt pledge to represent the interests of these vestries in parliament.[46] In Finsbury, Thomas Wakley also relied to a considerable extent on the support of radical parochial reformers. Prior to his election to parliament in 1835, Wakley had been churchwarden of the dual vestry of St Giles-in-the-Fields and St George's, Bloomsbury (Finsbury), and had become very closely involved in the radical struggle for parochial reform there. The radical Finsbury parochial reformer George Rogers had even been Wakley's election committee manager in 1835, and over the course of the following two years he did his best to keep him from abandoning parochial interests.[47] In Southwark, D. W. Harvey also relied heavily on the support of the borough's radical parochial reformers. From 1835 the radical St George-the-Martyr churchwarden Charles Anderson and his fellow vestry reformer John Day were particularly important to Harvey's support network. Both men were prominent members of a vestry reform organisation, the United Parishioners Society, to which Harvey himself also belonged.[48] During the mid-1830s these various reform networks,

---

[43] Murphy, *Letter to the radicals of the United Kingdom*, 6.
[44] Election voucher and letter, Hovendon to Hall, [1837?], Sir Benjamin Hall papers, Gwent Record Office, Newport, D.1210.203. Joseph Drake, yet another Barlow Street committee member, was secretary of Hall's committee.
[45] *The Vestryman*, 21 June 1834; *The Times*, 28 Feb. 1837, 6.
[46] E. Spiers, *Radical general: Sir George DeLacy Evans, 1787–1870*, Manchester 1983, 60.
[47] See S. S. Sprigge, *The life and times of Thomas Wakley*, London 1899, 310–11; G. Rogers, *A letter to T. Wakley ... being an answer to calumny, and a statement of reasons for not having supported Wakley at the recent Finsbury election*, London 1837; St Giles-in-the-Fields, and St George, Bloomsbury, Householder's Parochial Union, *An address to the members explaining the reasons for the expulsion of G. Rogers*, London 1837.
[48] *The Times*, 28 Sept. 1838, 3. The society had been founded in 1831 to combat the powers of the select vestry: C. Anderson, *An account of the alterations, reductions, exposures, etc. effected by the United Parishioners Society of St. George the Martyr, Southwark*, London

and the radical MPs who benefited from them, became increasingly integrated with one another. 'It is important upon all occasions, and under any circumstances', noted the *Parochial Gazette* in May 1837 'that there should be a constant communication kept up between the different localities – that each should be in possession of the condition of the others – and that they should all as far as possible adhere to the same principles of action.'[49] Harvey's close working relationship with Wakley throughout the 1837 election, and the unremittingly 'localist' tone of their joint campaigning, is evidence that such co-operation was often effected in a most powerful way.

Although the metropolitan radical movement of the mid-1830s cannot be said to have been entirely unified, working alliances had nevertheless begun to form between the vestry radicals, the metropolitan co-operativists, the members of the London Working Man's Association and other early Chartist organisations, and ultra-radical supporters of Wakley in Finsbury and of Daniel Whittle Harvey in Southwark.[50] In 1836 these various groups coalesced around the radical platform advocated by Harvey's *True Sun*, which played an important part in launching the LWMA, and around Harvey's and Wakley's combined agitation against the Newspaper Stamp Act and for increased suffrage.[51] Future LWMA directors, including John Cleave and Henry Heatherington, worked closely with Harvey and Wakley on the abolition of stamp duty as well as on vestry reform, which they supported from the pages of journals such as the *London Dispatch* and the *Weekly Police Gazette* and through co-operation with the Finsbury vestry radical (and future Chartist) George Rogers.[52] Like many other members of the vestry radical leadership, George Rogers's involvement in Chartism came via his links to the LWMA and West London Democratic Association. The St Pancras vestry reformer Thomas Murphy even acted as delegate of the LWMA during the Birmingham and Glasgow Chartist congresses of 1838. In Lambeth,

---

1833; *Rules and regulations of the society called the United Parishioners of St. George-the-Martyr, Southwark, established 13 January, 1831*, London 1833.

[49] *Parochial Gazette*, 8 May 1837, 4. Co-operation between parochial reformers from different vestries was common. For examples of co-operation between the Lambeth vestry reformers and Potter, Savage and Murphy of Marylebone see *The Ballot*, 17 Apr., 3 July, 25 Dec. 1831 and 22 Jan. 1832.

[50] See, for instance, the anti-poor law radical meeting held at the Crown and Anchor tavern in February 1837: *The Times*, 28 Feb. 1837, 6.

[51] Place papers, MS Add. 27827, fos 33–4; *True Sun*, 2 Jan. 1836, 3; J. Wiener, *The war of the unstamped: the movement to repeal the British newspaper tax, 1830–1836*, London 1969, 30, 141; G. J. Holyoake, *History of co-operation*, London 1879.

[52] See *The London Dispatch; and People's Paper and Social Reformer*, 16 Oct. 1836, and George Rogers to William Lovett, 14 Sept. 1838, William Lovett papers, BL, MS Add. 78161, fo. 98.

meanwhile, the prominent early Chartists William Carpenter and Thomas MacConnell were equally immersed in the movements for vestry reform and state retrenchment; whereas in Finsbury, George Rogers (Wakley's onetime campaign manager) balanced his agitation for the restoration of open vestries with a leading role in the Chartist locality and a close working relationship with the aristocratic Chartist champion Duncombe. William Carpenter's journal, *The Charter*, espoused the vestry radical agenda for 'local self-government' and contained frequent condemnations of Whig attempts to 'suffocate English liberty' through a programme of government centralisation.[53] John Cleave's *English Chartist Circular* advanced similar retrenching priorities, instructing its readers in Paine's view that 'government in its mildest form is an evil; society in its every state, a blessing'.[54] From July 1836 Cleave, Murphy, D. W. Harvey, Hetherington and the Marylebone parochial reformer Dr Thomas Wade all became leading lights in Daniel O'Connell's universal suffrage club.[55]

Like Henry Hunt, these radicals were said to be 'of the party [to which] parliamentary and parish reform, universal suffrage and open vestries, were considered as equally required to adjust the people's rights'.[56] Fundamental to this consideration was an understanding of the ways in which the ratepaying clauses of the 1832 Reform Act politicised vestry administrative control. By the terms of the act, registration for the parliamentary franchise in most boroughs was dependent on completed payment of the poor rates.[57] Because registration depended on payment of the rates, parish overseers of the poor, who were appointed by the vestry, became exceptionally important political officials, whose judgement and political preferences could potentially determine the political character of a borough's electorate. In addition to deciding who was eligible to pay the rate, it was left to the overseer's discretion to determine the manner in which a rate could be paid, and to draw up the lists of those who had successfully paid. It was the overseer of the poor, for instance, who determined whether rates could be compounded in his parish, and because compounding was common practice in metropolitan parishes

---

[53] *The Charter*, 17 Feb. 1839, 57; 3 Feb. 1839, 21; 31 Mar. 1839, 148; 27 Jan. 1839, 5.

[54] *English Chartist Circular* vol. 1, # 1 (1841), 1, and vol. 1, # 5 (1841), 17. See also James Watson and Henry Hetherington, *Socialism set to rest by the* Weekly Dispatch, London 1840, esp. pp. 2–6.

[55] *The Times*, 6 July 1836, 5.

[56] St Giles-in-the Fields and St George, Bloomsbury joint vestry, *Refutation of the charges against the select vestry*, London 1829, 45–6.

[57] For an excellent discussion of the relationship between the poor rate and registration for the parliamentary franchise see P. Salmon, *Electoral reform at work: local politics and national parties, 1832–1841*, Woodbridge 2002, 185–93.

with closed vestries, reformers were able to draw a direct link between popular control of the vestry and the proper working of the reform act. As Francis Place put it, the overseers had the power to 'disfranchise whom they please. They may also put down whom they please as qualified as £10 house-holders ... and they have done so to a great extent'.[58] At the first reformed parliamentary election, Lincoln Stanhope estimated that 4,000 out of a possible 10,000 electors in Tower Hamlets had been disfranchised through the practice of compounding.[59] The Finsbury radical MP Thomas Duncombe was also awake to the difficulties caused by this system for radical candidates. 'Most metropolitans', he complained in 1832, 'through apathy, ignorance, and poverty – have not qualified for registering and there is a devil of a row about it. 7000 are disfranchised in Marylebone ... I think these candidates for the metropolitan boroughs are much to blame in not seeing that their forces were in marching order.'[60] Whereas overseers appointed by radical vestries, such as St Pancras, ensured that rates were set low and collected in plenty of time to enable easy registration, those appointed by closed or Sturges Bourne vestries, such as Lambeth, effectively struck off many potential voters.[61] This arrangement ensured a healthy radical interest in vestry reform above and beyond the desire for low taxes and local self-determination. A core group of radicals therefore kept the localist agenda at the heart of almost every impor-tant metropolitan radical movement of the 1830s – from the National Polit-ical Union and the National Union of the Working Classes at the beginning of the decade, to the London Working Man's Association and the 'taxes on knowledge' agitation of the middle years, to Chartism in the later 1830s.[62] Moreover, it is no mere coincidence that the two most outspoken parliamen-tary critics of the ratepaying clauses of the 1832 act (Duncombe and DeLacy

58 Place to Brougham, 5 Apr. 1837, Place papers, MS Add. 35150, fo. 252.
59 The Times, 24 Oct. 1832, 3. Hansard 3rd ser.cvii.989, 26 July 1849.
60 T. S. Duncombe to Durham, 13 Aug. 1832, 1st earl of Durham papers, Lambton Park Archives, Chester-le-Street, D.P.13, box 3.
61 See the testimony of a Lambeth liberal named Slade, who, in a letter to Tennyson D'Eyncourt, complained that many within the borough 'have lost the right of voting owing to the neglect of the collector of the poor taxes': [?] Slade to Charles Tennyson D'Eyncourt, 29 Dec. 1834, Tennyson D'Eyncourt papers, IV/3/66.
62 Cleave, Wakley, Rogers, Murphy, Potter, Savage and the Lambeth vestry reformers William Carpenter and W. D. Saull were all founding members of the NPU. Moreover, Place's notes reveal that these men acted together within the Union. George Rogers proposed Wakley and Lovett for membership; Murphy proposed Rogers, Potter and Savage, and John Cleave proposed William Carpenter: Place papers, MS Add. 27791, fo. 222. See also NPU, A test for candidates, London 1831, which lists select vestry reform as one of its eleven key pledges. For the national importance of the NPU see N. LoPatin, Political unions, popular politics, and the Great Reform Act of 1832, Basingstoke 1999.

Evans) were members of metropolitan constituencies with strong vestry radical movements.[63]

Perhaps Greville was a little over-anxious about the gains being made by these radicals when he noted in early January 1835 that 'all the moderate Whigs are beat in the Metropolitan districts'.[64] However, his somewhat panicked and hasty observation reveals something of the extent to which metropolitan political culture was changing during the mid-1830s. The strange exception to the trend toward vestry-influenced radicalism was Tower Hamlets, which continued to return Whiggish members throughout the 1830s, and which retained a correspondingly Whiggish, populist and constitutionalist political culture. Tower Hamlets lacked many of the social and administrative structures that had enabled vestry radicalism to flourish in other parts of London. To begin with, the borough was perhaps the largest, most socially heterogeneous, and most artificial parliamentary constituency in London. It covered an area of twelve square miles and included no fewer than seventeen parishes – almost all of which were closed and many of which were exceptionally corrupt (the one exception was St Leonard's, Shoreditch, which in the mid-1830s fell under the control of the future Chartist leaders Gough and Pearce, and began to play an important part in the wider metropolitan vestry radical movement).[65] Partly as a consequence of borough radicals being so thoroughly excluded from vestry business, the conversion of Tower Hamlets to parochial radicalism was delayed until the 1840s, when a widespread agitation against church rates mobilised previously silent elements in the borough.[66]

The early progress of vestry radicalism in the Tower Hamlets was also inhibited by the borough's comparative poverty. By the 1830s Marylebone, Southwark and Westminster all contained thriving and comparatively wealthy commercial communities, and it was largely from these communities that the most successful radicals sprang. By imposing a £40 minimum property qualification on vestrymen, Hobhouse's act effectively ensured that the

---

[63] For Duncombe's position on the ratepaying clauses see *Hansard* 3rd ser. xxxii.1168–71, 18 Apr. 1836. Duncombe estimated that a further 95,000 men would be enfranchised in London alone if the rate clauses were dropped.

[64] *Greville memoirs*, iii. 139, entry for 9 Jan. 1835. In 1835 Henry Bulwer was returned in Marylebone and George Byng retained his seat in Middlesex.

[65] In Shoreditch, an open vestry was held at least every fortnight. Radicalisation of the vestry had much to do with discontent over the local arrangements of poor relief: *Shoreditch Observer*, 27 Feb. 1858.

[66] See *The Morning Advertiser*, 5 Oct. 1844 and 12 Jan 1850, and *The Parochial Expositor; or Anti-Church Rate Payers Gazette*, which became the *Parochial Chronicle* in 1852. This process is discussed in greater detail in chapter 4 below.

reformed vestries would be bastions of the 'shopocracy': recall, for instance, that in his letter to Hobhouse, DeVear described Whalley's supporters as 'the shopkeepers and clerks', and would consequently promote a commercialist libertarian agenda heavily informed by the necessity of keeping rates low. In Marylebone, Potter was a successful, if small-scale, tallow chandler; Savage was a linen-draper and then a publican; and Murphy was a coal merchant. In 1832 each of these men had been categorised as 'other than working man' members of the NPU.[67] In Finsbury, George Rogers (a successful tobacco merchant) and his fellow members of the Householder's Parochial Union were solidly middle class. In Tower Hamlets, however, the *petit bourgeoisie* were increasingly outnumbered by the type of sweated labourer whom Mayhew described as politically apathetic, and indeed Hobhouse vestries did not promote their interests. 'In passing from the skilled operatives of the west-end to the unskilled workmen of the eastern quarter of London', observed Mayhew in 1850,

> the moral and intellectual change is so great, that it seemed as if we were in a new land, and among another race. The artisans are almost to a man red-hot politicians. They are sufficiently educated and thoughtful to have a sense of their importance to the State … the unskilled labourers are a different class of people. As yet they are as unpolitical as footmen, and instead of entertaining violent democratic opinions, they appear to have no political opinions whatever; or, if they do, … they rather lead towards the maintenance of 'things as they are', than toward the ascendancy of the working people.[68]

'Titled radicals' in London, 1832–41

James Epstein, John Belchem, Patrick Joyce, Miles Taylor and Eugenio Biagini have each highlighted the importance of the 'gentleman leader' to nineteenth-century popular politics. The gentleman leader has been described by these historians as a 'romantic popular hero', always a great orator and often a demagogue, whose life and manner of public presentation 'dramatised and personalised' popular causes. By definition, the gentleman leader enjoyed an elevated social position *vis-à-vis* his audience, but his public *persona* often managed to transcend class distinctions by remaining populist. Although he was not 'of' the people, the gentleman leader was still

---

67 Place papers, MS Add. 27791, fo. 222.
68 H. Mayhew, *London labour and the London poor*, London 1884, 243. Green's *From artisans to paupers* endorses this geography of apathy.

clearly 'for' the people.[69] Although the 'gentlemen leaders' identified by Epstein (a group which includes Henry Hunt, Feargus O'Connor, John Bright, Ernest Jones and William Ewart Gladstone) were socially privileged, the metropolitan radical leadership was an altogether more rarefied bunch. In fact, London can be seen as the context within which elite leadership of popular politics reached its apex.[70] Bright, for instance, was in all respects a man of business, whereas the Lambeth radical MP Charles Tennyson owed his social and political authority entirely to inheritance, land and family connections. The same can be said for many of London's leading radical representatives. Unlike the progressive, dissenting, 'gentlemen leaders' of provincial origin, London's radical leadership appealed to notions of patriotism and chivalry, rather than to political economy and self-interest, in their disinterested defence of English liberty, and remained suspicious of philosophic radicalism, preferring instead a reactionary radical historicism. Indeed, notions of chivalry and honour seem to have compelled no fewer than five metropolitan MPs (Thomas Duncombe, Francis Burdett, Charles Tennyson D'Eyncourt, William Molesworth and George DeLacy Evans) to take part in public duels during their political careers. In many respects, these values and tendencies aligned London's reformed radical leadership with an earlier generation of 'Romantic radicals'.[71] The overwhelmingly patrician character of London's radical leadership, however, prompted the mid-Victorian satirist Edward Whitty to decry the emergence of an entirely new group: 'the titled Radicals', the electoral successes of whom convinced Whittey that the 'metropolitan boroughs have a good deal to learn – in self respect'.[72]

Burdett's paternalist and independent pose in unreformed Westminster has been noted. In the reformed metropolitan constituencies, Burdett's heirs could be found everywhere. In Lambeth, for instance, Charles Tennyson took the additional name D'Eyncourt in 1834 to advertise his genealogical connection to Edward IV, and thereby establish his patrician *bona fides*. A few

---

[69] See P. Joyce, *Visions of the people: industrial England and the question of class, 1840–1914*, Cambridge 1991, esp. pp. 39, 44–7; Biagini, *Liberty, retrenchment, and reform*, esp. ch. vii; Belchem, 'Orator' Hunt; J. Epstein, *The lion of freedom: Feargus O'Connor and the Chartist movement*, London 1982; J. Belchem and J. Epstein, 'The nineteenth-century gentleman leader revisited', *Social History* xxii (1997), 174–92; and M. Taylor, *Ernest Jones, Chartism, and the romance of politics*, Oxford 2003.

[70] Jon Parry has aptly described the metropolitan radical leadership as 'high bred romantics': *The rise and fall of liberal government in Victorian England*, New Haven 1993, 99.

[71] See Spence, *Birth of romantic radicalism*. The historian of English local government Josef Redlich used the phrase 'constitutional romantics' to describe the same set of men: *The history of local government in England*, London 1958.

[72] E. Whitty, *The governing classes of Great Britain: political portraits*, London 1854, 202.

years later he acquired the title of count palatine while playing with the idea of becoming a knight of Malta.[73] Yet, through each of these increasingly patrician and aristocratic transformations Tennyson continued to present himself as a romantic hero, a 'man of the people' and a champion of the peoples' ancient rights. The proud 'count' felt no compunction in declaring to audiences that 'we bear the stamp of freedom on our brow and scorn the recognition of the proudest peer who ever bore a coronet upon his. The aristocracy at large must be taught their proper places'.[74] In Marylebone, Benjamin Hall's concern for the well-being of his constituents was informed by a distinctly patrician understanding of the duties of a good landlord.[75] Hall, or Baron Llanover as he was later known, was a substantial landlord in Wales, yet in his metropolitan constituency he was a thoroughgoing radical champion of popular liberties and a scourge of the Anglican establishment. According to one political satirist, Hall 'insulted the Church for several successive sessions with such safe *eclat* that ––––– the furrier, ––––– the chemist, and ––––– the doctor, who manage these things [the vestries] for the great borough of Marylebone, took it for granted that Sir Benjamin must be a Radical'.[76] Sir William Molesworth in Southwark, Lord Dudley Coutts Stuart in Marylebone, and J. T. Leader in Westminster were equally grand at home and demotic in public. In particular, Molesworth, the romantic historian of Greece, was accused of adopting radicalism 'only for the sake of taking an artistic position in the House', causing at least one metropolitan local paper to lament the 'melancholy decadence in the character and ability' of the post-reform metropolitan representatives.[77]

Paradoxically, while the figureheads of the reformed metropolitan political culture retained and even extended many elements of Burdett's romantic and patrician flamboyance and fashionability, this culture none the less also became markedly more democratic and less paternalist. Especially with the rise of the vestry-based 'local self-government' movement from 1834, the foppish and high-born metropolitan radical leadership was forced to become both more mindful of, and responsive to, the wishes of their constituents and

---

[73] M. Girouard, *The return to Camelot: chivalry and the English gentleman*, New Haven 1981, 71.

[74] Tennyson D'Eyncourt papers, IV/64/51. Tennyson's aristocratic bearing generated confusion over his true political connections – some thought that he must be a Whig: ibid. IV/3/79.

[75] M. Fraser, 'Benjamin Hall, MP for Marylebone, 1837–1839', *National Library of Wales Journal* xiii (1964), 319.

[76] Whitty, *Governing classes*, 206.

[77] *Ratepayer or the London Borough of Lambeth … Journal*, 2 Sept. 1850, 4; Whitty, *Governing classes*, 204.

less reliant on their own 'independent' judgements and considerations when voting and debating in parliament. Indeed, during the mid-1830s, pledges, those tools of 'vulgar tyranny' despised and refused by Burdett in the pre-reform period, became commonplace in the metropolitan constituencies. Radical candidates simply could not hope to be returned for metropolitan constituencies without making fairly extensive electoral pledges.[78] As an upshot of this change, metropolitan MPs began to advocate constituency issues and interests within parliament with as much, if not more, energy as issues of national importance.

From 1834 the unpopularity of Whiggery within the metropolitan constituencies posed a new challenge to London's 'titled radicals'. Conflations of 'titled radicalism' and advanced Whiggery were easily made. Tennyson, for instance, was mistaken by no less an authority than Lady Holland for a 'zealous Foxite', and was frequently reminded by his election agent of the need to mingle more freely and more frequently with Lambeth electors. 'In your long silence to them', the agent warned Tennyson, 'all your rejection of Whiggery will be forgotten.'[79] Many 'titled radicals' quite simply looked like Whigs to the casual observer, and indeed the likes of Charles Tennyson and Dudley Coutts Stuart were completely, and often, at home within Whig society. In 1847, for instance, every metropolitan constituency bar the Tower Hamlets was represented by at least one radical who belonged to Brooks's Club.[80] A political premium was consequently placed on the ability of such men to put demonstrable distance between themselves and the hated Whigs whom they so closely resembled and with whom they mixed so freely. From the mid-1830s London's radical leadership began to advertise this distance by deploying increasingly romantic sensibilities. Tennyson, for instance, styled himself a medieval baron, characterised his crusade for popular rights as a chivalric undertaking, and did everything within his powers to convince his constituents that he found Whiggery odious.[81] At the same time, London's 'titled radicals' began to privilege romantic narratives of Saxon liberty over Country rhetoric and 'ancient constitutionalism', which Whigs and radicals

---

[78] Whalley managed to eschew pledges in 1833, but not 1834. For borough criticism of his 1833 refusal see *The Reformer, a Daily Evening Newspaper*, 15 Mar. 1833.

[79] Lady Holland to C. R. Fox, Dec. 1832, Holland House papers, MS Add. 51790, fos 24–5; Edward Burrow to D'Eynecourt, 26 Jan. 1835, Tennyson D'Eyncourt papers, IV/3/110.

[80] Duncombe (Finsbury), Hall and Coutts Stuart (Marylebone), D'Eyncourt (Lambeth), Bernal Osborne (Middlesex), Molesworth (Southwark), Evans and Leader (Westminster). William Clay (Tower Hamlets) was admitted to the club in 1852, but he was actually a Whig: V. A. Williamson, G. W. S. Lyttleton and S. L. Simeon, *Memorials of Brooks's from the foundation of the club, 1764, to the close of the nineteenth century*, London 1907.

[81] Girouard, *Return to Camelot*, 74–6.

had equally embraced in the pre-reform era. Benthamism, meanwhile, made very little impression, and certainly no positive impression, on the 'titled radicals'. The romantic political *personae* deployed by Duncombe in Finsbury and Tennyson in Lambeth owed more to Young England than the *Westminster Review*. Romanticism was, of course, an anathema to true Whigs.[82]

Thomas Duncombe's early career in Finsbury, which he represented in parliament from 1834 until his death in 1861, highlights many of the most striking features of 'titled radicalism' in early Victorian London. Duncombe was perhaps the most flamboyantly aristocratic, and certainly the most radical, of all the 'titled radicals' in London. As the nephew of the earl of Feversham, and as heir to the considerable Yorkshire estate of Copgrove, Duncombe was 'brought up with decidedly aristocratic inclinations'.[83] After Harrow, Duncombe was commissioned in the Coldstream Guards, but soon tired of peace-time garrison duty and returned to London to partake in clublife. Throughout the 1820s and '30s Duncombe frequented the Whig metropolitan salons and clubs, was a regular at Almack's, and generally cultivated a reputation as a 'beau, a wit, and a trifler' who luxuriated in 'transcendent dandyism and lavish expenditure'.[84] Like many Regency aristocrats, Duncombe was an extravagant gambler, losing much of his fortune at cards and roulette, and by the mid-1830s he had become notorious in the popular imagination for aristocratic fashionable excesses and debauchery. As *Fraser's Magazine* noted in 1834, Duncombe indulged in

> a habit of promiscuous intercourse with all kinds of women, married or unmarried; a patronage of places where the youthful heir is often reduced to beggary and impelled to suicide; and a readiness to take any man's life for a misplaced word or a misconstrued look – these are the 'follies of fashionable life'; and these habits, whether you choose to call them follies or crimes, are by common report ascribed to Mr. Duncombe.[85]

During his first years in Finsbury, these aristocratic dispositions and excesses, and Duncombe's obvious comfort in Whig society, caused considerable

---

[82] Mitchell, *Whig world*, 30–31.
[83] Duncombe, *Life and correspondence*, i. 2. In fact, Duncombe at one point suspected that his uncle, the earl of Feversham, was born out of wedlock and that Feversham's estates and titles therefore rightfully belonged to him: Duncombe to Durham, 23 Aug. 1836, 1st Earl Durham papers, D.P.13, box 3. Duncombe was also related to the earls of Carlisle, Onslow, Eldon and Galloway.
[84] Sprigge, *Thomas Wakley*, 247; P. W. Kingford, 'Radical dandy: Thomas Slisingby Duncombe, 1796–1861', *History Today* xiv (1964), 400. For Duncombe's commitment to fashionable trousers see Duncombe to Durham [n.d., letter #9], 1st Earl Durham papers, D.P.13, box 3.
[85] *Fraser's Magazine* (Oct. 1824) (10), 502.

confusion, and much suspicion, among borough radicals. Borough ultra-radicals questioned Duncombe's commitment to radical reform and critiqued his apparent lack of seriousness as a grave character failing. Duncombe's close social ties to Whiggery proved especially damaging to his reputation as a true reformer. Thomas Wakley in particular made frequent reference to Duncombe's prominence in Whig society and pointed to his past political ties to Hobhouse and Lord Cowper as evidence of Duncombe's links to political Whiggery. During the 1834 campaign for Finsbury, Wakley accused Duncombe of being a ministerial candidate, and confessed that he was first prejudiced against Duncombe upon learning that both Althorp and Brougham supported his candidacy.[86] At the following election it was the Tory sergeant Spankie who accused Duncombe of being a Whig in 'disguise'.[87] Although the Whigs had eagerly tried to enlist Duncombe during the early 1830s, he had repeatedly rebuffed their advances, and by 1834 he had become completely alienated from Whiggery. 'I have come to one conclusion with regard to the reconstruction and intentions of the present cabinet', wrote Duncombe to Lord Durham in 1834, 'namely, that it is one mass of hypocrisy and humbug, and I must convince you that no faith is to be placed in either "Bears or Big Wigs".'[88] Duncombe remained a strong 'independent' supporter of Durham throughout the 1830s, and stayed true to the radical platform first articulated by Horne Tooke and Cartwright during the 1770s and '80s.[89]

By 1837 Duncombe had won the confidence of the radical press, with *The Spectator* insisting that while he might popularly still be considered a Whig, he was in fact one of the few truly radical MPs in London.[90] Only in the early 1840s, with Duncombe's increasingly prominent contributions to the Chartist movement, did popular opinion come into alignment with *The Spectator*'s assessment.[91] At this fraught political moment, with other radicals

---

[86] *The Times*, 26 June 1834, 6; 1 July 1834, 3; 3 July 1834, 5.

[87] Ibid. 8 Jan. 1835, 3.

[88] Duncombe to Durham [n.d. 1834], 1st Earl Durham papers, D.P.13, box 3. 'My dear old friends', Durham noted two years later, 'now that they are in office, take care of themselves, and I don't suppose I shall see much of them until they are out again': Duncombe to Durham, 20 Feb. 1836, ibid.

[89] Duncombe, *Life and correspondence*, i. 69, 70, 112. Duncombe did his best to enhance Durham's reputation among the metropolitan radicals. See, for instance, Duncombe to Durham [n.d. 1834 – 'Tuesday'], 1st Earl Durham papers, D.P.13, box 3.

[90] *The Spectator*, 28 Jan. 1837, 86.

[91] Duncombe was a consistent parliamentary champion of Chartism, and he even presented the Charter to the Commons in 1842: D. M. Thompson, *The Chartists: popular politics in the industrial revolution* Aldershot 1984, 18, 58.

falling from public favour, George DeLacy Evans could observe that Duncombe 'alone of all the metropolitan members has the People's confidence'.[92] Indeed, Duncombe had been transformed from the 'best political comedy going' to the 'humorous and fascinating prophet of radicalism'. He was, as the Finsbury radical William James Linton once observed, 'an aristocrat by nature as well as by circumstance, yet ever on the people's side, as fearless as Roebuck and more popular, as Roebuck sided with the Whigs in their Poor Law policy: a man to be honored'.[93] Greville, for one, was shocked at Duncombe's success as a radical figurehead. 'It is not a little remarkable', he confided in his journal, 'that Duncombe is supported by all the Dissenters, even the Quakers, with whom austerity of morals and decent behavior are supposed to have weight.'[94]

Duncombe's successful transformation into a radical hero, and his simultaneous alienation from political Whiggery, was accomplished partly through his unstinting criticism of Whig policy on poor relief, as Linton's comparison with Roebuck illustrates, and his opposition to the church rates. However, Duncombe's opposition, within parliament, to Whig policy was on its own not enough to establish his reputation as a radical. The crucial factor was instead Duncombe's successful construction of a compellingly romantic public *persona* – a *persona*, it should be mentioned, which shared many similarities with Burdett's earlier romantic presentation as a people's champion. Like Burdett before him, Duncome presented himself as a voice for the voiceless and as a guardian of English liberty, willing to exploit his own social advantages on behalf of liberty regardless of the personal consequences. Burdett, for instance, had made his name by championing the prisoners at Cold Baths Fields in 1805; Duncombe generated enormous publicity for himself in 1840 by advocating the cause of the Newport prisoners. Duncombe's presentation of the Charter petition to parliament in 1842 was intended, like his Newport agitation, to display his 'fearless' championing of historic English liberty, and was an even greater piece of romantic stagecraft.[95] In the wake of this rather grand public statement of his commitment to radical reform, dandy Duncombe acquired the demotic popular sobriquet of 'honest Tom', and comparisons were made between Duncombe's brave stewardship of the petition, and Burdett's defence of free speech in 1810.

---

92 Duncombe, *Life and correspondence*, i. 344.
93 W. J. Linton, *James Watson: a memoir*, London 1879, 45.
94 *Greville memoirs*, iii. 140.
95 See chapter 4 below. See M. Chase, *Chartism: a new history*, Manchester 2007, 205–6, and P. Pickering, 'And your petitioners, &c.: Chartist petitioning in popular politics, 1838–1848', *EHR* cxvi (2001), 368–88.

Although the theatricality of Duncombe's guardianship of English liberty recalled a time when the cry of 'Burdett and liberty' rang through the Westminster streets, key differences between Burdett's 'cold patrician hauteur' towards radicals of lesser social standing and Duncombe's more egalitarian engagement with his constituents illustrate the extent to which metropolitan political culture had been radicalised during the mid-1830s. Unlike Burdett's princely position in Westminster, Duncombe's success in Finsbury was predicated on his willingness to make pledges and ultimately represent in parliament the wishes of his constituents. Whereas Duncombe repeatedly pledged support for the six points of the Charter and voted accordingly for any reform bill in parliament, Burdett remained unwilling to 'take orders' from his constituents on the issue of further political reform, and in fact became quite opposed to any further modification of the parliamentary franchise. Burdett's 1834 rebirth as a Tory was ultimately brought about by his inability to reconcile himself to an ever more demanding metropolitan radical culture, and to suffer the indignity of taking instructions from low-born vestry-based shopkeepers.[96] It is also revealing, however, that Burdett chose to throw in his lot with Peel when, in party terms, he had always been closer to Foxite Whiggery. The great unpopularity of Whiggery in the metropolitan constituencies might just have been decisive.

Whigs, radicals and 'Whig-Radicals' and London, 1837–8

By the later 1830s, vestry-based radicals such as Thomas Murphy and George Rogers had come to recognise 'titled radicals' such as Duncombe as allies in their fight against Whiggery. At the same time, Murphy and Rogers recognised the emergence, throughout the metropolis, of a new, and less acceptable, species of liberal: the 'Whig-Radical'. In an 1838 pamphlet Murphy described these 'Whig-Radicals' as moderate political reformers who entertained sympathies for Benthamism and who, crucially, co-operated with the Whigs on 'centralising' legislative measures such as the New Poor Law.[97] In

---

[96] Although Burdett did not officially stand as a Tory until 1837, there is compelling evidence that he had already converted by the early months of 1834. See Burdett papers, MS.Eng.hist.b.200, fos 199, 205, in which Burdett refuses to join his fellow metropolitan radicals in censuring Peel's ministry and in which he acknowledges rumours that he is in collusion with the new government. In her unpublished PhD thesis, Caroline Hodlin has argued that Burdett was a 'Country Tory' throughout his career: 'Francis Burdett'. However, prior to 1830, Burdett was close to political Whiggery, and it is worth pointing out that elements of the 'Country' mentality were common among Foxite Whigs.
[97] Murphy, *Letter to the radicals of the United Kingdom*, 16–24.

Middlesex, Joseph Hume was identified, as early as 1835, as a leading 'Whig-Radical'. William Molesworth, who in 1836–7 had his eye on a metropolitan seat of his own, led the rebellion against Hume, claiming that he had been compromised and degraded by his associations with the Whigs and that he 'would stand for Westminster against the devil himself if he had any Whig inclinations'.[98] It is revealing that even Francis Place, Hume's long-time associate and fellow Whiggish moderate, agreed, complaining that Hume should have 'cut the whigs' long before 1837.[99] Metropolitan radical newspapers such as the *London Mercury* were equally critical of Hume's co-operation with the government, and especially outraged over Hume's strong support for the New Poor Law. When Hume was defeated in 1837, the outcome was regarded by the *Mercury* as a triumph for 'true' radicalism over 'Whig-Radicalism'.[100] Just months prior to Hume's defeat, at a meeting of reform-minded metropolitan vestry officials, the future Chartist John Bell had won acclaim by advertising his own opposition to Whig-Radicalism, and by specifically criticising Hume's support of the New Poor Law. Bell

> hoped [that] the people would never be satisfied till they obtained a total repeal of this most barbarous measure [the new Poor Law]. He had never shrunk from denouncing the conduct of Joseph Hume and the rest of the party of hypocrites and impostors who called themselves friends of the people, and who supported this oppressive and tyrannical act in all its stages.[101]

Hume's public complaint that 'the radicals in London suspect the Ministers of insincerity, and do not give them either the support or approbation they deserve', did not help his reputation.[102]

From 1834 onward, the spectre of 'Whig centralisation' dominated radical and liberal discourse in London, and ensured that the crusade for 'local self-government' struck at the very heart of the radical agenda there. Hume's expulsion from Middlesex in 1837 merely confirmed that Whiggery's metropolitan reputation had been severely damaged by the New Poor Law. Unlike in provincial settings, harsh treatment of the poor was only a minor source of metropolitan objection to the New Poor Law.[103] The real cause of alarm and

---

98 William Molesworth to Place, 4, 5 Oct. 1836, Place papers, MS Add. 35150, fo. 167
99 Place to J. A. Roebuck, 3 Oct. 1836, ibid. fos 160–2.
100 *London Mercury*, 13 Aug. 1837, 680.
101 *The Times*, 28 Feb. 1837, 6. For Bell's low opinion of Hume see also *The Times*, 21 Mar. 1837, 6.
102 *The Spectator*, 17 June 1837, 563.
103 The moralistic tone of northern opposition to the Poor Law Amendment Act is conveyed in N. Edsall, *The anti-poor law movement, 1834–1844*, Manchester 1971;

opposition in London lay in how the legislation would impinge on the newly-won powers of the liberalised vestries.

> The measure is not [claimed the *Vestryman and Metropolitan Parochial Gazette*] a mere possession of the poor rates, it is not a simple pounds, shillings, and pence question ... but it is a deep laid Whig scheme, and nearest the hearts of its projectors, to stifle in the first hour of existence, the rising liberty of the parishes of England, and which the Whigs feel and dread would work as beneficial, as rapid a change in the present iniquitous elective system, in the return of members to the Commons House.[104]

Whereas Lord Althorp had foreseen Marylebone's objections and suggested that parishes with populations of 70,000 or greater (i.e. the 'Hobhouse parishes' of St Marylebone, St Pancras and St George, Hanover Square) be excluded from the New Poor Law, Edwin Chadwick resisted any exclusions and in fact felt that the Hobhouse vestries were in special need of an administrative overhaul.[105] According to Chadwick's thinking, Hobhouse's rejection of plural and proxy vestry voting had been both unjust and unwise. Taking power out of the hands of the large landlords, who were after all mainly responsible for providing the funds for poor relief, would lead to profligate and irresponsible expenditure. The franchise for the boards of guardians would correct this deficiency by introducing plural voting on a sliding property scale and by enabling non-resident landlords the same privileges as resident occupiers. Needless to say, this replication of the 1818 Sturges Bourne Act, and the changes that this would make to arrangements for appointing overseers of the poor, greatly antagonised the newly powerful metropolitan vestry radicals.

The St Marylebone vestry radical John Savage, for instance, condemned the measure as a 'repeal of the [Hobhouse's] Vestries Act ... it establishes

---

A. Digby, *Pauper palaces*, London 1978; F. Driver, *Power and pauperism*, Cambridge 1993; J. Knott, *Popular opposition to the 1834 poor law*, London 1986; M. E. Rose, 'The anti-poor law movement in the north of England', *Northern History* i (1966), 70–91, and 'The anti-poor law agitation', in T. J. Ward (ed.), *Popular movements, 1830–1851*, London 1970, 78–94; A. Brundage, *The making of the new poor law: the politics of inquiry, enactment, and implementation, 1832–1839*, London 1978; and E. C. Midwinter, *Social administration in Lancashire, 1830–1860, poor law, public health, and police*, Manchester 1969. Metropolitan anti-poor law priorities are neatly summed up by the motto of the (fiercely anti-poor law) United Parishioners Society of St George, Southwark: 'low rates, no extravagant salaries, and mercy at least to the old poor'.
[104] *Vestryman and Metropolitan Parochial Gazette*, 5 July 1834, 43.
[105] Brundage, *England's Prussian minister*, 57.

Sturges Bourne's Act all over the kingdom', and a fellow vestryman claimed similarly that the Poor Law Amendment Bill 'was intended to supersede the vestries act'. In neighbouring St Pancras the ultra-radical Thomas Murphy claimed that 'the object of the Poor Law Amendment Bill was to destroy the power of the vestries'.[106] Radical vestry protests against the New Poor Law were often couched in constitutionalist language and drew heavily on a patriotic historical narrative of English liberty. The measure was attacked by metropolitan radicals as an inherently 'un-English', and sometimes explicitly 'French', corruption of the 'ancient' or 'Saxon' constitution. The radical Southwark anti-poor law campaigner John Day, for instance, roused his fellow parishioners by asking: 'let Englishmen, tax-payers, and ratepayers see how they are degraded under this new poor law, and say will they be content that this scheme of wholesale taxation without representation should continue any longer? And will they be satisfied that their lawful and ancient right to control the expenditure of their own funds shall be taken away forever?'[107] Other critics looked to the reformed vestries to lead the fight against the corruption of these ancient rights: 'Will the various parishes endure to have their rights smuggled away?', asked one vestry radical, only to answer emphatically:

> No, their past resistance is the best guarantee for their future opposition ... the parishioners of St. Marylebone, St. Pancras, and St. James were roused on former occasions to determined resistance; will they now be more supine? Oh no, they have tasted the bitterness of this French centralisation-mongery, and will never endure to have every vestige of power purloined by a designing and interested clique ... while there is still time, let me exhort every parish not yet under the thrall of the triumvirate, to adopt that excellent act already adopted by the parishes in our own borough, called Hobhouse's Act, and to omit no opportunity of offering that strenuous resistance which Englishmen have been ever ready to make, when they see invasion attempted on their own privileges and the rights of humanity[108]

By framing their fight in this way, London's vestry radicals managed thoroughly to politicise the issue. 'The question of local taxation', observed the journalist James Williamson Brooke, had become 'magnified into one of national liberty.'[109] Given the radical and democratic nature of these

---

106 *New Vestryman*, 3 May 1834; *Vestryman and Metropolitan Parochial Gazette*, 28 June 1834, 34, 29.

107 J. Day, *A few practical observations on the new poor law*, London 1838, 8.

108 *Marylebone Journal and Metropolitan Register of News, Politics, and Literature*, 22 Apr. 1837, 9.

109 Brooke, *Democrats of Marylebone*, 30.

critiques, Nicholas Edsall's claim that metropolitan opposition to the New Poor Law was 'led and supported almost exclusively by overseers and church-wardens in the dozens of small parishes threatened by administrative ration-alisation', and 'the work of men who had done well out of the Old Poor Law and were afraid of losing their income or their jobs', appears entirely unjusti-fied.[110] The geography of opposition to the measure also bears this out. Like Hobhouse's act, the New Poor Law was permissive rather than mandatory, and a number of metropolitan parishes voted to opt out of the act. Those parishes which chose to remain outside of the metropolitan poor law unions – a group which included St George, Hanover Square; St Giles and St George, Bloomsbury; St James, Westminster; St Marylebone; St Pancras; and St Leonard's, Shoreditch, and which contained roughly one third of London's entire population – were precisely those in which the vestry radical move-ment was strongest.[111]

Anti-poor law feeling ran particularly high in London during 1837 and 1838, as the St Pancras vestry engaged in a well publicised fight with the poor law commissioners over the vestry's right to opt out of the system. Meetings were held throughout London in support of St Pancras's right to keep its own overseer of the poor, and resolutions were passed condemning the commis-sioners and the entire system of Whig centralisation. A pan-metropolitan meeting held in January 1837, for instance, resolved that 'the extent of the powers vested in the commissioners are most arbitrary and unconstitutional; that the giving of votes to owners of property not occupiers is destructive of the principle of self-government; that the scale of voting is unjust, and the mode of voting by proxy is most vicious'.[112] The *Marylebone Journal and Metropolitan Register of News, Politics, and Literature*, meanwhile, held up the New Poor Law as proof that the Whigs 'have shown but a limited inclination to leave the great Act of Reform to its legitimate working'.[113] In this context, Hume and fellow radical collaborators on poor law reform were exceptionally

---

[110] Edsall, *The anti-poor law movement*, 137.

[111] St George, Southwark, became part of a Union, but eventually its anti-poor law lobby won control of its board of guardians and refused to co-operate with the Poor Law Commis-sioners: St George the Martyr, Correspondence ... with the Poor Law Commissioners, 19 Aug. 1835; 19, 25 Mar. 1836, PRO, London, MH12/12300. In 1836 (shortly before St Leonard's, Shoreditch, opted out of the poor law apparatus) the Commissioner Charles Mott noted that 'at St. George, Southwark and Shoreditch, the right working of the new system is doomed': Poor Law Commission, assistant commissioners' and inspectors' corre-spondence, 28 May 1836, MH32/56.

[112] *The Times*, 20 Jan. 1837, 3. For details of other parish meetings see *The Times*, 8 Sept. 1836; 4, 19, 23 Apr. 1836; 2, 3, 4, 7, 18, 22 Feb. 1837; 1, 8, 15, 17, 21 Mar. 1837.

[113] *Marylebone Journal*, 22 Apr. 1837, 1.

vulnerable. Others, however, profited from anti-poor law sentiment. During the 1837 election Thomas Wakley and D. W. Harvey, in particular, topped the polls in their respective constituencies by running virulently anti-Whig campaigns, and by continually advertising their hostility to the New Poor Law, which they characterised as an 'unconstitutional' and 'un-English' innovation. Both men had publicly rejected the New Poor Law, and argued for its repeal on the grounds that this would 'place power in the hands of the parishes of England, instead of the hands of three men residing in Somerset House'.[114] From 1834 Harvey had been under considerable pressure from his Southwark constituents (and especially from his fellow members of the United Parishioners Society) to remain opposed to Whiggery's 'centralising tendencies'.[115] In 1836 Harvey came good, securing for the radical St George's vestry churchwarden Charles Anderson a personal audience with Lord John Russell at which an anti-poor law memorial was presented to the leader of the Commons. The vestry radical John Day, meanwhile, confessed that his support for Harvey was founded on a shared antipathy to the New Poor Law.[116] This dynamic was mirrored in Wakley's relationship to the Householder's Parochial Union of St George and St Giles, Bloomsbury, the unflagging support of which Wakley rewarded in June 1836 with a bill for the mandatory extension of Hobhouse's act to all metropolitan parishes.[117] In February 1838 Wakley became a founding member of the Central Anti-Poor Law Association.[118]

In Marylebone, opposition to both the New Poor Law and Whig-Radicalism peaked in 1838, at the by-election occasioned by Whalley's forced resignation from the borough.[119] Thomas Murphy's ultra-radical call to arms determined to

> appeal to the radicals of the borough, and the opponents of the New Poor Law, convinced that the time had come when the radicals must cut all connection with the Whigs and the Whig-Radicals, look upon them as branches of the Tory faction, seeking with them to rob the people of their rights and liberties as well as their purses.[120]

114 *London Mercury*, 30 July 1837, 663.
115 *The Times*, 10 Aug. 1836, 5; 24 Nov. 1836, 6; *London Mercury*, 6 Aug. 1837, 674
116 *The Times*, 21 Oct. 1836, 4. Day expressed his appreciation at Harvey's retirement: *The Times*, 25 Feb. 1839, 3.
117 *Hansard* 3rd ser. xxxiv.746–54, 22 June 1836.
118 *The Times*, 10 Feb. 1838, 6.
119 Whalley was unseated in 1838 after failing to prove that he possessed the requisite property qualification to sit in parliament.
120 Murphy, *Address to the radicals of the United Kingdom*, 16.

Hume's support for the Whig-Radical candidate William Ewart was contrasted to D. W. Harvey's championing of Colonel T. P. Thompson. Murphy, meanwhile, described the contest simply as one between 'a radical, a repealer of the New Poor Law ... [and] ... a Whig-Radical, an avowed supporter of the despotic principles of that atrocious act'.[121] Although Ewart described himself as an 'independent', and had come out forcefully against the church rates, he had committed an unpardonable sin by supporting the New Poor Law. Ewart's support for the measure was quickly and unambiguously portrayed by borough radicals as latent Whiggery. 'Mr. Ewart supported the Whig government in all their atrocious outrages upon the liberties of the people', claimed Murphy on the hustings, 'and when he went into the House of Commons, he went in as an avowed supporter of the Whigs.'[122] The ultra-radicals only required that Thompson swear that he bore 'a hatred and detestation of all centralisation of power' and he was given their unwavering support.[123] In Westminster, George DeLacy Evans also suffered for his cosying up to Lord John Russell. He had been lambasted as 'no better than a Whig' in the pages of *The Spectator* and identified as a 'Whig-Radical non-representative' by *The Times* in 1837, but had salvaged some popularity by coming out strongly in opposition to the New Poor Law.[124] Consequently, he retained his seat in 1837, although he lost some radical support to J. T. Leader, the romantic and charismatic associate of Lovett and Hetherington and an equally staunch critic of the Whig tendency to 'centralisation'. The new assistant poor law commissioner, James Kay, understandably reported in January 1839 that London 'is distinguished from every other district with which I am acquainted by a greater jealousy of central authority'.[125]

The elections of 1837 and 1838 marked a watershed in the development of metropolitan liberalism from a culture of Whiggish constitutionalism to one of retrenchment-obsessed anti-Whiggery. As the defeats of Hume and Ewart show, by the late 1830s it was not enough for radicals merely to support the traditional radical platform of expanded suffrage, triennial parliaments, the abolition of taxes on knowledge and the repeal of the church rates. Unless these pledges were accompanied by one to uphold the principle of local self-government, metropolitan radicals could not be assured of the support of radical communities. The fact that even Joseph Hume, perhaps the most effective and committed of all the metropolitan radicals, could be turned out

---

[121] Ibid, 17.
[122] *The Times*, 2 Mar. 1838, 5.
[123] Ibid.
[124] *The Spectator*, 28 Jan. 1837, 86; *The Times*, 3 July 1837, 4.
[125] Poor Law Commission, assistant commissioners' and inspectors' correspondence, 14 Jan. 1839, PRO, MH 32/50.

because of his co-operation with the Whig government on the New Poor Law illustrated a fundamental shift in London's radical culture – from a position of relative moderation and co-operation with Whiggery to one of outright hostility and resistance. Most important, it signified the arrival of a new force in the metropolitan radical agenda – the cry for 'local self-government' and the language of retrenchment.

Writing in 1844 one metropolitan radical reflected on the momentous events of the early 1830s and meditated on the effect that these had had upon the transformation of London's political culture. Little mention was made of parliamentary reform:

> In 1830, when men in England were generally expecting great political changes, one of the most practical and sagacious of our public men was reproached by his friends that he did not join them in the discussion of the constitutional questions then in agitation. His reply is very nearly our text – 'let me have the legislating for the parish; I leave to the boys in the debating societies the remodeling of our constitution.' Few persons will readily acquiesce in his conclusion; for comparatively few are aware of the vast extent of interests immediately involved in local government ... those, however, who are practically aware of these facts know, at the same time, that the great offices of the Home government, with the exception of the judiciary, are stations, comparatively, of idle show; and that when their occupiers are actively engaged, it is rather in parliamentary warfare than in the administration of civil government ... the more this fact is considered, the more it will become apparent that the real government of the country is carried out by functionaries themselves obscure and unobserved, but the aggregate of whose duties vastly exceeds those of the central government.[126]

---

[126] *The Municipal and Poor Law Gazette and Local Functionary*, 13 Jan. 1844, 1.

3

The Polarisation of Metropolitan Political Culture, 1842–1855

At the fall of Melbourne's second government, vestry reformers still wielded significant electoral influence in the metropolitan boroughs. In Marylebone, the Barlow Street committee, although smarting from the 1838 by-election return of the Tory Lord Teignmouth, was still powerful enough in 1841 to engineer the return of its preferred candidate, Admiral Sir Charles Napier. Like Duncombe, Tennyson and so many of his fellow metropolitan MPs, Napier cut an aristocratic and romantic figure. In addition to a reputation for military heroism (at sea rather than on land – Napier was sometimes mistaken for his namesake, the conqueror of the Sind, whose own military 'heroism' is commemorated with a bronze statue in Trafalgar Square), Napier possessed a clutch of honorary titles. He was, for instance, a Knight Commander of the Bath, a Knight of the Tower and Sword in Portugal, a Knight of St George in Russia, a Knight of Maria Teresa in Austria, and a Knight of the Red Eagle in Prussia.[1] Unlike Tennyson and Duncombe, however, Napier was far from an out-and-out political radical. Although he vigorously advocated the protection and extension of vestry rights and powers, Napier could not, for instance, bring himself to endorse either universal suffrage or annual parliaments. Under the protection and guidance of the Barlow Street committee, he instead promoted a programme of government retrenchment through tax and trade reform while offering lukewarm support for moderate political reform. As Napier's example suggests, whereas retrenchment and 'local self-government' had once been understood by the vestry reformers as a means to the larger end of parliamentary reform, by 1841 'local self-government' was fast becoming a great end in itself.

Although Napier's Marylebone victory confirmed the survival of vestry radical influence, 1841 was nevertheless a year of setbacks for Hobhouse's

---

[1] N. Williams, *The life and letters of Admiral Sir Charles Napier, K.C.B.*, London 1917, 214.

children. The first blow came during the run-up to the 1841 general election, when D. W. Harvey's decision to vacate his seat in order to become Commissioner of Police for the City of London deprived Southwark's vestry radicals of their parliamentary mouthpiece. Harvey's replacement, Benjamin Wood – brother of the City radical hero Alderman Wood, was significantly less popular among Southwark's vestry reformers. His reluctance to denounce the New Poor Law alienated many borough radicals from his campaign and split the Southwark Reform Association between those who could overlook Wood's Whig-Radicalism and those who could not. In the immediate wake of the split, John Walter, proprietor of *The Times* and strong opponent of 'Whig centralisation', took his opportunity to stand for the borough as a 'Tory radical'.[2] Charles Anderson and John Day, among other prominent members of the SRA, were vigorously courted by Walter's election committee. Although Anderson could not bring himself to support either Wood or Walter, John Day threw his full support behind Walter.[3]

In Westminster, DeLacy Evans's conduct created similar problems for the borough's vestry radicals. Although Evans was more popular than Wood and more fully committed to the promotion of 'local self-government' – indeed his strong opposition to the New Poor Law enabled him to fend off all accusations of Whig-Radicalism and endeared him to the St James vestry radicals – his frequent absences from both the borough and parliament (required, it must be said, by his duties as a major-general) upset many of his supporters, particularly those who demanded his regular attendance at vestry meetings. By 1837 the relationship between Evans and his radical constituents had been severely damaged, forcing Evans to confide in Palmerston that, after a long absence in the Basque country, he was almost too embarrassed to show his face in Westminster, 'without doing which I fear I shall lose my seat and (what I am more vexed about) gives just grounds of offence to my indulgent constituents'.[4] Four years later, Evans had fallen so completely from grace with these constituents that he lost his seat to the Tory military man Henry John Rous.

Losses in Southwark and Westminster were accompanied by the inability of vestry radicalism to make inroads in Tower Hamlets, which continued in its support of Whiggery by replacing the retiring Whig placeman Stephen Lushington with Charles Richard Fox, first son of the late 3rd Baron Holland and surveyor-general in Melbourne's second government. Throughout the Tower Hamlets election campaign, Fox's committee repeatedly advertised

---

2 *The Times*, 10 Jan. 1840, 6.
3 Ibid. 23 Jan. 1840, 5.
4 George DeLacy Evans to Palmerston, 4 Jan. 1837, Palmerston papers, GC/EV/25, fo. 2.

their candidate's Whig credentials and lineage. At a meeting of electors in Whitechapel, for instance, those in attendance were reminded of the great accomplishments of Fox's 'illustrious' father and uncle, while at a meeting in Hackney one week later the event chairman initiated proceedings by reminding the assembled crowd that Fox

> was descended from a family well known and highly respected, and who had stood forward and dared to be honest in the worst of times, who were always the zealous advocates of civil and religious liberty, and whose high and patriotic characters would, he thought, be in some measure a guarantee to the electors for the faithful and honest discharge of his duties if sent to parliament – of the descendant of the House of Holland![5]

Whereas Fox's return was interpreted by Lady Holland as a popular triumph of Foxite ideals, *The Times* rather less charitably characterised Fox's victory as evidence that the Tower Hamlets had become nothing more than a 'Whig rotten borough'.[6]

Towards a metropolitan social reform movement

Although Rous's Westminster return, Harvey's Southwark defection and Fox's Tower Hamlets triumph were setbacks for the vestry radicals, the greatest challenge to vestry radical authority and influence came in July 1842 with the publication of Edwin Chadwick's *Report on the sanitary condition of the labouring population of Great Britain*. The investigations which informed Chadwick's *Report* were prompted by the coldly pragmatic, and ultimately accurate, suspicion that poor public health was responsible for keeping rates 'unnaturally' and unsustainably high. Put simply, Chadwick believed that dirt caused disease, which in turn resulted in dependency, which in turn led to ever increasing levels of public aid.[7] Consequently, the *Report* made five

---

[5]   Lady Holland to Henry Holland, 2 July 1841, *Lady Holland to her son, 1780–1880*, 193. *The Times*, 10 June 1841, 6; 17 June 1841, 6.
[6]   *The Times*, 5 July 1841, 4.
[7]   Chadwick's thinking was heavily informed by two earlier investigations into the nature and causes of ill health in the most impoverished neighbourhoods of London's 'east end': Neil Arnott and James Kay, 'On the prevalence of certain physical causes of fever in the metropolis, which might be removed by proper sanitary measures', in *Fourth annual report of the poor law commissioners*, London 1838, 103–53, and Southwood Smith, 'On some of the physical causes of sickness and mortality to which the poor are particularly exposed, and which are capable of removal by sanitary regulations', in *Fifth annual report of the poor law commissioners*, London 1839, 160–71.

central arguments. A lengthy opening section (especially chapters i, ii and iv) aimed to correlate insanitation, defective drainage, inadequate water supply and overcrowded housing, with disease, high mortality rates and low life expectancy. This first section was counterbalanced by a lengthy chapter vi, in which Chadwick detailed the advantages to be gained when employers and landlords provided sanitary workplaces and dwellings for their employees and tenants. Employers who behaved as benevolent patriarchs, argued Chadwick, were more likely to profit from a well-behaved, healthy and productive workforce. Over the course of only twenty pages chapter v quickly detailed the economic repercussions of poor public health, while chapters iii and viii exposed, to great effect, the social cost of squalor, particularly the many ways in which squalor damaged public morality. Here Chadwick made an unequiv-ocal statement on the causal link between poorly constructed, unhealthy and inadequate housing, on the one hand, and intemperance, immorality and disease on the other. Chapter vii, meanwhile, detailed the inherent ineffi-ciency of the existing local administrative and governmental machinery, and argued that the public health could only be improved through radical admin-istrative overhaul. Each of the *Report*'s five main themes: (1) the correlation of poverty, squalor and death; (2) paternal obligation to tenants and employees; (3) the economic consequences of squalor; (4) the moral conse-quences of squalor; and (5) the administrative underpinnings of squalor, were powerful and singular condemnations of existing social and administrative conditions. Taken together, they constituted a comprehensive and devas-tating analysis of urban suffering.

Although many of the *Report*'s arguments were made through statistical comparison and analysis, it was neither dry, nor inaccessible, nor even a 'spe-cialist' document. Many of its most important passages were highly emotive, and most of its charts and statistical comparisons were easily accessible to a wide public audience.[8] The *Report* conveyed its statistical and technical evidence, for instance, in novel and highly engaging ways, including the use of 'sanitary maps' of places such as Bethnal Green and Liverpool in which black crosses (signifying high death rates) crowded thickly in the poorest and most densely populated areas. Beyond these grim geographies of death, the *Report* was very effective at spelling out the high economic and social costs of ill health. Chadwick argued that Britain's existing urban administrative apparatus was not sufficiently sophisticated to prevent poor public health,

---

[8] For a sample chart in which the life expectancy of poor labourers in Bethnal Green is compared, with devastating effect, to that of poor labourers in rural Rutland and Manchester see E. Chadwick, *Report on the sanitary condition of the labouring population of Great Britain*, ed. M. W. Finn, Edinburgh 1965, 154–61, 223.

and that the existing legal system was incapable of redressing the social problems occasioned by poor public health. Many of the 'centralising' administrative solutions proposed by Chadwick in his *Report* in fact owed a great debt of inspiration to the work of continental medical reformers such as Villerme, Mohler and Liebig.[9] Indeed, at the very heart of the *Report* lurked the very forceful suggestion that only a unified and centralised public health infrastructure (and especially one run by trained 'experts' according to 'scientific' principles), could save the public health, and purse, from the existing system of local meanness, incompetence and corruption.[10] Vestry government had been placed squarely in a Benthamite vice.

Chadwick's investigations and proposals informed a wide spectrum of British opinion and shocked many readers whose only previous glimpse of urban slum life had come through the humorous caricatures found in Egan's *London life* and Bee's *Living picture of London*, or by way of the fleeting, often moralistic and artificially theatrical, glimpses provided by 'middle-class' literature such as *Sketches By Boz*.[11] According to R. A. Lewis, the 'first great service' of Chadwick's *Report* was to

> dispel by the hard light of its revelations the darkness of ignorance which hid from bourgeois eyes the domestic condition of the workers. The lanes and alleys of the poor … the rookeries of St Giles, Villiers Square, and Golden Square, were as remote from the experience and imagination of the great majority of the middle and upper-classes as some Punjab village or South African kraal.[12]

In addition to the massive amount of attention given to the *Report* in the

---

9   Finer, *Life of Chadwick*, 209–10.

10 See especially Chadwick, *Report*, 380–96.

11 Deborah Epstein Nord has argued that Dickens's *Sketches*, like Egan's *London life*, ultimately distanced their middle-class readerships from the harsh realities of slum life by continually lapsing into comic theatricality and romanticism. The 'seven dials' section of the *Sketches*, the only point at which Dickens's ventures into the slum world, is a good example. According to Nord, 'far from convincing his readers that this, like Newgate, is a real place, he [Dickens] offers them a benign stage performance and the entertaining world of squalor, which Cruikshank captures in his accompanying illustration of scrapping slum women': *Walking the Victorian streets: women, representation, and the city*, London 1995, 50–66. One is reminded of Tom and Jerry's visit to the 'All–Max' gin haunt in *London life*, a scene which was also memorably illustrated by Cruikshank, and which ends in comical brawling.

12 Lewis, *Edwin Chadwick*, 46–7. S. E. Finer, meanwhile, notes that the *Report* 'burst on a startled middle-class public. Its immediate success was electric': *Life of Chadwick*, 209. For further discussion of the *Report*'s impact on middle Britain see D. Owen, *English philanthropy, 1660–1960*, London 1965, 374.

newspaper media, Chadwick also arranged to have the *Report* published in quarto form. This ensured that its evidence and conclusions would reach as wide an audience as possible; indeed Chadwick himself claimed that more than 20,000 copies of this quarto edition had been purchased by 24 July (just two weeks after its initial publication).[13] Harriet Martineau, meanwhile, believed that the *Report*'s 'private influence' would be almost as great as any prospective legislation.[14]

Martineau was prescient. The *Report* did generate as much, if not more, interest among private citizens as it did among public figures. In the wake of its publication, a thatch of societies and associations were established in London by men and women who had been touched by Chadwick's research. Initially, such organisations tended to exhibit purely philanthropic, rather than political, characters. The Metropolitan Visiting and Relief Association, for example, was founded in December 1843 as a direct consequence of Chadwick's *Report*.[15] Its mission was both philanthropic and 'evangelical', as it sought to improve London's religious and moral health while also enabling sanitary and other social improvements. The association responded to the *Report*'s call for renewed paternalist responsibility by encouraging its wealthy and socially prominent members (including Lord Ashley, the marquis of Westminster and Thomas Baring) to 'promote kindly feelings between those classes of society which are kept so far asunder by the difference of their worldly conditions'.[16] The Metropolitan Association for Improving the Dwellings of the Industrious Classes, meanwhile, ignored London's spiritual shortcomings and focused instead purely on remedying the physical barriers to working-class social progress. Like the Visiting and Relief Association, MAIDIC had been inspired into life by chapter vi of Chadwick's *Report*, which implored landlords, employers and other patricians to honour their social obligations to tenants, employees and various other 'dependants'. The *Report* claimed, for instance, that

> the only conspicuous instances of improved residences of the labouring classes found in the rural districts are those which have been erected by opulent and benevolent landlords for the accommodation of the labourers of their own estates; and in the manufacturing districts, those erected by wealthy manufac-

---

13 Edwin Chadwick to Brougham, 24 July 1842, Sir Edwin Chadwick papers, Special Collections, University College London, 378.

14 Harriet Martineau to Edwin Chadwick, n.d., ibid. 1362.

15 Owen, *English philanthropy*.

16 Metropolitan Association for Promoting the Relief of Destitution and for Improving the Condition of the Poor, by Means of Parochial and District Visiting, *First annual report*, London 1844, 1.

turers for the accommodation of their own work-people. As in England, so in Scotland, the most important improvements have been effected through enlightened landlords.[17]

Urban life, Chadwick argued, had corrupted and impaired the natural bond between the landlord and his dependant. During the early 1840s MAIDIC attempted to re-forge these 'organic' social bonds by building labourers' housing blocks in St Pancras and Bethnal Green. Each of these blocks was named after a prominent MAIDIC benefactor.[18]

Although MAIDIC and the Visiting and Relief Association had been inspired by the *Report*'s call for paternal reinvestment in the lives of the urban poor, neither organisation incorporated this paternalism into any sort of political agenda. Yet Chadwick's *Report* was a thoroughly political document, and it was as a political call-to-arms that organisations such as the Health of Towns Association read it. According to its first address, HOTA was formed

> for the purpose of diffusing among the people the information obtained by recent enquiries, as to the physical and moral evils that result from the present defective sewerage, drainage, supply of water, air, and light, and the construction of dwelling houses: *and also for the purpose of assisting the legislature to carry into practical operation any effectual and general measures of relief, by preparing the public mind for the change.*[19]

Among Chadwick's biographers, much has been made of HOTA's political bi-partisanship (i.e. its mixed, 'Whig' and 'Tory' membership), although little mention has been made of the fact that HOTA's 'bi-partisan' membership was drawn from the paternalist and interventionist wings of both 'parties'.[20] Whigs such as Russell, Morpeth, Grosvenor, Ebrington might indeed have rubbed shoulders with the Tory likes of Ashley, Disraeli and Lord John Manners, but both Peelites and liberals were noticeably absent from HOTA's membership. Moreover HOTA's most active and influential members (Lord Robert Grosvenor and Lord Morpeth, for instance) were key originators of social policy in Russell's first ministry. By the time of HOTA's merger into the Metropolitan Sanitary Association in early 1849, it had become an almost completely Russellite organisation. With the arch-Russellite Lord

---

[17] Chadwick, *Report*, 233.

[18] *Charter of incorporation of the Metropolitan Association for the Improvement of the Dwellings of the Industrious Classes*, London 1845, and *Supplemental charter*, London 1850.

[19] Health of Towns Association, *Abstract of proceedings of a public meeting, held at Exeter Hall, 11 December, 1844*, London 1844, 1.

[20] See, for instance, Finer, *Life of Chadwick*, 238–9.

Robert Grosvenor at its head, MSA used its *First report* to announce a commitment to Chadwick's original vision of a rationalised, centralised and interventionist sanitary administration for all of London:

> under such an authority, competent officers, now employed under the district commissions, would at once act with confidence, in the exercise of an increased and efficient power, and submit views of detailed measures of relief or prevention which might be speedily tested, and if found efficient, would be immediately put into operation *throughout* the whole of the metropolis. They could, without confusion as to districts, make early agreements with several water companies for the necessary supplies of water.[21]

Given this agenda, MSA was unstintingly critical of London's parochially administered system of local government. The reformed vestries, MSA claimed, were 'composed for the most part of a small number of individuals belonging to the middle classes ... [and] are pervaded by private and sinister interests of all sorts, opposed to the interests of the public, and particularly to the well being of the lower classes'.[22] Chadwick, still in 1849 the motivating force behind MSA, himself strongly agreed with this assessment, claiming in a letter to Delane that:

> the small landlords whose houses require drainage work are the most active opposers of sanitary measures in the Common Council, and they are the same in the other parishes. The declaration of the speculators that the Public Health Bill was a great humbug, was the sentiment that was cheered in the Common Council. The question is however not whether money shall be expended without representation but whether the great minorities as well as the majority of the inhabitants of the metropolis will not have more responsible representation through Parliament than through a parochial parliament. In the metropolis, we think the former responsibility will really be the greater, of which the example of the City municipality appears the decisive evidence. The natural interests of the metropolis are moreover we think more fully respected in the national assembly than in any such body as that which the vestrymen propose ... personally, I have no other interest in the question than that of seeing sanitary measures executed. But the metropolitan parochial boards and parochial representation are equally fatal to any systematic progress.[23]

---

[21] MSA, *First report of the commissioners*, London 1847, 24.
[22] MSA, 'Considerations as to house and town drainage', 9; Chadwick papers, 54.
[23] Chadwick to John Thadeus Delane, 27 Nov. 1850, ibid. 608, fos 58–60.

From the mid-1840s Charles Cochrane's National Philanthropic Association, which, despite its name, was a wholly metropolitan organisation, joined HOTA in its crusade for better public health and established the political critique of London's 'self-interested' vestry shopocrats which MSA would later take up. Like HOTA and MSA, the leadership of NPA was dominated by paternalist social elites. Early vice-presidents included the duke of Grafton, the earl of Devon, Lord John Russell, Lord Robert Grosvenor and the bishop of Durham.[24] In 1844 NPA established formal links with HOTA, and in the following years it helped to establish metropolitan Russellite reform organisations such as the Health of London Association, the Westminster Sanitary Committee, the Lambeth Anti-Cholera and Dwellings Improvement Committee and the St Pancras Committee for Improving the Dwellings of the Poor. Through these organisations the NPA regularly castigated vestry radicals for making political capital out of human suffering. The association claimed, for instance, that working men had been 'taught to trace all their misfortunes to Political mismanagement!' If their 'homes were uncomfortable, the towns in which they resided unhealthy, – their social condition in a backward state', claimed the association, then

> the Government or Legislature was invariably blamed and considered responsible: – it scarcely ever entered their imaginations, that these were objects entirely under their own control! It may here be stated that under the peculiar Constitution of our Country, the welfare of the People is committed principally to the charge of municipal and [in London to] parochial authorities, who have ample powers to regulate the social state of the community: – but, curiously enough, whilst these authorities have lamentably neglected their duties, we have been indebted entirely to the government and Legislature for repairing such negligence.[25]

In contrast to the spite heaped upon London's inactive 'parochial authorities', HOTA was showered with compliments. 'Their labours', proclaimed NPA, 'have led to the public being made aware of the vital importance of sanitary improvements; and to the passing of important Acts of Parliament, which place at the command of Householders and Lodgers a large amount of power to remedy the evils arising from parochial and municipal indifference.'[26]

---

[24] For membership lists see NPA, *Report of the National Philanthropic Association (instituted March, 1842) for the promotion of social and sanitary improvements and the employment of the poor*, London 1847.
[25] NPA, *Sanitary progress: being the fifth report of the NPA*, London 1850, 1–2. See also C. Cochrane, *An address to the business-like men of Westminster on their present candidates*, London 1847.
[26] NPA, *Sanitary progress*, 2.

Professionals, the Chadwickian programme and Whiggery in London, 1841–52

The Chadwickean reform agenda promoted by organisations such as HOTA and MSA appealed enormously to the metropolitan professional middle class. The appeal was two-pronged. First, the Chadwickean programme exploited elements of philanthropic culture, which boomed in the years following the publication of Chadwick's *Report* and which were promoted with particular vigour by high-order professionals such as physicians, barristers clerics and members of metropolitan literary bohemia – a group that Harold Perkin once characterised as 'ready made social crank[s] who could be relied on to come to the aid of any class but their own'.[27] For many of these professionals, susceptibility to philanthropic culture translated easily into support for Chadwick's, and later Russell's, attempts at 'state paternalism' through administrative centralisation. Consequently, at the height of the agitation against the Public Health Bill in 1847, Howitt's *People's Journal*, an important articulator of professional values and mentalities, declared that

> there must be a system of centralisation, combining the freedom from petty and sectarian interests, and intelligent superintendence of a central authority, with the administrative energy and aptitude of local boards ... we shall hear much of centralisation, the rights of property, of vested interests, and so forth; but we must trust that there is sense enough in the people of England to explode these follies and fallacies, to drown these selfish cries in a louder cry for health and life.[28]

The Chadwickean reform agenda did indeed facilitate the rise of an 'expert' bureaucracy – an administrative innovation that held special appeal for 'lower order' professionals such as surgeons, who by the mid-nineteenth century were fighting hard for professional recognition.[29] Consequently, the *Lancet*, for instance, is to be found endorsing Russell's early sanitary reform programme explicitly on the basis that it aimed to utilise medical expertise.[30] The metropolitan civil engineer Henry Austin supported the work of the

---

[27] Perkin, *Origins*, 256–7. See also G. Stedman Jones, *Outcast London: a study in the relationship between classes in Victorian society*, Oxford 1971, 268–9.
[28] *People's Journal* iii (17 Apr. 1847), 218–19. *Punch* promoted a similar position, and its individual editors and writers promoted sanitary reform from the pages of publications such as *London life and the London poor* and Dicken's 'Our vestry'.
[29] M. J. Peterson, *The medical profession in mid-Victorian London*, London 1978, 284–7.
[30] See *Lancet* i (1848), 216, 169.

Chadwickean Society for the Promotion of Metropolitan Improvements for precisely the same reason, confessing in a *Westminster Review* piece his hope that 'the proper authorities' would soon be enabled to take metropolitan sanitation in hand on 'some good and *broad* principle'.[31]

From 1846 professional support for the Chadwickean reform programme translated into significant electoral support for Russellite Whiggery within the metropolitan constituencies. Early Victorian London contained more doctors, lawyers and journalists than the rest of the country put together, and was the undisputed centre of the Anglo professional world.[32] By 1851 nearly 30 per cent of all professionals employed in England and Wales (or 84,738 in gross numbers) was employed in London.[33] Moreover, as home to the Inns of Court, the Royal Collages, the great teaching hospitals and central government, London was also the institutional nerve centre of the professional world. Peter Earle has estimated that as much as one-third of the early Georgian metropolitan middle-class was composed of professionals. A century later, professionals accounted for a slightly lower proportion of the expanding metropolitan middle-class, but wielded perhaps even more social and political clout.[34] From 1832 'the new London Gentry', as Gareth Stedman Jones memorably called London's mid-Victorian professional community, began to exercise a particularly strong influence over metropolitan electoral politics.[35] The Webb Street and London University 'medical electorate', to take just one metropolitan professional subgroup, was able almost on its own to ensure the legislative success of Chadwick's sanitary reforms.[36]

In London, this 'medical electorate' organised itself and spread its political message through societies such as the Health of London Association and the MSA, fully one-third of whose lay, non-titled membership was composed of medical practitioners of some description.[37] Indeed, it is little wonder, in light of professional interest in the Chadwickean reform agenda, that sceptics

---

[31] H. Austin, *Metropolitan improvements*, London 1842, 2. See also *Westminster Review* lxxi (Oct., 1842).

[32] P. Corfield, *Power and the professions on Britain, 1700–1850*, London 1995.

[33] Schwarz, *London in the age of industrialisation*, 4, 263.

[34] P. Earle, *The making of the English middle-class: business, society and family in London, 1600–1730*, London 1989, 60. In 1851 professionals made up around 6% of the entire metropolitan labour force. See also Schwarz, *London in the age of industrialisation*, 23.

[35] Stedman Jones, *Outcast London*, 269.

[36] A. Desmond, *The politics of evolution: morphology, medicine, and reform in radical London*, Chicago 1989, 27, 163–4.

[37] See, for instance, the membership list attached to MSA, *Public health a public question: first report of the Metropolitan Sanitary Association on the Sanitary Condition of the Metropolis*, London 1850. The council membership of the NPA was also dominated by medical practitioners.

often described HOTA, MSA and like-minded organisations as being dominated by a 'coterie of patientless doctors, briefless barristers, and better employed engineers'.[38] The example of the aural surgeon Joseph Toynbee is indicative of the ways in which such organisations politicised their professional memberships and by so doing created extensive and influential metropolitan support networks for the first Russell government's legislative programme of administrative centralisation. Before joining MSA in 1845, Toynbee had been an enthusiastic, if politically apathetic, supporter of organisations such as the National Philanthropic Association and the Metropolitan Association for Ventilation for the Poor. In his engagements with these organisations, Toynbee confessed that he worked merely to 'confer a good deal of happiness ... on the labouring classes', but not to effect any kind of legislative implementation of the wider Chadwickean reform programme.[39] In 1845 Toynbee joined the executive committee of the Society for Improving the Conditions of the Labouring Classes and in the same year he became a general committee-member of both the Health of Towns Association and the Metropolitan Sanitary Association. In the following year, he became treasurer of the Metropolitan Association for the Improvement of the Dwellings of the Industrious Classes, in which capacity he began to work closely with Lord Morpeth.

From this point on Toynbee's philanthropy became strongly politicised, and when Morpeth introduced his Chadwickean Public Health Bill in March 1847, Toynbee threw all of his weight behind it.[40] He believed Morpeth's bill to be a 'very comprehensive one', and revealed further the extent to which his involvement in social reform had been politicised by warning that while the bill would 'do great good ... if it passes; it will no doubt create great opposition in interested parties, but we must break it down'.[41] In the wake of the bill's passage through parliament, Toynbee confessed to finding Chadwick's appointment to the Board of Health a source of 'great satisfaction'.[42] At around this time Toynbee began to characterise the radical cry for 'local self-government' as a self-interested ruse used by the shopocracy to keep rates

[38] R. Braun, *Extramural interment and the Metropolitan Sanitary Association*, London 1852, 10.

[39] Joseph Toynbee to Charles Toynbee, 1 Mar. 1844, Toynbee family papers, Bodl. Lib., MS Eng.lett.c.535, fo. 1.

[40] It is a measure of Toynbee's politicisation that he hoped that the public health movement would weaken Chartism: J. Toynbee to Chadwick, 25 Apr. 1846, Chadwick papers 1981, fo. 6.

[41] J. Toynbee to Arnold Toynbee, 30 Mar. 1847, Toynbee papers, MS Eng.lett.c.535, fo. 6b.

[42] J. Toynbee to Chadwick, 3 Oct., 1848, Chadwick papers 1981, fo. 8.

low, whatever the social costs. Toward the end of his life, he recalled with regret how a fundamentally middle-class commercialist 'anti-centralisation' lobby had blinded working men to their true interests. Speaking of the radical rebellion against the Russellite social reform programme, Toynbee claimed that

> after blandly smiling at all our commissions, committees, lectures, evidence, speeches, books, and statistics, which showed the evils arising from defective sanitary legislation John Bull suddenly became alarmed ... so he jumped up, cudgel in hand, beating about him right and left, and of course threw blame on the wrong parties.[43]

But Toynbee's support for Russell's centralising legislation was in its own way also inspired by self-interest. Toynbee hoped, for instance, that his tireless advancement of the Chadwickean programme from within organisations such as the MSA, the medical expertise which he had lent to these organisations and his public defence of Russell's government in the face of the radical onslaught, would be repaid with bureaucratic appointments to whatever sanitary authorities Russell's government might establish.[44] During the mid-1840s this same expectation was widespread among lower order professionals, who looked forward to the creation of a civil service based on merit and specialised knowledge rather than social connections. In London, no Chadwickean organisation embodied this expectation more fully than the Health of London Association, which explicitly and repeatedly advertised its professional character by claiming to speak on behalf of London's surgeons, solicitors, architects and surveyors, and which benefitted from the uncompromising Benthamite leadership of Thomas Southwood Smith, R. A. Grainger and Henry Austin. Although the HLA admired the work carried out by MSA and HOTA, it none the less 'considered that the idea of endeavouring to obtain the sentiments and opinions of that portion of the public who were, from their professions or avocations, best fitted to afford information, had not been sufficiently carried out'.[45]

In 1847 the HLA issued a report which claimed to represent the opinions of more than 3,000 professionals from across the metropolis on how London's existing sanitary provision, and the network of local government which

---

[43] J. Toynbee, *The breath of life and the breath of death and a people without a country*, London 1866, 4.

[44] G. Toynbee (ed.), *Reminiscences and letters of Joseph and Arnold Toynbee*, London n.d., 18.

[45] HTA, *Report of the Health of London Association, on the sanitary condition of the metropolis*, London 1847, p. ix.

provided it, ought to be reformed. The report's conclusions, which were drawn from an extensive survey of professional opinion, were a ringing endorsement of the Russell government's policy of administrative centralisation and a stinging condemnation of metropolitan vestry government, which the report suggested should be replaced by a centrally administered 'council of health' to preside over London's water provision, sewerage and waste collection. The professional respondents to the Association's survey 'universally declared', claimed the report,

> to be essentially necessary for the benefit of the community at large that such a central board be constituted ... many express their surprise that government has never yet instituted such a council, or that the philanthropic portion of the public has not insisted on it ... sanitary measures, in order to be effectual, must be carried out on a large scale; and unless the Legislature gives encouragement to public bodies to carry out efficient measures for sanitary improvements, they will never be effectually promoted, for it is impossible for private contractors to undertake very extensive works. The powers invested in the various existing commissions are wholly inadequate for the purpose of promoting the public health. The legislature should encourage sanitary improvements in every possible way, either by giving more power to the existing boards, controlled by a central board, or by creating new powers.[46]

The report's conclusions illustrate both the widespread support which Russell's first government enjoyed among London's lower order professionals and the very low view which this professional community took of London's system of vestry government. At the same time, they also suggest that while professional support for the Chadwickean programme may have been motivated by a desire to improve the living conditions of London's poor, it was also inspired in no small measure by the expectation that such as programme would establish a centralised bureaucracy of specialists which might reward their particular expertise. From the later 1840s, the professional endorsement of Russellite policies for administrative centralisation helped to create an increasingly bifurcated metropolitan political culture, the central dyad of which was composed of interventionist, statist professionals on the one hand and retrenchment-minded artisans and traders on the other.

[46] Ibid. 22, 63.

The 1847 general election

At the same time that the Russellite social reform programme inspired and organised professional critics of metropolitan vestry government, it also, quite unintentionally, revived and gave new purpose to the nearly moribund metropolitan vestry radical movement by providing a succession of new measures of 'Whig centralisation' for it to rally and unite against. The vestry radical movement had been nearly dormant since losing the parliamentary advocacy of D. W. Harvey and Samuel Whalley in 1840. Peel's curtailment of poor law proxy and plural voting in 1844 further enfeebled the movement by removing two of its motivating grievances. In 1847, however, a rejuvenated metropolitan vestry radical movement began to coalesce around opposition to Russell's public health and education policies, and began once again to promote the virtues of 'local self-government' and voluntarism as libertarian alternatives. Moreover, the revived movement emphasised the continuities between the Whig legislation of 1834 and the new round of Whig 'centralising' legislation. The *Ratepayer or London Borough of Lambeth ... Journal* asked its readers, for instance, whether

> the usurpations and asperities of that first memorable specimen of centralisation – the original poor law – been forgotten? Are the labours, the toils, the unceasing devotion of those who directed their skill, position, and talents to destroy those usurpations, to remove those asperities, and to redress these grievances become lost to memory, and been buried in oblivion?[47]

Although the revived movement also endorsed a considerable series of political reforms, its libertarian agenda was dominated by the promotion of administrative and economic retrenchment rather than further political reform.

Charles Pearson's 1847 electoral triumph in Lambeth neatly advertises the voluntarist, yet politically moderate, priorities of the rejuvenated metropolitan radical movement. Although Pearson has been described as an 'uncompromising radical', his commitment to political reform was not as strong as such a description might suggest.[48] Pearson's overriding interest lay in tax reform and government retrenchment, and his views on franchise reform

---

[47] *Ratepayer or London Borough of Lambeth ... Journal*, 1 May 1850, 4.
[48] Taylor, *Decline of British radicalism*, 82. Simon Maccoby, meanwhile, has described Pearson as a 'City sham radical', an accusation equally wide of the mark: *English radicalism*, 386.

were distinctly less advanced than those put forward by D. W. Harvey and Samuel Whalley during the 1830s. In the course of his 1847 campaign, Pearson qualified his support for franchise reform by telling the Lambeth electors that he 'was favourable to universal suffrage when the people should become universally enlightened, and when it would be thereby expedient to effect practically what was theoretically just'.[49] Many metropolitan ultra-radicals were understandably disappointed by Pearson's relative moderation on political reform, and he was considered by most to be 'too genteel for Chartism'.[50] Pearson advanced rather more wholeheartedly the radical critique of Whig centralisation and state enlargement, and in fact his Lambeth candidacy was motivated primarily by a desire to unseat the borough's ministerialist incumbent, the under-secretary for war Benjamin Hawes, whose support for Russell's centralisation programme had been unflagging. In his nomination speech Pearson severely criticised Hawes's servile relationship to Russell and suggested that this ministerial obsequiousness deprived Lambeth of true parliamentary representation. 'Mr. Hawes qualified his votes', claimed Pearson,

> having stated that inasmuch as he held an office in the Ministry, he was obliged to sink his own opinions (expressions of disapprobation) and defer to the majority of his colleagues ... such a state of matters showed the propriety of giving members of the Government a seat in Parliament without the right of voting. The course which Mr. Hawes had taken placed him at the pinnacle of these officials who ought to have a seat without a vote[51]

Pearson's return has been interpreted by historians as a victory for Protestant voluntarism in the face of Russell's plans to establish a system of national education.[52] According to this analysis, George Thompson's return for Tower Hamlets, Charles Lushington's return in Westminster, and Thomas Duncombe's growing popularity in Finsbury were also due to the growing influence of Protestant voluntarism in wake of the Maynooth Grant.[53] There is certainly some validity to this view. A high proportion of the parliamentary advocates of Protestant voluntarism in 1847 were metropolitan MPs, and

[49] *The Times*, 28 July 1847, 6.
[50] Ibid. 26 Oct. 1847, 5.
[51] Ibid. 30 July 1847, 2.
[52] For this view see particularly R. Cowherd, *The politics of English dissent*, London 1959; G. I. T. Machin, 'The Maynooth Grant, the dissenters, and disestablishment, 1845–1847', *EHR* lxxxii (1967), 61–85; and N. Gash, *Reaction and reconstruction in English politics, 1832–1852*, Oxford 1965.
[53] See especially Machin, 'Maynooth Grant', 82–3.

fully fourteen out of the fifteen candidates recommended by the Dissenting Deputies were elected in the metropolitan constituencies.[54] Moreover, in the wake of his defeat by George Thompson, C. R. Fox was unequivocal in his opinion that his support for national education had been his downfall and that the defection of the constituency's dissenting community into Thompson's camp had made all the difference.[55] In defeat Fox also reflected on the fact that a distinguished Whig lineage was no longer a ticket to success in the metropolitan boroughs.[56] Duncombe's rising star, meanwhile, was propelled to a significant degree by his high-profile parliamentary advocacy of voluntarism.

Yet in 1847 the type of voluntarism promoted by metropolitan radicals was far more expansive, and far less focused on the question of religious endowments, than the type promoted by most Protestant voluntarists. Duncombe's approach to the voluntarism debate, for instance, was very wide ranging. Where it engaged with the issue of national education it did so as part of a wider critique of the expansion of central government. Duncombe's objection to the Russellite scheme for the state training of teachers hinged on his belief that such a scheme would 'enormously increase the influence of the Crown and the patronage of the Government'. National education, Duncombe maintained, was simply the latest in a long string of policies (which included the establishment of the Board of Health) aimed at enhancing the powers of central government at the expense of local self-government.[57] The scheme's exclusion of Catholics was for Duncombe only a secondary concern. Benjamin Hall's reaction to the measure proceeded from a similar ideological opposition to state enlargement. Although he admitted that national education worked well in some continental nations, Hall ultimately found it incompatible with English liberty. Hall 'did not think that it would do for a country like this, where the people had been taught for many years to depend upon their own exertions, and they saw the proud result of those exertions'.[58]

In Tower Hamlets, George Thompson also endorsed a wide-ranging agenda of retrenchment which extended far beyond objections to the state Church and state education. Thompson strongly courted London's vestry radicals, often praising 'the period when our Saxon Ancestors held their local

---

[54] See, for instance, idem, *Politics and the Churches in Great Britain, 1832–1868*, Oxford 1977, 191.
[55] *The Times*, 27 July 1847, 8; 2 Aug. 1847, 2.
[56] Ibid. 2 Aug. 1847, 2.
[57] *Hansard* 3rd ser. xci.995, 19 Apr. 1847.
[58] Ibid. 3rd ser.xci.1297, 23 Apr. 1847.

meetings of Representatives in the various parks of England', and acknowledging his desire that 'the People of this great nation ... acquire a just knowledge of their local and civil rights, and, as the consequence of all these, increase their power to carry out their wishes'.[59] Charles Lushington's return for Westminster has also been interpreted as victory for voluntarism, when, in fact, it probably had as much to do with vestry opposition to his opponent Charles Cochrane, who was president of the National Philanthropic Association, and to the support provided for Lushington by the Westminster Reform Society (the last re-incarnation of the Westminster Committee).[60] William Molesworth's victory over Edward Miall in an 1845 Southwark by-election provides perhaps the most striking example of how, in the metropolitan constituencies, voluntarism was subsumed by the wider radical agenda for retrenchment. As editor of the *Nonconformist* Miall's voluntarism was dominated by opposition to the Anglican establishment and only incidentally concerned with abolition of the poor law. Molesworth, on the other hand, understood voluntarism as central to a wide-ranging libertarian programme for state retrenchment. His Southwark campaign therefore made great play of the need for free trade and a general retrenchment of central government alongside of Anglican disestablishment. Although he endorsed the Maynooth Grant, Molesworth none the less described himself as 'decidedly in favour of the voluntary principle'.[61] Despite the strong support given by the voluntary press to Miall's candidature, Molesworth's expansive voluntarism proved far more attractive to the Southwark electors.[62]

As each of these cases suggest, in 1847 metropolitan voluntarism simply comprised part of a wider libertarian agenda that had been fundamental to metropolitan radicalism since 1834. The contributions of Protestant dissent were correspondingly minimal. This was recognised by William Howitt's *People's Journal*, which characterised the metropolitan opposition to Russell's education scheme as a part of the wider vestry radical agenda for retrenchment and low taxes. According to the *People's Journal* the metropolitan critics of the government appealed to

that vulgar prejudice and senseless clamour against government interference

---

[59] George Thompson to Amelia Thompson, 20 Nov. 1847, Raymond English Anti-Slavery Collection, John Rylands University Library, Manchester, REAS/2/2/9. Thompson's diary entries for 1847 (REAS/7/2) record his various meetings with the St Marylebone and St James vestrymen.

[60] See J. Winter, 'The "agitator of the metropolis": Charles Cochrane and early-Victorian street reform', *LJ* xiv (1989), 36.

[61] *The Times*, 19 Aug. 1845, 5. Perhaps unsurprisingly, Miall accused Molesworth of being inconsistent in his advocacy of voluntarism: *The Times*, 26 Aug. 1845, 7.

[62] *Eclectic Review* (Sept. 1845), 491; *Nonconformist*, 17 Sept. 1845, 645.

and so-called centralisation, which now threatens to reduce the education of the people to a dependence on the tender mercies of the voluntary system, and would with equal cruelty and injustice leave the health of the people to the sleepy system of laisses faire. These are they who dignify local license by the lofty name of liberty ... and throw the veil of patriotism over every form of petty sectarian prejudice, and all the revolting corruption of local jobbery and intrigue. These are the men who are most active at elections ... fostering all their idle prejudices in favour of that local tyranny which they would persuade [the electors] is self-government, and filling the House of Commons with living mirrors of their own deformity[63]

Like Moleworth, Thompson and Duncombe, Pearson profitably applied the principles of voluntarism well beyond education and religious endowments to a wide range of Russellite social policy. In the wake of Pearson's Lambeth return, the 'titled radical' and Lambeth MP Charles Tennyson D'Eyncourt acknowledged that Pearson's victory over Hawes owed rather more to Pearson's wide-ranging ideological opposition to 'Whig centralisation' in general than it did to any particular opposition to religious endowments. To D'Eyncourt's mind

[the elector's] opinion was, that no man was fit to be connected with the government who was their representative ... these demonstrations, made from time to time, would show the real opinions of the great mass of the People, and he trusted that these hints would induce the Government to take away from their educational measure its party and sectarian tendency, *and to hold their hands in their centralisation policy, which was calculated to place the superintending control of the country in the hands of commissioners instead of local functionaries.*[64]

Indeed, Pearson's campaign pronouncements on sanitary reform were unfailingly voluntarist. Pearson promised the Lambeth electors, for instance, to

vote for the repeal of the window tax, and considered that the concession of such a measure would have shown a more sincere desire for the sanitary improvement of the people than all the talk about a Health of Towns Bill, which would give a great many petty places to a great many petty people.[65]

---

[63] *People's Journal* iii/68 (17 Apr. 1847), 238.
[64] *The Times*, 2 Aug. 1847, 2. Despite the strong recommendation of his campaign advisors, D'Eyncourt himself voted with the government to increase the Maynooth Grant in 1852 and was consequently defeated in the borough: H. Hersee to Tennyson, 5 Mar. 1852, Tennyson D'Eyncourt papers, IV/3/126.
[65] *The Times*, 28 July 1847, 6.

Like Benjamin Hall, Pearson characterised Russellite reforms in health and education as inimical to English liberty. Pearson's *First letter to the electors of Lambeth,* for instance, asserted that

> the centralising system which prevails in despotic states is fast gaining ground in this nation. Feeble as may be my powers, I will, if returned to Parliament, do my best to expose its evils and impede its progress. The power and patronage which the centralising system confers offer temptations too powerful for any Ministers to resist, and too valuable for any place holders or place seekers to oppose.[66]

In response to Morpeth's Public Health Bill, Pearson appealed to 'the independent conduct and action which was the glory of our Saxon institutions' and wondered how far England would stray before its heritage of local self-government would be restored.[67]

Pearson's strong desire for a 'restoration' of 'Saxon' local rights dated back more than thirty years to his election, on radical principles, to the City Court of Common Council. In the City Pearson agitated for a democratic reform of the Corporation, and through this pursuit he became a close ally of the arch-localist, and unrivalled glorifier of Saxon liberty, Joshua Toulmin Smith.[68] Indeed, Pearson's 1847 Lambeth candidature came about through his friendship with the City solicitor, and radical Lambeth vestryman, John Hunt. According to one contemporary observer of Lambeth politics, Hunt

> embraced the first opportunity of introducing Mr. Pearson to a club composed mainly of parochial gentlemen, who contributed five shillings each, yearly, to a fund to relieve any case of sudden or extreme distress recommended by a member ... the club were charmed with their new and distinguished acquaintance. A vote of thanks was proposed, and, in responding to the compliment, Mr. Pearson adroitly suggested that he might some day be a parliamentary candidate in Lambeth, and there and then he received a pledge of support from his admirers. Thus he established the nucleus of support of an election party.[69]

Once he had been successfully returned for the borough, Pearson repaid his debt by faithfully promoting the interests of these 'parochial gentlemen' in parliament. In June 1850, to take just one example, Pearson attended an

---

66 C. Pearson, *Mr. Charles Pearson's first letter to the electors of Lambeth,* London 1847, 6 (Tennyson D'Eyncourt papers, IV/3/110).
67 *Hansard* 3rd ser.xcviii.771, 8 May, 1848.
68 P. Claus, 'Languages of citizenship in the City of London, 1848–1867', *LJ* xxiv (1999), 23–37.
69 Hill, *Electoral history of Lambeth,* 72–3.

important vestry session and 'begged of the meeting that he might well understand their precise opinion upon the Bill under consideration [metropolitan interments], in order that he should properly represent them in another place'.[70]

Like D. W. Harvey in the 1830s, Pearson came to metropolitan parliamentary politics by way of the City, and brought some of its entrepreneurially influenced radicalism with him. Both in Southwark and Lambeth, vestries under threat from the spectre of Chadwickian administrative centralisation were grateful that their defence would be made by such popular and capable men. Returns in other metropolitan constituencies added to the ranks of the parochial radicals and opponents of Russellite policy. Like Pearson in Lambeth, Osborne proposed middle-class rationalism and good sense as the antidote to paternal government. To Osborne's mind, the middle class was the essential feature of metropolitan political culture. It was thanks to middle-class sensibility that London had not been over-run by Chartism, and indeed it was 'that class which, uniting the ornamental and polished superstructure [the aristocracy] to the more rude and solid foundation [the working class], is in fact the cement which insures the stability of the glorious fabric [of British politics and society]'.[71]

Liberals, Radicals and popular opposition to the Russellite programme, 1847–55

From 1847 three related developments lent support to the libertarian agenda promoted by Pearson, Duncombe and other metropolitan radicals. Firstly, a new generation of metropolitan non-conformists coalesced around the *Leader* newspaper and the movement to promote European liberalism and nationalism. Secondly, 'localist' ideologues such as Joshua Toulmin Smith and Francis Newman became increasingly central to the metropolitan radical movement during the later 1840s. Finally, vestry-based reformers throughout London were rejuvenated through their common opposition to Russellite public health and sanitation policy. Moreover, these developments grew from a common synergy. From 1848 *Leader-* and *Reasoner*-affiliated metropolitan radicals such as G. J. Holyoake, James Stansfeld and William Ashurst began to find common cause with City-affiliated vestry radicals such as Pearson, Apsley Pellat and Joshua Toulmin Smith. Toulmin Smith, for instance, counted Holyoake as a close associate and found in Stansfeld a kindred spirit.

---

70 *The Ratepayer, or Borough of Lambeth … Journal*, 1 June 1850, 6.
71 *Hansard* 3rd ser. c.168, 6 July 1848.

'I certainly have looked on Stansfeld', Smith confided to Holyoake, 'as one of the very, very few in Parliament who are there for principle's sake and who would appreciate the sort of aim striven after in the "Remembrancer".'[72] For his part, Holyoake believed that Smith had 'no compeer or any master, amid his predecessors in the same field'.[73] The emergence of this new radical matrix all but ensured the complete polarisation of metropolitan political culture.

Unitarian and freethinking radicals such as Peter Alfred Taylor, William Ashurst, Francis Newman, William Shaen, James Stansfeld and William James Linton were particularly instrumental in binding London's various radical groups into a coherent libertarian movement during the later 1840s. William Ashurst's 'Muswell Hill brigade' and the South Place Chapel group, which found a salon in Taylor's Aubrey House, were in some respects radical alternatives to the Whig Devonshire and Holland House sets.[74] Moreover, many members of the *Leader* and *Reasoner* circles also had close connections to the City of London and its unique heritage of local democracy. Ashurst, for instance, was a City solicitor and an active common council member throughout his life. Before becoming involved in the wider metropolitan reform movement, Ashurst had also filled the post of City undersheriff for a short time and had published pamphlets on the need for reform of the City Corporation.[75]

Such affiliations acted as bridge between *Leader* and *Reasoner* radicals on the one hand, and post-1847 metropolitan radical MPs such as Pearson of Lambeth, Thomas Challis of Finsbury, Apsley Pellatt of Southwark, and Charles Salisbury Butler of Tower Hamlets, each of whom carried deep attachments to the City. Apsley Pellatt, for instance, was a Southwark industrialist, but he was also an active member of the City's common council, which informed his entrepreneurial and libertarian radical priorities. As a leading member of the National Constitution Association, which included among its supporters Peter Taylor, the Southwark radical vestryman John Day, and the St Marylebone vestryman John Nicholay, Pellatt argued against both universal suffrage and the principle of aristocratic and paternalist

---

72 Joshua Toulmin Smith to George Jacob Holyoake, [n.d., 1862?], G. J. Holyoake papers, Co-Operative Archive, Manchester, GJHCC/1463.

73 Holyoake, *History of co-operation*, 251–2.

74 See M. D. Conway, *Autobiography: memories and experiences*, London 1904, ii. 51; B. Hammond, *James Stansfeld: a Victorian champion of sex equality*, London 1932, 10, 16; G. Mazzini, *Mazzini's letters to an English family*, London 1920; F. B. Smith, *Radical artisan: William James Linton, 1812–1897*, Manchester 1973, 13–14, 58.

75 For Ashurst's criticisms of the City Corporation's court of aldermen see W. H. Ashurst, *Corporation register*, London 1832.

government, and in favour of political leadership by the middle classes.[76] Thomas Challis, who first stood for Finsbury in 1852 after receiving a deputation from prominent parochial reformers who had been impressed by his defence of local self-government, harboured even stronger connections to the City.[77] At the time of his election, Challis was an alderman for Cripplegate, and became Lord Mayor of the City shortly afterwards. Unsurprisingly, given his City credentials, Challis made opposition to 'Russellite Centralisation' a central plank in his election platform, telling an audience of Finsbury electors that, 'to every system of centralisation I am strongly opposed, believing that local self-government, whether municipal or parochial, is most equitable, inexpensive, and useful'. Like Pellatt in Southwark and Pearson in Lambeth, Challis was above all else a moderate, middle-class reformer.[78] By the early 1850s these City men, and their glorification of the 'City model' of local self-government, had fundamentally altered the nature of metropolitan vestry radicalism. By this time, vestry-affiliated papers such as the *Ratepayer* began to heap praise upon the City and even began to suggest that the metropolitan parishes incorporate themselves as quickly as possible.[79]

This change was partly due to the rising influence of *Leader-* and *Reasoner*-affiliated radicalism. From its inception, the *Leader* promoted a wide-ranging agenda of political, economic and administrative reforms, many of which extended far beyond the solutions offered by leading reformers within parliament. Linton asserted that his 'purpose' at the paper was to be 'at once an organ of the European republicans and the centre of the English republican party'.[80] The tone of republicanism promoted by Linton and his associates within *Leader* and *Reasoner* circles was both entrepreneurial and libertarian.[81] Schemes for centralised government of all descriptions – from Russellite 'paternal' liberalism to O'Connorite land nationalisation and Blancian socialism – were severely criticised.[82] Although many *Leader-* and

---

[76] *Morning Advertiser*, 24 Feb. 1855, 5; 28 Feb. 1855, 3; 5 Mar. 1855, 3; 2 May 1855, 5.

[77] T. Challis, *Government majorities: letter to the right honorable Lord John Russell, M.P., on the ministerial device for the subversion of local self-government*, London 1851.

[78] Idem, *To the electors of Finsbury*, London 1852, refuses, for instance, to endorse universal suffrage.

[79] *Ratepayer or the London Borough of Lambeth … Journal*, 1 May 1852, 4; 1 July 1851, 4.

[80] W. J. Linton, *Memories*, London 1895, 120.

[81] It is worth noting that, as chairman of the Metropolitan Anti-Corn Law Association, the *Leader* circle radical P. A. Taylor severely criticised monopolies of all kinds and advocated much greater deregulation of the market: Metropolitan Anti-Corn Law Association, *Resolutions of the Metropolitan Anti-Corn Law Association, passed 18th of August, 1842; address of the Metropolitan Anti-Corn Law Association to their fellow citizens*, London 1842.

[82] *Leader*, 19 Aug. 1854, 781; 18 May 1850, 179; G. J. Holyoake, 'The *Leader* and its rela-

Reasoner-affiliated radicals, and Holyoake and Ashurst in particular, promoted co-operation, they did so according to the same voluntarist, anti-statist priorities which prompted Toulmin Smith to call himself a co-operativist.[83] Holyoake himself described co-operation as both a system of 'self-help' and a 'supplement to political economy', and was quick to spell out the great differences between English co-operation and continental communism.[84] 'The self-managing scheme', proclaimed Holyoake

> under which working people create profits and retain them among themselves, Mr. Owen had not foreseen. His idea was to organise the world, co-operation attempts the humbler work of organising the provision store and the workshop. This is the distinction between communism and co-operation which public men of no mean discernment continually confound together. Von Sybel defines the Communist proper as 'those who desire to transfer every kind of property to the State'. This is the continental craze upon Socialism and has nothing to do with anything English.[85]

The editorial position of the *Reasoner*, meanwhile, was heavily influenced by the freethinker, co-operativist and polymath Francis Newman, whom Holyoake described, in the pages of the *Reasoner* no less, as 'a man of reputation, genius, and attainments ... [whose ideas would] shape this age and rule the next'.[86] According to Linton, the radicals of *Leader* and *Reasoner* circles looked on Newman as 'a man of culture and fine thought, with excellent sympathies and intentions'.[87] Newman was an outspoken admirer of Toulmin Smith's work on 'local self-government'. Shortly after arriving in London to take up a chair in Latin at University College, Newman became personally acquainted with Toulmin Smith and convinced that his œuvre comprised

---

tion to free discussion' (1850), part of *Reasoner tracts*, no. 8 (1850), 3; *People's Journal* xxi, 284. Unsurprisingly, the *Leader* and *Reasoner* radicals associated Catholicism with centralisation. See Society of the Friends of Italy, *Address of the Society of the Friends of Italy*, London 1851, 12–14, and G. J. Holyoake, *The polity and resources of freethinking*, London 1848, 2–3. F. Newman, *An appeal to the middle-classes on the urgent necessity of numerous radical reforms, financial and organic*, London 1848, is another forceful articulation of the *Leader* circle's entrepreneurial and anti-paternalist republicanism.

[83] B. Weinstein, ' "Local self-government is true socialism": Joshua Toulmin Smith, the state, and character formation', *EHR* cxxiii (2008), 1193–228.

[84] Holyoake, *History of co-operation*, i. 5–6.

[85] Ibid. ii. 69.

[86] *Reasoner*, 2 Nov. 1853. For Newman's influence over Holyoake and the editorial position of the *Reasoner* see E. Royle, *Victorian infidels: the origins of the British secularist movement, 1791–1866*, Manchester 1974, 158.

[87] Linton, *Memories*, 159–160.

'the most important political work, as to me appears, which the nineteenth-century has produced in England'.[88] From 1849 the two men codirected the London Hungarian Committee, and from this mutual endeavour Newman became even more convinced of the validity of Smith's views on 'local-self-government'. In the course of the following year, Newman began to argue, in a manner familiar to those acquainted with Toulmin Smith's writings, that

> however much the Parliamentary franchise needs reform, yet a *greater* need is that of limiting the functions of Parliament, and giving them to County Assemblies or Town Motes. That word *Mote* is almost obsolete ... the modern substitute 'meeting,' has no taxing powers, no legal officers, no constitutional power any more than the mob ... the sands of the Whigs run fast out, and it is high time for the radicals to have a creed.[89]

Five years later, at the height of the struggle to de-centralise London's local government, Newman had lost none of this commitment to local self-government. In fact, his vision had become even further radicalised in some respects. With the Hungarian Association defunct, Newman joined Smith and Charles Elt in the Anti-Centralisation Union. On 29 March Newman wrote to Smith suggesting that their agitation become more aggressive:

> I think that you will feel with me that so long as the Anti-Centralisation Union is a mere <u>defensive</u> society, it will derive vigour solely from active attempts of centralisers, and will ... die when they (from any cause) are languid: after which, to revive it will be impossible. Is not the present a good opportunity of assuming the offensive? I should like to see the Union publicly claim of parliament the abolition of those acts which prevent a real militia in every locality under the proper local officers, (not crown appointed) and not under martial law. We know that London once had trained bands under the Lord Mayor: I want to claim this again.[90]

For all of Newman's faith in local democracy, he remained unwilling to endorse the parliamentary enfranchisement of the working classes. 'Rich men should have more power than poor men', he argued in 1848, 'partly because on average they are more intelligent, as a result of leisure and education; that

---

88 F. Newman, *Lectures on political economy*, London 1851.
89 *Memoir and letters of Francis W. Newman*, ed. I. G. Sieveking, London 1909, 369.
90 Francis Newman to Toulmin Smith, 29 Mar. 1855, Francis Newman–Joshua Toulmin-Smith correspondence, BL, R.P. 831 (2).

is, they are generally more fit for power.'[91] Newman confided to Thornton Hunt, meanwhile, that he was

> exceedingly far from being able to believe that Universal Suffrage is the cure needed by England just at the present, or that any socialistic system is possible on such a scale as sensibly to effect national affairs ... have you seen Toulmin Smith's pamphlet on the Reform of the Corporation of London? I look more to the channel of reform which he is opening than to any Parliamentary Franchise.[92]

Newman remained sceptical of parliamentary reform for some time. In 1853, for instance, he confessed to Holyoake that 'I believe the democracy of America to work better for their nation, than our mixed government for our nation; yet I also believe that the effort to superimpose their democracy upon us, would only cause convulsion and misery: for this reason I cannot simply call myself a democrat.' Newman also warned the parliamentary reformers to be careful not to 'alarm our aristocracy with the idea of conspiracy'.[93] These cautious and moderate views on the necessary extent of political reform endeared Newman to the new generation of libertarian reformers represented in parliament by Pearson and George Thompson. So, for that matter, did Newman's tendency to characterise Whiggery as a fundamentally aristocratic creed which had 'no future in England'.[94]

Unsurprisingly, given his intellectual influence, Newman's views on the importance of local self-government, and the repugnant nature of government centralisation, were shared by most members of *Leader* and *Reasoner* circles. The Finsbury radical engraver W. J. Linton, a frequent *Leader* contributor, for instance made explicit the connections between the European struggles for self-government and those taking place at home in England.[95] 'Centralisation is despotism', insisted Linton,

> now dominant in France, under Whig auspices it is creeping into England ... democracy [meanwhile] holds the family inviolate. It is the first association ...

---

91 Newman, *An appeal*, 24.
92 Newman to Thornton Hunt, 7 Mar. 1850, Leigh Hunt papers, BL, MS Add. 38110, fo. 261.
93 Newman to Holyoake, 1853, Holyoake papers, GJHCC/616.
94 'I begin to think that Whiggery has no future in England. It looks as if the Whigs and Tories must sink their differences (under Lord Stanley?) and the new party will be avowedly Aristocracy with feudal landed power against democracy undisguised (perhaps I am wrong: that is Whiggery. Toryism only will perish)': Newman to Holyoake, 30 Apr. 1866, ibid., GJHCC/1672.
95 It has been claimed that Linton was among the *Leader*'s three most important contributors: A.T. Kitchel, *George Lewes and George Elliot: a review of records*, New York 1933, 65.

then comes the parish or commune. There are duties to that, interests of that, local characteristics of that, best worked out, best understood, best developed and harmonised, by that parish or commune. Each little parish is a family, inviolate in its own home. Each little parish is a sovereign state, only account-able to its neighbors for its conduct toward, its influence on, them. With its special life they have no right to interfere: they could not understand it ... this is democracy: the very opposite of centralisation, whether that centralisation be the 'despotism' of one, the 'oligarchy' of the few, or the 'mob rule' of the many.[96]

Of equal importance was Linton's rejection of 'the "mob rule" of the many'. Such views highlighted Linton's rejection of Communism, which he described as 'but a reaction ... without faith or powers of organisation, it will be but an extreme in reaction to an extreme'. Linton's support for Mazzini grew out of his admiration for the Italian's commitment to liberalism.[97]

This view, in which centralisation was portrayed as a continental and particularly a Catholic practice, was universal among the *Leader* group. The equation of Catholicism with continental despotism and domestic centralisa-tion (which was often characterised as a 'French influence'[98]) was particularly pronounced in the agitations of the Friends of Italy and the Subscription for European Freedom, membership of which was drawn largely from the *Leader* group.[99] Just as in their objection to the New Poor Law, metropolitan radicals stressed the Gallic character of Russellite health policy in contrast to the Saxon pedigree of local self-government. Some went further still, arguing that the English aristocracy, and therefore all Cousinhood Whigs, carried in their blood a Norman predilection for centralised forms of government. Linton, for instance, made this association in his poem, *Bob Thin, or the poor house fugitive*. Written in 1845, it characterises the New Poor Law as a Norman innovation:

> Time was when every man was free
> to manage his own cookery:
> whether he got it in the chase
> or grew and eat it in the same place.
> this was the Old Time, long 'ere these days
> when 'merrie England' basked in the blasé

---

[96] This is quoted in G. Claeys, 'Mazzini, Kossuth, and British radicalism, 1848–1854', *JBS* xxviii (1989), 240.

[97] Ibid. 239, 241.

[98] For a fairly typical metropolitan radical critique of the French origins of centralisation see, for instance, *The Spectator*, 13 Dec. 1851.

[99] See Finn, *After Chartism*, 167, and *Reasoner*, 25 Feb. 1852, 230–1; 10 Nov. 1852, 346–7.

... the days of Natural Equality and property for all;
there were no Poor Laws, for this good
reason that no man wanted food;
and no one's neighbor any ravages
committed; till at length some savages,
a Lordly idle set of stoats,
seized peaceful husbandmen by throats,
and over natures gentlest code,
on roaring rapine rough-shod rode.
... now to apply the application
to the back of our own happy nation: –
we've had our scions of misrule, of the illegitimate Norman School,
who've laid our husbandmen in bond.[100]

Linton's poem invokes a romantic Saxon past in which individuality and self-sufficiency were prized over all else. The Southwark radical MP William Molesworth also seems to have understood local self-government as a uniquely English achievement. In the immediate aftermath of the 1848 revolutions, he rejoiced at the 'advancement of the human race', but felt doubtful whether 'the genius and character of the people [of France] will enable them to have those forms of republican government which are but limited to the Anglo-Saxon races. I am grieved, likewise, to see those struggles of races (especially in Austria) out of which no good can come'.[101] From 1847 metropolitan radicals, from within the vestry and without, began to characterise their crusade for local self-government' as a fight to preserve 'Englishness' itself at the very heart of the empire.

---

100 W. J. Linton, *Bob Thin, or the poor house fugitive*, London 1845.
101 William Molesworth to Richard Cobden, 22 Oct. 1848, Richard Cobden papers, BL, MS Add. 43667, fo. 228.

4

Redefining the State, I: Rates and Taxes, 1834–1853

Few grievances mobilised the metropolitan radical opposition to Whiggery quite like the church rates and assessed taxes. It was Whig prevarication over the window tax, it will be remembered, that ultimately cost J. C. Hobhouse the support of Place's Westminster Committee and his Westminster seat to boot. The assessed taxes fell heavily on Londoners and there was no shortage of commentary from the metropolitan radical press on London's disproportionate suffering under the house and window taxes in particular.[1] In the House of Commons, the Westminster MP George DeLacy Evans frequently characterised the window tax as a uniquely metropolitan burden.[2] Moreover, like other metropolitan radicals, Evans consistently linked his criticism of both the assessed taxes and the church rate to support for administrative retrenchment and the supposed rights and privileges of 'local self-government'.[3] This was precisely how Evans framed his opposition to the window tax in 1834, for instance, when he presented to parliament a series of anti-window tax petitions from London's reformed and reforming vestries.[4] As Evans's example suggests, from the mid-1830s metropolitan radical critiques of the assessed taxes and church rate became central to the construction of a broader opposition to Whig centralisation. By 1850 the window tax was frequently invoked by metropolitan radicals alongside the New Poor Law and London's quasi-centralised health authority as institutional proof of Whig debasement of 'local rights'. At the same time, sustained

---

[1]   See, for instance, *The Spectator*, 26 Apr. 1834, 395, and United Parishes of Westminster, *Facts (founded upon parliamentary returns) illustrative of the great inequity of the taxes on houses and windows, shewing how unjustly and oppressively the bear upon the middle and industrious classes*, London 1834, esp. pp. 7–8.
[2]   *Morning Advertiser*, 9 Jan. 1851, 3.
[3]   G. DeLacy Evans, *A letter to the electors of Westminster*, London 1833, 23, 35–6; *Morning Chronicle*, 8 May 1833, 2; *The Freeman's Journal*, 13 May 1833, 2.
[4]   *Hansard* 3rd ser. xxi.264–72, 13 Feb. 1834. See also *The Times*, 8 Feb. 1834.

controversy over the nature of the church rate fuelled an important debate over the legitimate location of the power to set rates, and over the proper role and sphere of central government generally.

In London, the 'localist' critique of rates and taxes was articulated by reformers of all religious stripes from within the radical vestries, and was driven primarily by political, rather than moral, considerations. Although the Unitarians of South Place chapel and the freethinkers of the *Leader* and *Reasoner* circle were particularly forceful metropolitan advocates of abolition of the church rate, it is by no means clear that Unitarian opposition to the church rate was motivated by religious considerations, rather than by a gener-ally 'volunteerist' political ideology.[5] Hugh McLeod, Edward Royle and Eric Hobsbawm have rightly identified secularism and rationalism as defining features of the metropolitan radical tradition, and indeed from the mid-1840s London's secularist reformers, along with their rationalist counterparts from the South Place chapel, promoted church rate reform with as much fervour as any provincial Congregationalist or Baptist.[6] Although many of London's leading vestry radicals and 'localist' ideologues also happened to be either nonconformists or secularists, the metropolitan anti-church rate crusade, in particular, was in many ways less concerned with ending the religious imposi-tions of the established Church than with 're-establishing' the rights and powers of local government. Many reformers understood Russell's protection of the Anglican establishment, and more to the point Whig unwillingness to grant vestries the power to refuse to set a church rate, as simply another feature of the Whig commitment to government centralisation.

Church rates, 1834–55

Whiggery's declining metropolitan popularity during the 1830s, and its growing reputation as the party of 'centralisation', had much to do with the passage of the 1834 Poor Law Amendment Act. However, even before the

[5] R. Brent, 'The Whigs and Protestant dissent in the decade of reform: the case of the church rates, 1833–1841', *EHR* ci (1987), 897–909; Machin, *Politics and the Churches*, 8–27; Briggs, *Victorian cities*, 68–9.
[6] H. McLeod, *Class and religion in the late-Victorian city*, London 1974, 42–68. See also Royle, *Victorian infidels*, 191–5, and Weiner, *Radicalism and freethought*. Eric Hobsbawm has also rightly identified secularism as an important thread linking successive generations of nineteenth-century metropolitan radicals: *Primitive rebels*, London 1959, 128. For the closeness of freethought and Unitarianism see *Reasoner* xxxiii (1850), 40–2; *South Place Magazine* xi (Mar. 1906), and G. J. Holyoake, *Secularism distinguished from Unitarianism*, London 1855.

storm over the New Poor Law erupted in June, the Grey administration had already alienated metropolitan radicals by fudging an attempted church reform. Many of the concerns eventually raised by radicals in relation to the New Poor Law (most notably, the threat that the measure presented to vestry self-determination and local democracy) were first aroused in April 1834, following the publication of Lord Althorp's abortive church rate reform measure. In the months leading up to the presentation of Althorp's bill, the bulk of metropolitan dissenters and radicals remained fairly optimistic that the government plan, whenever it arrived, would be satisfactory.[7] However, from January 1834 a group of metropolitan vestry radicals became restless over the government's timeline for reform and decided to take matters into their own hands. In that month, the St Pancras vestry, which had already fallen under the direction of the ultra-radical Irish Catholic Thomas Murphy, successfully refused to set a church rate, justifying their action by appealing to the 'immemorial rights' of institutions of local government to set and reject all rates and taxes.[8] Finsbury vestry radicals under the leadership of the Wakleyite George Rogers attempted a similar refusal. In the course of a tumultuous vestry sitting, Rogers instructed members of his Householders' Union of St Giles-in-the-Fields and St George's Bloomsbury to imitate the St Pancras radicals by making use of their vestry votes to undermine the rate.[9] Lambeth radicals also attempted to imitate the St Pancras radicals, as the Chartist publisher and vestry radical William Carpenter joined forces with prominent local dissenters to simultaneously reject the rates and assert the principle of local self government. Acting in concert with a fellow Lambeth Presbyterian named Thomas McConnell, Carpenter urged the ratepayers to reject each new rate suggested by the Lambeth churchwardens and asked them to promote the voluntary principle instead. Although Carpenter's anti-church rate motions and amendments were ultimately defeated by the plural votes of wealthier Anglican vestry members, the Lambeth vestry radicals continued to look to their vestry, rather than to parliament, as their best hope of 'defeating' the church rate. The Lambeth Anti-Church Rate Association, which came into being as a direct consequence of the vestry agitation, took precisely this course of action – urging its membership to take matters into their own hands at vestry meetings rather than wait for parliament to abolish the church rate.[10] In defeat, the Lambeth agitation received substantial coverage in the radical press and became something of a sensation in the

---

7   B. L. Manning, *The Protestant dissenting deputies*, Cambridge 1952, 36.
8   *True Vestryman and Borough of Marylebone Gazette*, 4 Jan. 1834, 42.
9   *The Patriot*, 29 Jan. 1834, 39.
10 *True Sun*, 23 Jan. 1834, 2.

radical community. It is significant that much of the ensuing radical media coverage focused as intensely on vestry plural voting and the 'evils' of the Sturges Bourne Act (which still applied in Lambeth), as on the question of the church rates *per se*.[11]

By mid-March 1834 high-profile metropolitan vestry rebellions like those in Finsbury, Lambeth and St Pancras had helped to pressurise the government into announcing its intention to introduce a church rate measure in the coming months. The legislation finally produced by Lord Althorp on 21 April, 1834 was almost universally unpopular and met an exceptionally quick death in the Commons.[12] However, despite its short and unsuccessful parliamentary life, Althorp's bill remained an important touchstone in the metropolitan fight against the church rates for years to come. In his speech introducing the bill, Althorp admitted his own view that dissenters were justified in their opposition to the church rates, and that parliament was 'bound so far to relieve them'. He also repeatedly advertised his understanding that dissenters objected primarily to the principle of paying church rates, rather than to the financial burdens imposed by these rates.[13] His plan therefore sought to abolish the rates while simultaneously preserving the church establishment by replacing the rates with an additional annual sum of £250,000 from the land tax which would be used to maintain and repair the fabric of parish churches and chapels. These new tax revenues would be administered by a permanently established, centrally appointed, Commission for Building and Repairing Churches. Althorp hoped that by taking decision-making away from vestry officials, and placing it in the hands of disinterested central government officials, he would solve the problems of wasteful, extravagant and corrupt church rate management.[14]

Many metropolitan reformers found Althorp's proposal to be even less palatable than the maintenance of the *status quo*. In the first place, commentators were bemused by Althorp's claim that the new legislation would relieve dissenters from their 'principled' objection to the church rates. *The Spectator* poked fun at the plan while wondering 'how Lord Althorp, who is perfectly aware that the dissenters objected to the principle, not to the cost, of supporting a church they disapprove of, could fancy that his measure could satisfy their honest scruples, is not to be comprehended by common intellects'.[15] Reformers also entertained more serious reservations over Althorp's true intentions for administrative centralisation. Coming so soon after the

---

11 See, for instance, *Poor Man's Guardian*, 1 Feb. 1834, 459.
12 Machin, *Politics and the Churches*, 44.
13 *Hansard* 3rd ser. xxii.1013–14, 1018, 1057, 21 Apr. 1834.
14 Ibid. 3rd ser. xxii. 117–18, 21 Apr. 1834.
15 *The Spectator*, 26 Apr. 1834, 381.

high-profile radical vestry campaign to refuse to set rates, many reformers saw in Althorp's plan an underhanded Whig plot to rein in vestry powers and enhance the role of central government. D. W. Harvey's *True Sun* character-ised the measure as a sinister threat to the legitimate powers of local self-government, and asked bitingly 'what but Whiggism can come of Whiggism?'[16] The *Patriot*, meanwhile, also pointed to dangerous administra-tive 'innovations' contained within the bill, noting that

> Lord Althorp's plan deprives the parishioners of the control they can now exercise over the rate, takes away the prerogative of taxing themselves for the support of the church, and places a dangerous and discretionary power in the hands of commissioners, whose office is already sufficiently unpopular if the bill passes, the power of resistance, now exercised by parishes, often so effectu-ally, will be taken away. Thus ... the bill will be obviously a new rivet of church and state.[17]

This widely held interpretation of Althorp's bill exerted a lasting and powerful influence on the metropolitan struggle against the church rates and ensured that, from April 1834, the nature of metropolitan agitation would be heavily informed by the struggle between local self determination and central control.

Although Althorp's measure dented metropolitan faith in legislative solu-tions to the church rate issue, many reformers continued to hold out hope that a liberal government would eventually concede rate abolition and even disestablishment.[18] By the early months of 1836, radicals and nonconformists were again anxious to see movement on the question of church rate repeal.[19] Moreover, the revived anti-church rate movement was particularly active in London. Whereas the 1835 municipal reform had partly satisfied noncon-formist anti-church rate reformers in provincial centres, London's exclusion from the measure ensured that the metropolitan agitation would continue to

---

16 *True Sun*, 23 Apr. 1834, 4.

17 *The Patriot*, 23 Apr. 1834, 136–7. Indeed, strengthening the Church establishment seems to have been the real aim of the Grey administration, and Althorp's 1834 bill was just the first intimation of this. Russell was particularly commited to strengthing these bonds, and was not averse to enlarging central government to do so. In August 1834, for instance, he advised Melbourne that the government should 'resist the separation of church and state and all propositions having that end in view': Holland House papers, MS Add. 51677, fo. 123. See also J. P. Ellens, 'Lord John Russell and the church rate conflict: the struggle for a broad Church, 1834–1868', *JBS* xxvi (1987), 232–57.

18 Cowherd, *Politics of English dissent*, 92.

19 See, for instance, *Patriot*, 29 Feb. 1836, 69.

press for the dual goals of local self-government and rate abolition.[20] In the wake of Althorp's abortive bill, metropolitan anti-church rate agitation began to recruit from a broader, decidedly non-sectarian, support base and began increasingly to find its *raison d'etre* in state retrenchment and opposition to paternal, centralised government. Organisations such as the Church Rate Abolition Society embodied these explicitly political priorities and values. From its establishment in October 1836, CRAS drew together metropolitan radicals and liberal churchmen with the Dissenting Deputies and the sponsors of the nonconformist *Patriot*.[21] Soon after its first meeting, the society published a pamphlet outlining the concerns of a broad based anti-church rate movement. Chief among these was the belief that the Whigs would use church rate reform to weaken the position of the vestries. CRAS promised to fight this threat with as much energy as it would fight the continuation of the church rates itself. 'To any measure of commutation on the principle proposed to parliament by LORD ALTHORP', began CRAS's first address,

> the objections are insuperable. Deeply as we deplore local divisions and party strife, we should prefer, *decidedly* prefer, with all its evils, the continuance of the present system of parochial taxation, to any Legislative Enactment providing for the erection or repairs of Ecclesiastical Buildings from the general revenue of the country. Such a measure would present a temptation alike to selfishness and extravagance, by placing the sums expended beyond the salutary influence of popular control; – would tend to perpetuate that system of injustice which is now, in many parishes, legally resisted with complete success ...
>
> While Law continues to give its sanction to this evil, [one should] employ all legal measures to prevent its infliction; and, when these are unavailable to mitigate its force, attend parochial vestries, and there appeal to the kindness and justice of your neighbours; and if such means fail, and numbers prove against you, carefully examine the validity of the rate, scrutinise the expenditure of Churchwardens, and firmly resist the *illegal* application – a case not unfrequently occurring – of the Church Tax. We need to inform you, that by this course Church Rates have already been abolished in many parishes.[22]

Agitation within metropolitan constituencies revealed similarly political priorities. In Southwark, for instance, opposition to the church rates was

---

[20] Cowherd, *Politics of English dissent*, 91.
[21] Ellens, 'Russell and the church rate conflict', 238.
[22] Church Rate Abolition Society, *Address of the committee to the people of Great Britain and Ireland*, London 1836.

located firmly within the vestries and was decidedly non-sectarian. When, in March 1837, the St Saviour's vestry voted to reject the rates, the agitation was reported to have been led by a 'busy, factious knot of radicals' rather than by local dissenters. In order to help the vestry in their struggle to reject the rates, the doyen of the Muswell Hill Brigade and *Leader* circle, William Henry Ashurst, published a series of handbills that instructed local radicals to 'act like Britons, and keep yourselves clear of the bondage of this jobbing [Church] faction'.[23] Thus, the rates agitation was framed as a straightforward radical fight against a wasteful and excessive government. At one vestry meeting convened to reject the rate, a man distributing the CRAS pamphlet was asked whether he belonged to 'the Dissenting body, as he made himself so exceedingly active in opposing the church rates'. His reply was revealing. 'Belong to the dissenters?' he scoffed, 'to be sure not; it will save our pockets, that's all; that is the only reason why we oppose the church rates.'[24] As Stephen Lushington observed in March, 'many who belonged to the church objected to the expenses gone to on account of the new churches, and joined the dissenters in their efforts to get rid of the rates'.[25]

As non-sectarian popular opposition to the church rates increased, and as elections drew nearer, the government began to feel a growing pressure to address the issue with some piece of legislation that would prove more popular among liberals than Althorp's bill. The resulting bill, which owed its character primarily to Russell's input, proposed to abolish the rates completely and to maintain the fabric of the church by better management of church lands. Regardless of whether, as Ian Newbould has maintained, the Whig bill was a cynical ploy to placate the dissenters before an election, the new plan met with almost universal approval from the metropolitan radical community, largely because its effect was retrenchment without the loss of vestry rights.[26] Reaction to the bill again revealed the radical and localist, rather than sectarian, priorities of the anti-church rate movement. As the government bill was being debated in parliament, the Marylebone radicals celebrated what they deemed to be a worthwhile bill, and noted that a substantial portion of metropolitan support for the bill came from right-thinking Anglican vestrymen. 'We are glad to perceive', wrote the *Marylebone Journal*,

---

[23] Madame Venturi, *Mr. Morris's 80th birthday party*, London 1904, 88; *The Times*, 17 Sept. 1838, 7.
[24] *The Times*, 17 Sept. 1838, 7.
[25] *Hansard* 3rd ser. xxxvii.378, 13 Mar. 1837.
[26] Newbould, 'Whiggery and the dilemma of reform', 233–4.

that the inhabitants of several parishes of the metropolis have, on the question of church rates, met and passed resolutions in favour of their abolition. It is very creditable to the churchwardens in some of these parishes, that they have taken the lead in demonstrations made in support of the ministerial measure … this was particularly the case in the parish of St. Andrews, Holborn, and in that of St. Pancras … the assertion that the hostility to the church rates is all on the side of the dissenters, and exercised from factious motives, is thus shown to be utterly untrue.[27]

Indeed, in 1837 two of the most outspoken advocates of church rate abolition within parliament were not dissenters, but the London-based Anglican 'localist' radicals Thomas Duncombe and D. W. Harvey.

Unfortunately for those metropolitan radicals who supported the government's proposal, the administration, and Russell in particular, soon came to the conclusion that the bill could not pass. In early August a decision was made to jettison the legislation.[28] Melbourne, however, seems to have counselled Russell not to abandon the bill outright. Instead, he and Russell continued to promise a select committee on the bill, all the while remaining conscious that it would in due course be defeated in the Lords. The bill's eventual death in 1837 was a heavy blow to the anti-church rate movement, which had put so much faith in Russell's intentions. After the great disappointment occasioned by its defeat, metropolitan radicals began to come round to the view promoted by newspapers like the *Parochial Gazette*. In the *Gazette*'s opinion, as long as the bishops sat in the House of Lords and Russell remained opposed to the voluntary principle, parliament would never be able to deliver church rate abolition. The paper consequently advised ratepayers throughout the metropolis to utilise their parish vestries and to take the question into their own hands by voting within the vestry against setting rates.[29] Of course, this method of vestry control had already been advocated by radicals in Lambeth, St Pancras and Christ Church. But in 1834, when these vestries staged their high-profile rebellions, radicals had still hoped that a parliamentary solution might be forthcoming. From 1838 radicals and dissenters began to explore completely vestry-based solutions.

During the debates over Spring Rice's 1837 bill, Thomas Duncombe had managed to raise his profile within the metropolitan, and indeed the national, anti-church rate movement. His prominence in organisations such

[27] *Marylebone Journal and Metropolitan Register of News, Politics, and Literature*, 22 Apr. 1837, 4.
[28] Ellens, 'Russell and the church rate conflict', 241.
[29] *Parochial Gazette*, 27 May 1837, 28.

as the Church Rate Abolition Society was matched by his outspokenness in the Commons on issues relating to church reform.[30] Greville, for one, thought that Duncombe, who was notorious for his gambling, womanising and generally lax morals, was the last person who should be championing the dissenting cause in parliament. 'It is not a little remarkable', he wrote in 1837, 'that Duncombe is supported by all the Dissenters, even the Quakers, with whom austerity of morals and decent behavior are supposed to have weight.'[31] Of course, Duncombe was also supported (and perhaps supported more fervently) by Finsbury's Chartists and vestry ultra-radicals. Not surprisingly, the vestry was central to Duncombe's vision of church reform. By early February 1840 Duncombe had incorporated his twin desires for local democracy and church rate reform into a single bill that, he thought, would resolve the question for good. The bill contained an important innovation that would come to characterise the metropolitan anti-church rate movement throughout the 1840s and '50s. Unlike previous radical solutions, Duncombe's bill did not legislate for the abolition of the church rates. Instead, it sought merely to retain vestry control over the setting and collection of the church rate, while exempting non-Anglicans from payment of rates set by the vestry.[32] Although Duncombe's proposal was not quite a voluntarist solution, Russell none the less rejected it immediately. Russell believed that by exempting dissenters, the measure would fatally undermine the church establishment and, consequently, endanger the 'common good'. After his brief advocacy of church rate repeal in 1837, Russell had now returned to his staunch defence of the establishment principle.[33]

Duncombe's agitation on behalf of church reform in 1840 was partly inspired by the case of John Thorogood (of Chelmsford, Essex), who had taken part in his vestry's attempted rejection of the rate, refusing to pay his local church rate, only to be imprisoned as a consequence.[34] During the later months of 1839, Thorogood became notorious in radical and dissenting circles, and Duncombe positioned himself as his main champion in parliament. Thorogood had become the latest in an already long line of so-called 'vestry martyrs' – men whose vestry-based anti-church rates agitations were undermined by plural voting and other conditions of the Sturges Bourne Act,

---

[30] *London Mercury*, 23 Oct. 1836, 1; *The London Dispatch; and People's Political and Social Reformer*, 16 Oct. 1836, 36–7. D. W. Harvey, Thomas Challis and Apsley Pellat were also founding members of the Church Rate Abolition Society.
[31] *Greville memoirs*, iii. 140.
[32] *Hansard* 3rd ser. lii. 89–92, 11 Feb. 1840.
[33] Ibid. 3rd ser. lii.97.
[34] Ibid. 3rd ser. lii.88.

and whose property was spoiled or whose liberty was taken away as a result.[35] 'If', declared Duncombe in early February 1840, 'it was a fault for an individual to differ from others in political feeling, or in religious creed, such certainly he believed were the only crimes of Mr. Thorogood.'[36] The sacrifices made by 'vestry martyrs' were celebrated during the 1830s by periodicals such as the *Poor Man's Guardian*, *True Sun* and the *Patriot*.[37] More often than not, the attention given to vestry martyrdom by the radical media focused on the necessary injustices of select, closed or Sturges Bourne vestries. Thorogood's case again brought these issues before the public, and revived the anti-church rate movement during a period of relative complacency and quiet. In London, this revival led to some important developments.

By 1841, as Richard Brent has observed, 'the campaign against the church rates had taken the form of local and direct action'.[38] In Tower Hamlets, which throughout the 1830s remained relatively uncritical of Whiggery and distant from the metropolitan vestry radical movement, the local church reform movement helped to bring about parochial awareness and vestry politicisation. At St Leonard's, Shoreditch, the ultra-radicals Gough, Pearce and M'Douall began in 1837 to lead their vestry in persistent criticism of both the 'centralising' New Poor Law and the remaining corn laws.[39] Such vestry-organised criticism of Whig policy prepared the way for the Shoreditch Parochial Association, which sought to protect the vestry from the Poor Law Commissioners and preserve its right to refuse to set a church rate.[40] From early October 1843 members of the association, led by a solicitor named Peter Thomas, conducted a series of vestry-based rebellions against the setting of a church rate. The militant and chaotic nature of these rebellions brought national publicity to the St Leonards radicals.[41] Perhaps even more important, the anti-church rate agitations of the Shoreditch radicals also seem to have inspired other Tower Hamlets vestry reformers, and particularly those in East Hackney and Stepney, to use their own vestries for similar ends.[42] The

---

[35] Machin tells the story of a vestry martyr named Nunn, who was resident in St John's, Hackney: *Politics and the Churches*, 103.

[36] *Hansard* 3rd ser. lii.89, 11 Feb. 1840.

[37] For a typical treatment of 'vestry martyrs' see *Poor Man's Guardian*, 1 Feb. 1834, 459.

[38] Brent, 'The Whigs and Protestant dissent', 909.

[39] *The Times*, 28 Feb. 1837, 6; 24 Sept. 1841, 4.

[40] *Morning Advertiser*, 5 Oct. 1844, 3; 20 Dec. 1842, 3. This organisation should not be confused with the 'Shoreditch Parochial Reform Association', which was founded in 1850 to alter the appointment of the parish's trustees of the poor: *Shoreditch Advertiser*, 5 June, 26 July 1862.

[41] *The Times*, 5 Oct. 1843, 5; 24 June 1843, 6.

[42] In July the Hackney reformers used their vestry to defeat the rate: *Morning Advertiser*, 13 July 1844, 3.

Stepney Anti-Church Rate and Parochial Reform Society made the connection explicit in its double-barrelled mission to defeat 'any future attempt to
saddle the parish with church rates; and [to promote] the furtherance of
parish reforms, and to watch over parochial expenditures'.[43] From 1842
Tower Hamlets vestry radicals began to promote this agenda by publishing
newspapers such as the *Parochial Expositor; or Anti-Church Rate Gazette*,
which grew directly out of the Shoreditch church rate rebellions, and which
linked church rate reform closely to the empowerment of local government.

At the same time, parliamentary candidates such as T. E. P. Thompson
began to recognise the increasing overlap between vestry radicalism and the
church rate reform movement in Tower Hamlets. Thompson's 1841 Tower
Hamlets campaign advocated widespread governmental retrenchment
(including the repeal of the corn laws) alongside the abolition of the church
rates and the imposition of the six points of the Charter. Thompson also
spoke out strongly in favour of local self-government: the 'English right to
local self-government' provided the central theme of his nomination speech,
which condemned successive Whig ministries for trampling this right and for
introducing what Thompson called the 'great evil [of] the system of centralisation'.[44] Although Thompson's campaign ended in crushing defeat (he
polled only 830 votes to C. R. Fox's over 4,000) it was none the less a watershed moment for the borough. For the first time, 'local self-government' and
anti-Whiggery appeared in Tower Hamlets as election issues, and they owed
their appearances to the unpopularity of the church rates. In years to come
(as the result of the 1847 election proves) localists and critics of Whiggery
would become much more successful.

With the Tower Hamlets vestries now joining the rest of London in challenging their local rates, and with Duncombe's bill setting the tone of debate,
the metropolitan solution to the church rates seemed to lie increasingly with
the vestries. Yet the vestries remained in a precarious position. Although the
metropolitan radicals had led numerous vestry rebellions against the rates in
the 1830s and '40s, the question of whether vestries could legally refuse to set
a rate remained unsettled until 1853, when a final judicial decision was
reached concerning vestry obstructionism. In fact, from the late 1830s steps
had been taken by both the Melbourne and Russell administrations to outlaw
vestry refusal to set a church rate. Responding to an increasingly pronounced
establishment fear that parish churches throughout England might be left to
decay if their funding was controlled by radical vestries, the newly appointed
Ecclesiastical Commissioners advised that vestry majorities opposed to

---

[43] Ibid. 21 Mar. 1846, 3.
[44] *The Times*, 1 July 1841, 3.

setting church rates should be considered invalid. In 1837 this view launched a famous and ultimately decisive test case over vestry control of the church rates, when the Braintree (Essex) vestry was persuaded by the metropolitan Unitarian and *Leader*-affiliated radicals Samuel Courtauld and P. A. Taylor to vote against setting a church rate for the following year. Faced with Courtauld's substantial vestry majority, the Braintree churchwardens recalled the advice of the Ecclesiastical Commissioners and decided to set a church rate themselves. When a local dissenter named Burder refused to pay this 'illegal' rate, the churchwardens took him to the Consistorial Court of London, where Stephen Lushington (the Russellite MP for the Tower Hamlets) ruled in favour of the churchwardens. This decision infuriated a group of prominent metropolitan radicals (including the freethinkers and Unitarians William Ashurst, Peter Alfred Taylor, W. J. Fox and Aplsey Pellat), who started a subscription to fund Burder's further legal battles.[45] The sustained support and agitation of this group enabled the eventual reversal of the initial decision in August 1853, when the House of Lords ruled that a rate must be made by a majority in vestry, and that no other rate was valid.[46]

Samuel Courtauld, whose support was especially important to the ultimate success of the Braintree cause, publicised the agitation as a straightforward fight for the extension and empowerment of 'local self-government'. While giving evidence to a parliamentary select committee on church rates in 1851, for instance, Courtauld made it clear that he promoted the Braintree cause merely as a vehicle for promoting voluntarism and vestry power. Asked by the select committee-man Alexander Hope whether 'a mixed minority of Churchmen and Dissenters taxing a mixed majority of Churchmen and Dissenters is, in your mind, a great grievance?', Courtauld responded that

It is a great grievance that they should do so; it is not, in my mind a great grievance that they should have the power of doing so; that is the grand distinction. If I were in a vestry in which there were only a dozen Dissenters and hundreds of Churchmen, and the question came to be considered, 'Shall we lay a compulsory rate including the Dissenters', I would argue against it, and I would say, 'it is not right for you to tax the minority under these circumstances'; but I have no objection to their having the power of considering that question. I have a very great regard for that remnant of our Saxon institutions which under these parochial arrangements gives to a parochial community a power of

---

[45] S. Courtauld, *The Braintree church-rate case: report of the proceedings on the occasion of the presentation of a testimonial to Samuel Courtauld*, London 1857; Venturi, *Mr. Morris's 80th birthday party*.

[46] G. Martin, *A brief statement of the effect of the judgments given in the Braintree case on the law of church rates*, Exeter 1854, 5.

self-government, though they may not always exercise that power well ... I do not know that I should be at all opposed to the law of church rate, so far as it devolves upon a parish the power of dealing with that church rate; I am not the less opposed to any imposition, of church rate, upon Dissenters; and more- over I would say, for myself and others, that we should deprecate above all things any legislative settlement of this vexed question of church rates, which would throw any portion of the church rate charges upon the public revenues, having in our own mind the separation of what I call Church and State.[47]

According to Courtauld, the issue of local self-government, and not the propriety of having Dissenters pay for the upkeep of the Anglican fabric, was the truly important issue at the bottom of the church rate controversy. As with Duncombe's 1840 plan, Courtauld's evidence rejected any legislative solution involving commutation or even abolition, and endorsed instead a system of complete vestry control as the best solution. This was, according to Courtauld, a voluntary solution.[48] The strong support given to this view by Stansfeld, Taylor, Shaen and other members of the South Place community again suggests the political, rather than moral, priorities of many metropol- itan Unitarians and freethinkers. The localist Southwark MP Apslet Pellat, who was also questioned by the same select committee, agreed with Courtauld's analysis and articulated the vestry radical view that the greatest obstacle blocking the satisfaction of the dissenters was not the church rates themselves, but the Sturges Bourne Act, which often prevented vestry radi- cals and dissenters from being able to refuse the rates.[49] Pellat's criticism of the Sturges Bourne Act in relation to the church rate controversy was not unusual. In 1834 William Carpenter and Thomas M'Connell had made the same criticism in the course of their failed church rate rebellion in Lambeth. Given the perceived relevance of vestry plural voting, it should come as little surprise that the church rate debate was often tied together with the poor law debate. Courtauld and his South Place Unitarian radical friends, for instance, conceived of the church rate debate in similar terms to the New Poor Law controversy:

the Church Rate is 'a Tax' with which 'Parishioners' (not Lands) are lawfully charged, when by a majority, parishioners levy such a tax upon themselves ... in respect of its nature as a Tax, Church Rate stands upon the same ground as

---

47 *Report from the select committee on church rates together with the proceedings of the committee, minutes of evidence, appendix and index*, PP, ix (1851), qq. 620–1.
48 Ibid. q. 993.
49 Ibid. qq. 1732–4.

Poor Rate, which every lawyer knows is not a charge upon Lands, but a tax upon Persons, distributable according to their relative means as indicated by the Lands they occupy; the only distinction between the nature of the Poor Rate tax and the Church rate tax being this, that the one, having its origin in Act of Parliament for the support of the poor, Overseers can levy the tax without consent of the *taxed*; while the Church Rate, – originating in free will offerings, and devoted to purposes for which by law the tithes were liable – can only be imposed by churchwardens with the consent of the *taxed*.[50]

By 1855 the centrality of the metropolitan vestries to the church rate reform debate was universally acknowledged. Even William Clay, who had long harboured a Russellite suspicion of 'that bogey local-self government', was careful not to alienate his newly-radicalised Tower Hamlets vestry reformers. Clay's church rate abolition bill of 1856 made sure 'not to touch, except in one particular, the rights or constitution of the vestries'.[51] Clay's new-found deference to the institutions of local government illustrates the extent to which London's political culture had changed by 1855. Samuel Courtauld, who conceived of the church rate as a straightforward tax, summed up the metropolitan anti-church rate agitation by airing his view that

> I should have no objection if the consideration of these questions [church rate reform] were transferred from the Imperial parliament to the parochial parliament; I should have no objection if a parish in the exercise of their own self-government, and in the determining of those things in which their own interests are concerned, had a power by law of determining whether they would lay a tax for this, that, or the other purpose which they deemed to be right, whether a lighting tax, a tax for mending a bridge, for sewerage, or even for church rate.[52]

By 1855 Palmerston had come out publicly in support of the abolition of the church rate while Russell remained vigorously opposed to such a dangerous undermining of the church establishment.[53] Metropolitan Russellites like Sir Robert Grosvenor made very few concessions to the voluntarist and localist attitudes that motivated the metropolitan anti-church rate movement.[54]

[50] S. Courtauld, *At a meeting of the friends of civil and religious liberty*, London 1840, 2–3.

[51] W. Clay, *Speech of William Clay on moving the second reading of the church rate abolition bill*, London 1856, 16.

[52] *Report of the select committee on church rates*, ix, q. 993.

[53] Ellens, 'Russell and the church rate conflict', 250.

[54] R. Grosvenor, *The only compromise possible in regard to the church rate*, London 1861.

Palmerston's seeming endorsement of these attitudes, however, went a long way towards winning him metropolitan radical support. At the same time, metropolitan radicals understood Russell's attempts to strengthen the church establishment (and his various unsatisfactory proposals for church rate reform) as yet another indication that he would happily trample 'local rights' in pursuit of a centralised, paternalist state.

The window tax, 1851

In 1834, just as London's parochial radicals began to despair over Whig policy on the church rate, there emerged a widespread hope that Althorp's budget would finally rid London of the hated window and house taxes. Like the metropolitan anti-church rate movement, opposition to these duties originated in the vestries and revealed the anti-statist, anti-paternalist and fundamentally entrepreneurial attitudes of its promoters. In Marylebone, Barlow Street committee radicals such as William Hovendon and John Savage attacked the window and house taxes on the grounds that they injured commercial interests. At a succession of St Marylebone vestry meetings in February, Samuel Wilson spoke about the harmful effects of these duties on the glass industry, while others objected that the taxes imposed an 'intolerable burden on the trading and the middle-classes of the community', and fell 'with particular and grievous effect on the housekeepers, tradesmen, and shopkeepers in London'. In lieu of the taxes, the Marylebone radicals called for 'strict economy' and government retrenchment. 'Let the government only do its duty', proclaimed the Marylebone radicals, 'let economy and retrenchment be carried much further than at present ... let every reduction that could possibly be made be carried into effect.'[55] The petition that grew out of these vestry meetings emphasised with equal force the necessity of drastic state retrenchment. 'In praying your honourable House for the repeal of these taxes', wrote the petition's author Thomas Potter, 'we do not suggest any new taxes to supply their place, because we think that no new taxes ought to be imposed until economy and retrenchment have been carried to their utmost limits.' Retrenchment was to be preferred even to the implementation of a

---

[55] *The Times*, 4 Feb. 1834, 5. This view of the window and house taxes being taxes upon the metropolitan middle class is also put forward in L. J. Marshall, *Substance of a speech delivered by Lawrence J. Marshall, Esq. at a parish meeting at Hackney, on the 28th February, 1833 for the repeal of the house and window tax*, London 1833, 4. 'I advocate the repeal of those taxes', argues Marshall, 'because I consider them to press unfairly on the middle-class, and the metropolis and the districts surrounding it.'

land tax, which had also gained some support among metropolitan radicals and had grown out of the widespread impression that the house and window duties benefited the rural population, and especially the aristocracy, at the expense of the urban industrious classes.[56]

In the wake of the February meetings, the *True Sun* was delighted to report widespread public opposition to the assessed taxes. 'We rejoice', proclaimed the paper, 'to mark the spirit of determined opposition to these most infamous and oppressive imposts. Let there be no compromise with the *explanation-giving* ALTHORP and his coadjutors. These men never yet conceded any thing to justice – nor will they now.'[57] As with the church rates, Althorp's 1834 budget proved a great disappointment on the assessed taxes. Although the house tax was done away with, the budget ultimately retained the even less popular window tax. Radical outrage over the Whig failure to abolish this tax was acute, and in the wake of the budget the commercially-oriented criticisms originally raised by the Marylebone radicals during the vestry meetings of February 1834 set the tone for the ensuing debate. Noting the great surplus in the exchequer, the St Marylebone vestry again characterised the window tax as a prejudicial levy on the productive classes. 'It might be said', claimed one vestryman, 'that the window tax ... ought not to be abolished, because it did not rest upon the lower classes of society as other taxes did. To this he would reply, that it pressed grievously on the middle-class, to which he himself belonged, and that therefore it ought to be repealed.'[58]

Despite a sustained campaign of respectable commercial objections such as these, the first real opportunity finally to repeal the window tax did not present itself until February 1851, at a time when the Exchequer contained a record surplus. Throughout January various metropolitan vestries met to instruct their respective borough MPs on how to go about effecting repeal of the tax.[59] In the course of these meetings, the tax was variously characterised as 'oppressive', 'tyrannical', 'wasteful' and 'ridiculous' coming from a government that professed commitment to sanitary reform.[60] In early February a deputation from the leading radical metropolitan vestries was presented to Charles Wood by a group of more than 300 delegates who had made their way to Whitehall in a procession of sixty carriages from the Marylebone court-

---

56 *The Spectator*, 26 Apr. 1834, 395.
57 *True Sun*, 4 Feb. 1834, 3.
58 *The Times*, 23 Feb. 1837, 6.
59 *Morning Advertiser*, 9 Jan. 1851, 3; 17 Jan. 1851, 3; 18 Jan. 1851, 3; 25 Jan. 1851, 3; *The Times* 23 Jan. 1851, 3.
60 *The Times*, 28 Jan. 1851, 8.

house via Oxford Street, Regent Street, Pall Mall and Charing Cross. Each of the carriages displayed its own parish livery, and each carried a large placard reading 'unconditional repeal of the window tax'.[61] As in 1834 the tax was characterised by the delegation as a burden on commerce endured primarily 'not [by] the owners of extensive, magnificent, and splendid mansions with ample means and princely incomes – but [by] retail shopkeepers and the occupants of shops and warehouses'.[62]

Monster meetings in Westminster, Marylebone and Southwark followed closely on the heels of the deputation. 'The Chancellor of the Exchequer had told them', declared a St James radical named Nelson at a Westminster meeting, 'that no proposition could be successful without popular agitation. He thought the right hon. gentlemen would have plenty of it there.'[63] At the meetings, as at previous ones, speakers issued direct challenges to Whig sincerity over sanitary reform. Lord Duncan, for instance, railed against 'that miserable humbug the Sanitary Commission', while the prominent Westminster radical Henry Geesin exclaimed, 'how inconsistent and absurd to talk of introducing sanitary measures while this tax, obstructing the light of Heaven, and destructive of healthful ventilation, remained upon the statute-book!'[64] In Marylebone radicals took the argument one step further, calling for the resignation of the government if the window tax remained. The prominent radical, and later Palmerstonian, J. A. Nicholay, who chaired a meeting at the Marylebone courthouse on 20 February, made it clear that 'that [courthouse] assembly was a council of war; and they [the participants] meant to show the Chancellor of the Exchequer that they meant war, and no mistake … the game was in the hands of the people of the metropolis. The position of the ministry was so tottering that the metropolitan members could turn the balance'. Toulmin Smith, who had been moving ever closer to the Marylebone radicals on reform of metropolitan local government, was also in attendance and vigorously denounced the window tax and the Whig government.[65] Each of these meetings stressed the need for strict economy and further government retrenchment, and many of them (especially Marylebone and Southwark) expressed hostility even to any proposed income tax. In Southwark, local radicals went so far as to ask 'were there no men who had the spirit of the late Sir R. Peel?'. William Molesworth responded that 'he followed the policy of the late Robert Peel'.[66]

61 *Morning Advertiser*, 7 Feb. 1851, 6.
62 United Parishes of Westminster, *Facts illustrative of the great inequity of the taxes*, 8; *The Times*, 7 Feb. 1851, 8.
63 *The Times*, 13 Feb. 1851, 5.
64 Ibid.
65 Ibid. 20 Feb. 1851, 8.
66 Ibid. 27 Feb. 1851, 5.

Throughout the agitation against the window tax, vestries exerted remarkable powers over the parliamentary representatives of their boroughs. While presenting the 1851 deputation to Charles Wood, for instance, Wakley joked that if repeal of the window tax was not achieved the metropolitan electorate might refuse the supplies, but would certainly refuse to send their present members back to parliament.[67] Ultimately, the parochial agitation convinced Wood to repeal the window tax in 1851. Although he renewed the house tax in its place, this was a significant victory for the vestry reformers. As the *Ratepayer and Borough Chronicle: Tower Hamlets Reporter* put it,

the conduct of the metropolitan parishes in opposing the continuation of the window tax, and in endeavoring to obtain from her Majesty's ministry a repeal of that most obnoxious measure, is worthy of all praise. Not satisfied with denouncing it at their private and public meetings, and in numerous petitions to parliament, they have waited by deputation on the Chancellor of the Exchequer, and pressed upon him personally, the necessity and the justice of a repeal of a law which by tending to exclude the light and air of heaven, has had more victims sacrificed to its continuance than ever stained the altar of Juggernaut.

This agitation will, it is to be hoped, be productive of a further good: it will serve to convince the most confiding, that no tax will ever be repealed, unless at the urgent demand of the people, and that if further good is to be effected, the parochial bodies must by the perseverance of the ratepayers become so many bodies whereby the wishes of the nation may be learned and their wants redressed.[68]

---

67 *Morning Advertiser*, 7 Feb. 1851, 6.
68 *Ratepayer and Borough Chronicle: The Tower Hamlets Reporter*, 1 Mar. 1851, 8.

5

Redefining the State, II:
The London Government Problem

1834 was a decisive year in the deterioration of Whiggery's relationship to the metropolitan radical movement. In addition to being the year of maturation for London's Hobhouse vestries, 1834 played host to the heated debates on church rate and poor law reform which initiated a polarisation between vestry-based libertarians and Whig centralisers. From 1835 this was crystallised by debates on the reform of municipal government. London's omission from the Municipal Corporations Act lent further force to the metropolitan radical critique of Whiggery as the party of centralisation while simultaneously undermining such a critique in the provinces. The same was true of succeeding local government legislation. Whereas provincial opposition to the 1848 Public Health Act, for instance, revived the language of 'Whig centralisation' in places such as Leeds and Birmingham, the measure was none the less aimed at giving existing provincial municipal corporations more fully developed sanitary powers, and in fact the act's author, Lord Morpeth, maintained that the 1848 bill could be called a measure 'for consolidating, strengthening, and making more effectual the functions of local bodies in the various municipal towns of England and Wales'.[1] Russell agreed, and claimed that 'the essential object of the bill ... is giving local bodies the power of making sanitary laws'.[2] London, to which the Public Health Act did not apply, faced an altogether different level of central intrusion. From 1847 the implementation of Chadwick's 'London Programme' meant that the metropolitan sewers would be administered by a commission almost wholly appointed by central government. In the years following the establishment of

---

[1] See *Hansard* 3rd ser. xci. 624–31, 639–40, 30 Mar. 1847. For the radical argument against the Public Health Act see J. Toulmin Smith, *Centralisation or representation? The laws relating to public health*, London 1848. See also *Hansard* 3rd ser. xcviii. 713–15, 5 May 1848. Roberts, *Victorian origins*, also provides an overview.
[2] *Hansard* 3rd ser. xci. 624–31, 639–40, 30 Mar. 1847.

that commission, London's interment regime and water supply came under constant threat of central state control. The process of administrative centralisation was facilitated by the fact that London's sewers, graveyards and water had never been subject to any kind of municipal control. Prior to 1847 the sewers, for instance, had been administered by eight separate *ad hoc* boards of commissioners. None of these was accountable to vestry or any other form of representative local government. The great and central difficulty of the so-called 'London government problem' was that there was no 'London government' to speak of.

The 'London government problem' played a central part in the construction of early Victorian metropolitan political culture. Contrary to F. D. Roberts's claim that northern radicals 'took a much more hostile attitude to central government than did the London Liberals', London's unsettled administrative arrangements inflamed the anti-statist prejudices of many metropolitan radicals by nurturing among them a heightened vigilance against any encroachments on local prerogative.[3] It was precisely the unresolved nature of the metropolitan local administration that promoted such an astonishing sensitivity to the growth of a centralising state. At the same time, the open-endedness of the 'government problem' provided radicals with myriad opportunities to advance their own schemes for the extension and development of local self-government beyond its existing parish organisation. Moreover, contrary to the orthodox historiographical view, most of the localist solutions were not motivated by a narrowly self-interested concern for keeping rates low whatever the cost.[4] Rather, vestry-based radicals used the London government problem to advance a democratic reform agenda informed by an ideological opposition to both landowner and state paternalism. Whereas issues such as the church rate and the New Poor Law were exploited by radicals in a merely negative fashion to preserve the supposed prerogatives of parish government, the threat posed by the Russellite agenda for central control of metropolitan municipal government jolted radicals out of this reactionary pose. To put it another way, while Whig policy on the poor laws and church rates helped to galvanise metropolitan ideological commitment to 'local self-government', the 'government problem', and sanitary reform in particular, provoked radicals into constructing their own positive visions of precisely how 'local self-government' should work in prac-

---

[3] Roberts, *Victorian origins*, 79.
[4] For this orthodox portrayal of vestrymen see especially J. Firth, *Municipal London*, London 1876; Webb, *English local government*, especially ch. vii; Finer, *Life of Chadwick*; W. A. Robson, *The government and mismanagement of London*, London 1939; and Francis Sheppard's introduction to Owen, *Victorian London*.

tice. During the twenty years following the passage of the Municipal Corporations Act, London's vestry radicals promoted a series of municipal solutions to the 'government problem'. Some of their solutions promoted entrepreneurial interests, privileged the rights of private capital and sought to restrict as far as possible the scope of state interference (whether local or central) in the provision of utility services. Others argued for the establishment of powerful and interventionist municipal institutions which would do more than simply enable private enterprise to solve the problems of urbanisation. All were in agreement, however, that the central state had no legitimate role to play in administering metropolitan affairs. From the mid-1840s this consensus brought metropolitan radicals into a more direct and sharper conflict with Whiggery.

Reform and resistance, 1835–47

Although the 1831 Hobhouse Act politicised many of London's largest and wealthiest vestries, its impact on wider metropolitan political culture was vitiated by patchy application. Five metropolitan parishes adopted the act; a further seventy-three, however, were technically unaffected by it. For most metropolitan vestries, Hobhouse's measure was little more than an aspiration. Consequently, throughout the early 1830s Whig-Radicals such as Joseph Hume and Francis Place – both of whom had been prominent supporters of Hobhouse's measure – hoped that a second dose of local government reform might rationalise London's local government in a more comprehensive fashion.[5] The appointment in July 1833 of a royal commission to investigate the state of English and Welsh municipal corporations seemed a promising sign of government intention to do just this. Place in particular savoured the prospect of a democratic metropolitan municipal corporation.[6]

London's exclusion from the 1835 Municipal Corporations Act was a disappointment to those reformers who had heralded Hobhouse's act as the first step toward a comprehensive system of metropolitan representative local government.[7] The reform measures of 1835 sprang from the same set of moti-

---

[5] For Place's expectations see, for instance, Place papers, MS Add. 35149, fo. 236.

[6] Place was especially enthusiastic about the possibilities of municipal reform, and he even published a short-lived periodical entitled the *Municipal Corporation Reformer*: Wallas, *Life of Place*, 341–3.

[7] For the Municipal Corporations Act see W. I. Jennings, 'The municipal revolution', in H. Laski (ed.), *A century of municipal progress: 1835–1935*, London 1935, 58; B. Keith-Lucas, *The English local government franchise*, Oxford 1952; Keith-Lucas's introduction to

vations as Hobhouse's, and both acts belonged to the same legislative lineage. Whereas Hobhouse referred to his Select Vestries Act as the 'pilot balloon for the great reform Act', Joseph Parkes described the Municipal Corporations Act as 'the postscript to the reform bills of 1832'.[8] Both measures also benefited from the enthusiastic support of Francis Place, who acted as silent partner to both Hobhouse in 1831 and Parkes in 1834–5. Despite the importance of Place's input, Parkes's personal contribution to the electoral reforms of the 1830s, and to the character of the 1835 reform in particular, cannot be understated.[9] Although he maintained strong Whig connections, Parkes's views on local government were essentially those of a vestry radical.[10] This meant that while many Tories understood municipal corporation reform as a party measure designed to boost Whig parliamentary electoral fortunes, Parkes himself seems to have rejected the notion that the act would promote Whiggery in any way.[11] 'Whigs', he wrote to Place shortly after the reform had been passed, 'will of course rouse their bidding with the People's growing power and demand. They are an unnatural party standing between the People and the Tory aristocracy chiefly for the pecuniary value of offices and vanity of power. Their hearse is ordered.'[12] Fittingly, as the Municipal Corporations Bill was being debated in the House of Lords, Parkes began to collaborate closely with the Marylebone vestry radicals on a series of addresses to parliament in favour of the full bill and in condemnation of the obstinacy of the peers.[13]

S. Webb and B. Webb, *English local government from the revolution to the municipal corporations act*, London 1963; and Salmon, *Electoral reform at work*.

[8] Parkes to Place, Place papers, MS Add. 35150, fo. 99; Hobhouse, *Recollections of a long life*, i, 130.

[9] G. Finlayson, 'The municipal corporation commission and report, 1833–1835', *BIHR* xxxvi (1963), 40–1.

[10] William Thomas has described Parkes as a 'radical by conviction, [but a] Whig by interest and temperament': *Philosophic radicals*, 251–3. The same could be said of Hobhouse.

[11] For the bill's party dimension see especially G. Finlayson, 'The politics of municipal reform, 1835', *EHR* lxxxi (1966), 673–92; J. Phillips and C. Wetherall, 'Parliamentary parties and municipal politics: 1835 and the party system', *PH* xiii (1994), 48–85; and P. Salmon, 'Local politics and partisanship: the electoral impact of municipal reform, 1835', *PH* xix (2000), 357–76.

[12] Parkes to Place, Place papers MS Add. 35150, fos 100–2.

[13] In addition to being well known and respected by the vestry radicals, Parkes was prominent and well connected within London's South Place Chapel Unitarian community, the very social epicentre of the *Leader* circle of retrenchment-minded radicals and liberals: J. K. Buckley, *Joseph Parkes of Birmingham*, London 1926, 8, 124–5. Of course, Parkes was not the only 1835 commissioner with localist sympathies. His fellow commissioner, Francis Palgrave, shared Toulmin Smith's romantic view of Saxon institutions of local government in works such as *Observations on the principles to be adopted in the establishment of new*

Given London's omission from the 1835 reform, Parkes's Marylebone friends would have to wait a further two years before a separate royal commission turned its attentions to the operation of the City Corporation and the wider possibilities for metropolitan municipal government. Although the 1835 act did not apply to London, the widespread publicity given to it none the less inspired a series of movements for incorporation in parts of the metropolis. In Southwark the St Olave's vestryman George Richard Corner teamed up with D. W. Harvey, John Day and the Southwark Reform Association to argue for the advantages of either merging with the City Corporation or alternatively reorganising Southwark into a municipal corporation of its own.[14] This movement in turn prompted a separate group of Southwark householders to petition the City for admission to its Corporation.[15] Although the petition was ultimately rejected by the Common Council, Southwark's desire to be incorporated within the City did grab the attention of the 1837 commissioners, who wondered in the pages of their *Report* why the City had refused Southwark's request.[16] In fact, Southwark's desire to become part of a single enlarged City Corporation was entirely in keeping with the recommendations made by the 1835 commissioners for extending existing corporation boundaries to include developed areas on their outskirts.

Elsewhere, in metropolitan districts which lacked Southwark's unique historical relationship with the City, reaction to the 1835 act took different forms. In Finsbury, Thomas Wakley capitalised on heightened public awareness of local government issues by proposing an extension of the Hobhouse Select Vestries Act. After mounting a petitioning drive throughout May and early June, 1836 Wakley called on the Commons to nullify the terms of the second Sturges Bourne Act by applying the Hobhouse Act to every English vestry. If the principles promoted by the Sturges Bourne Act were just and desirable, why, Wakley asked his parliamentary colleagues, were they absent from both the 1832 Reform Act and the 1835 Municipal Corporations Act? Wakley's proposal demanded that London's vestries should enjoy the same 'representative principle' and the same freedoms from plural and proxy voting

---

municipal corporations, London 1832, and *The rise and progress of the English commonwealth: the Saxon period*, London 1832.

[14] G. R. Corner, *A concise account of the local government of the borough of Southwark, and observations upon the expediency of uniting the same more perfectly with the City of London or of obtaining a separate municipal corporation*, London 1836.

[15] An inhabitant of Southwark, *Statements of the inhabitants of Bridge Ward Without*, London 1836.

[16] *Municipal corporations in England and Wales: London and Souwark, London companies*, PP, xxv (1837), 17–18.

as the reformed corporations now did.[17] The government's hostile response (which, it should be noted, was grounded in a concern that extension of the Hobhouse act would interfere with the operation of the hugely unpopular poor law) further antagonised radical feeling toward Whiggery and prompted Daniel O'Connell to accuse Russell of opposing the measure out of a desire to protect his family interest in Bloomsbury, where the Sturges Bourne Act helped to keep the local administration in the hands of the largest landlords.[18] Despite strong support from London's leading radical MPs, Wakley's measure was ultimately defeated. Yet, in defeat, the measure still advertised the widespread feeling within London, touched off by the success of the 1835 act, that the question of metropolitan local government would need to be resolved sooner rather than later. Moreover, because it hinged on preserving the hated New Poor Law, the Whig rejection of Wakley's bill was doubly obnoxious to promoters of local self-government. At the very moment that local self-determination had been won for the provinces, the London government problem was perhaps further than ever from resolution.

By October 1837, when a second royal commission on municipal reform (this time operating without Parkes) finally presented its long-awaited *Report* on the City Corporation, recent vestry campaigns against the poor law and church rates had crystallised the metropolitan radical belief that Whiggery was inimical to the advance of local self-government. The findings of the 1837 *Report* did little to alter this belief. At its core lay a list of recommendations concerning the Corporation's relationship to the rest of the metropolis. The relationship was characterised by the commission as one 'of primary importance and difficulty' to the reform of the Corporation itself.[19] Consequently, although formally it was concerned only with investigating the corporation of London, the 1837 *Report* actually had much to say about the state of metropolitan governance generally. The commissioners discussed the precedent for expansion of the Corporation, as enshrined in the 1835 act, only to arrive at the conclusion that similar steps could not be taken in London.[20] The boundaries of corporations that had been extended in 1835, reasoned the commissioners, belonged to municipal boroughs in which the 'nucleus of the town' remained the most important part of the whole district. In the vast majority of provincial towns, the areas that had been newly incorporated did not threaten to destroy the primary importance of the older municipal area. The relative importance of London's 'suburbs' *vis-à-vis* the

---

[17] *Hansard* 3rd ser. xxxiv. 747–8.
[18] Ibid. xxxiv.750.
[19] *Second report of the municipal corporations commission*, 2.
[20] Ibid.

City presented a different dynamic. Obviously, any extension of the Corporation to the rest of London would fatally undermine the powerful and independent position now occupied by the City.[21]

What, if anything, could be done to remedy the difficulties caused by the
City's relationship to the rest of the metropolis? London's social singularity
called for a singular solution. The *Report* refused to entertain the idea that, for
the purpose of removing the appearance of singularity, 'the other quarters of
the town should be formed into independent and isolated communities, if
indeed the multifarious relations to which their proximity compels them
would permit them to be isolated and independent. This plan would, as it
seems to us, in getting rid of an anomaly, tend to multiply and perpetuate an
evil'.[22] Solutions to the 'anomaly' of metropolitan government were further
complicated by the fact that London was the seat of the national, and indeed
the imperial, government. In the commission's view, London's unique relationship to parliament raised the question of whether London should have its
own municipal government at all. Perhaps, they suggested, London would
more profitably be governed by a semi-permanent royal commission. The
1837 commission supported its argument by appealing to a recent precedent.
'In one particular', stated the *Report*,

> and that a most important and practical one, the opinion of Parliament [as to
> the administrative status of London] has been already declared by the estab-
> lishment of a Metropolitan Police, under the orders of the Commissioners
> appointed by, and immediately dependent upon, Your Majesty's Executive
> Government ... Other topics suggest similar conclusions, as the paving sewer-
> age, and lighting of the streets, which, as it seems to us, can never be so eco-
> nomically and efficiently performed in one town as when superintended by an
> undivided authority; and the only real point for consideration is, how far these
> duties for the whole metropolis could be placed in the hands of a metropolitan
> municipality, or how far they should be entrusted to the Officers of Your
> Majesty's Government. With respect to sewerage, indeed, there is an obvious
> absurdity in placing the City, and any large district which drains into it from a
> higher level, under different superintendence.[23]

The commissioners had already made known their opposition to the creation
of a single metropolitan municipality. Only the second option therefore
seemed possible.

[21] Ibid. 4.
[22] Ibid.
[23] Ibid. 4–5.

This suggestion guided Whig thought on the London government problem for most of the next two decades. As late as 1851, for instance, the Whig sanitarian F. O. Ward argued in the pages of the *Quarterly Review* that, in municipal terms, London was a special case which required special measures. As the seat of imperial power, London could never be considered a mere locality. To Ward's mind, the interests of London were indistinguishable from the interests of the entire country and were therefore eminently national. 'The parishes of London', declared Ward, 'stand, therefore, in an exceptional position; and their sanitary well-being claims the solicitude, not merely of their respective guardians, but of Parliament, and of the Crown.' On top of this consideration, Ward also repeated the concern of the 1837 *Report* that an elected metropolitan municipal council would surely rival the imperial parliament in power and persuasion, and that this would 'tend to uncentre the balance of national and local powers, and might in periods of political excitement, exert a most inconvenient and unconstitutional pressure on the councils of the Queens government'.[24] A royal commission seemed to Ward the most appropriate solution to this issue of truly national import.

In 1837, in the face of intense radical criticism (led, it should be noted, by Wakley and Harvey) the government equivocated on metropolitan local government reform.[25] Perhaps also fearful of the City's clout, the Melbourne government never attempted to translate the *Report*'s suggestions into legislation. But while this saved the government from further radical abuse in the short term, the unresolved London government problem was allowed to fester and became even more entrenched. Perhaps more important, although the recommendations made by the 1837 commission were not immediately acted upon, they nevertheless provided the bedrock of Russellite policy towards the problem for the next two decades.

Consolidation, 1847–8

Throughout the later 1830s and 1840s, as provincial cities such as Manchester (1838) and Bradford (1847) were incorporated under the terms of the 1835 act, London's position became ever more anomalous. Rather than rectifying this situation, the public health legislation of 1847–8 estranged London still further from the national system of local government. Although Morpeth had originally intended to include London in the 1848 Public Health Act, and proposed the creation of an elective metropolitan munici-

24 *Quarterly Review* lxxxviii (1851), 461–2.
25 *The Spectator*, 2 Dec. 1837, 1135; *Hansard* 3rd ser. xxxix. 37–47, 81–91, 20 Nov. 1837.

pality through which the act might operate, Chadwick's opposition to such a policy ensured that London was left out.[26] By equipping corporations with a vast range of sanitary powers, the Public Health Act completed the process of local government rationalisation that the Municipal Corporations Act had started. The omission of London meant that, once again, a separate metro-politan measure would be needed. Again, there was a separate royal commis-sion of inquiry for London, to work in parallel with the Health of Towns Commission. The First Royal Commission on the Health of the Metropolis, which convened on 24 September 1847, was charged not with reforming metropolitan local government *per se*, but with investigating London's system of house drainage and main drainage, street cleansing and paving, scavenging and water supplies, and with recommending the best means of using existing works and erecting new ones, and of finding the most equitable means of rating and assessment.[27]

While superficially concerned with the preservation of public health, the investigation was also thoroughly political, as its recommendations would potentially affect the powers enjoyed by institutions of local government. The composition of the commission reflected this. In parliament, the Finsbury radical Thomas Wakley sensed a central government land grab.[28] Unlike the 1835 commission, this new inquiry was largely free from the influence of localist input. In fact, the City Common Councillor Richard Lambert Jones was the sole representative of the metropolitan vestry radical interest. Arch-Russellites such as Morpeth and Robert Grosvenor, on the other hand, assumed influential positions. Grosvenor in particular had been appointed expressly for the purpose of knowing 'what is likely to go down with the general metropolitan feeling'. In practice, however, he was out of touch with metropolitan feeling, as the subsequent Sunday trading fiasco proved, and it is very likely that his appointment was chiefly the result of his closeness to Russell.[29] Just as earlier royal commissions had been accused of promoting party ends, so this one came to be regarded as a Whig party job. Its conclusions were consequently regarded as anything but objective. There was 'no opinion, however absurd', claimed Toulmin Smith from the pages of the newly Peelite *Morning Chronicle*, 'no scheme, however mischievous, we

---

[26] George Howard (Lord Morpeth) to Chadwick, 21 Feb. 1848, Chadwick papers, 1055; *Hansard* 3rd ser. xci. 642, 30 Mar. 1847.

[27] *First report of the commissioners appointed to inquire whether any and what special means may be requisite for the improvement of the health of the metropolis*, PP, xxxii (1847–8).

[28] *Hansard* 3rd ser. xcvi. 414, 10 Feb. 1848.

[29] Morpeth to Chadwick, 25 July 1847, and Chadwick to Morpeth, 18 Nov, 1847, Chadwick papers, 1055.

might almost add, no "fact", however fictitious, for which [the commission] could not make up a fair-looking case'.[30] The disproportionate contribution of Benthamites such as Chadwick, Southwood Smith and Austin also signalled a revival of the type of commission that had been so integral to the 'scientific legislation' produced during the early and mid-1830s.[31] Chadwick, who was already reviled in metropolitan radical circles because of his association with the New Poor Law, was appointed secretary of the new body.

Ten years had passed since the publication of the 1837 *Report*. Throughout this decade, and particularly since his 1842 *Sanitary Report*, Chadwick had clung to the same rigid set of beliefs over how the London government problem ought to be solved.[32] To Chadwick's mind, the greatest obstacle to the good and efficient administration of London was not vestry parsimony and narrow-mindedness (although he repeatedly and savagely criticised these failings of the vestry 'shopocracy'), but rather the lack of a unified system – which made concerted effort on sanitation next to impossible.[33] The findings of the 1847 royal commission reflected this opinion completely, and echoed the recommendation first made by the 1837 *Report* that the establishment of a crown-appointed commission of experts would be the best solution to London's administrative chaos.[34] The *Report* went so far as to recommend that the City be included in a single metropolitan sanitary jurisdiction. The installation of a single crown-appointed commission for the entire metropolis would do more than just help flush the sewers. It would, in the commission's view, ultimately lead to fairer and lower rates.[35]

Although the 1847 *Report* received strong backing from both the Health of Towns Association and the *Times*, and although Morpeth lent his full weight to the drive to include the City in a unified system, important members of Russell's government remained unconvinced.[36] Charles Wood

---

[30] *Morning Chronicle*, 28 Apr. 1848, 3. Toulmin Smith made further attacks on the partisan nature of Whig investigations in *Government by commissions illegal and pernicious*, London 1849.

[31] See R. Johnson, 'Educating the educators: "experts" and the state, 1833–9', in A.P. Donajgrodski (ed.), *Social control in nineteenth-century Britain*, London 1977, 77–107; Brundage, *Making of the new poor law*; Finlayson, 'Municipal corporation commission'; and H. M. Clockie and J. W. Robinson, *Royal commissions of inquiry*, Stanford 1937.

[32] Finer, *Life of Chadwick*, 297–314.

[33] For a taste of Chadwick's views on the social unsuitability of the vestrymen see Chadwick to Delane, 27 Nov. 1850, and Chadwick to Delane 24 Mar. 1848, Chadwick papers, 608.

[34] *First report on the health of the metropolis*, 48–9.

[35] Ibid. 49.

[36] HOTA, *Report of the sub-committee on the state of towns*, London 1848; HTA, *The*

and George Grey were particularly uncomfortable with the *Report*'s recommendations and each man lobbied hard for an alternative solution which might accommodate the City's 'special interests'.[37] Moreover, many ministers were uncomfortable with the suggestion that the commission be entirely appointed. Even Chadwick's staunchest ally, Lord Morpeth, believed that the Consolidated Metropolitan Commission of Sewers should be at least partially elective and representative. Writing to Chadwick in August 1847, Morpeth admitted that he 'certainly had always leaned to the suggestion of giving somewhat of the principle of representation to it [the new authority], with the view of commending it at the outset to popular feeling'.[38] Morpeth was awake to the political dimensions of the measure and mindful of the need to placate vestry radical opinion. This course, he repeatedly told Chadwick, would greatly reduce opposition to the measure. At the same time, however, Morpeth was also sympathetic to Chadwick's view that a representative body would not be up to the task of carrying out the works and improvements required on the ground. In his view, any successful reform would unite 'efficiency with the *appearance* of freedom and local agency' and by doing so would 'disarm the foolish prejudice about what they term centralisation, without any undue sacrifice to efficiency; let it appear if possible as if the localities are doing the work themselves'.[39] But Chadwick could not allow even this. By 1847 he had become thoroughly disgusted by the 'hypocrisy' of the vestry radicals. The 'representative vestries', Chadwick complained to Delane, were not representative at all:

> In respect to the meeting of representatives of the Parishes, for putting the sewers of the metropolis under parochial or representative management let me call your attention to the fact that at the meeting some seven or such small number were represented not of upwards of one hundred and forty – (140). I believe you will find that the proceeding is one of a very small agitation consisting of very large parishes but by no means countenanced even in those parishes by the inhabitants at large. I have been informed of several parishes having been requested to join in the agitation but that they refused, often having fairly discussed the matter, and determined that however insufficient the present Commission might be they, the parishioners, were incompetent to

sanitary condition of the City of London, London 1848; *The Times*, 11 Sept. 1847, 4; 2 Dec. 1847, 4; 8 Dec. 1847, 4; Chadwick to Lord John Russell, 1 May 1848, and Chadwick to Delane, 24 Feb. 1848, Chadwick papers, 1733, 608.

[37] Chadwick to A. Doyle, 2 Dec. 1847, Chadwick papers, 648.

[38] Morpeth to Chadwick, 9 Aug. 1847, Chadwick papers, 1055. See also, Morpeth to Chadwick, 25 Jan. 1848, ibid.

[39] Morpeth to Chadwick, 25 July 1847, and Morpeth to Chadwick, 23 Aug. 1847, ibid.

judge either of the plans ... what a new metropolitan municipality would be is shown by what the municipality of the City is now ... The question is however not whether money shall be expended without representation but whether the great minorities as well as the majority of the inhabitants of the metropolis will not have more responsible representation through Parliament than through a parochial parliament. In the metropolis, we think the former responsibility will really be the greater, of which the example of the City municipality appears the decisive evidence.[40]

Chadwick's strong resistance to giving even token representation to the ratepayers found support from Russell, who declared himself in no uncertain terms to be 'against Municipalities for London. They would be bad for local purposes, still worse for general purposes ... the police are under Government Commission – Metropolitan roads ditto – Sewers ditto'.[41] Grosvenor advanced similar views. In fact, as chairman of the Metropolitan Sanitary Association, he repeatedly praised the newly centralised Parisian sewer system and suggested that it be used as a model for London's.[42] Given the strong support of Russell and Grosvenor, Chadwick declined to include the representative principle in any plans, and the life of the nominated commission was extended in June 1848. This was a significant political miscalculation on Russell's part. An elected sanitary authority would have been both much more acceptable to radical opinion and much more effective at bringing metropolitan administrative arrangements (and perhaps metropolitan political culture) into line with those enjoyed by the rest of the country.

Throughout the late 1840s and early 1850s the MCS remained an isolated, unaccountable, and alarmingly 'executive' body. If Whiggery's metropolitan critics had ever entertained doubts over whether the Whigs were the party of centralisation, these were forever dispelled by the establishment of the new sanitary authority. Toulmin Smith, for one, could not resist noting in the wake of the establishment of the Consolidated Commission that

---

40 Chadwick to Delane, 27 Nov. 1850, ibid. 608. In a pamphlet Hugh Fortescue echoed Chadwick's view, claiming that 'Sir George Grey ... intimated to the Anti-Centralisation gentlemen of Marylebone and St. Pancras, that, if they would only get the signatures of a majority of the inhabitants to a petition for the grant of a charter of incorporation, no impediment would be offered to their having the Municipal Corporation Act applied to them in the usual way. But the majority they have not got yet, and know they cannot get; though there was nothing to prevent their obtaining it at once, had the public feeling of those parishes been what it was represented to be': *Representative self-government for the metropolis: a letter to Viscount Palmerston*, London 1854, 29.

41 Lord John Russell to Seymour, 30 Oct. 1851, Muncaster papers, Muncaster Castle, Cumbria. Russell proposed 'a Government Commission with 3 paid and 4 or 6 unpaid Commissioners'.

42 Lord Robert Grosvenor to Chadwick, 25 Sept. 1847, Chadwick papers, 899.

the Metropolitan Sanitary Commission professes to have been appointed for the purpose of inquiring 'whether any and what special means may be requisite for the improvement of the health of the metropolis.' Its real end would appear to have been to forward the ceaseless attempts of a liberal government towards engrossing under one central patronage the actual control over all local institutions, works, and arrangements, small as well as great, to the destruction of the local representative institutions on which the security, independence, welfare, and character of England and Englishmen entirely depend.[43]

The radical rejection of the 'London programme'

Although the establishment of the Metropolitan Commission of Sewers can now be seen as the (rather premature) high point of Chadwickian achievement in metropolitan sanitary and administrative reform, Chadwick himself understood it as a means to an end rather than as an end in itself. Replacement of the six ancient sewer commissions was for Chadwick merely the first step towards the accomplishment of a wider 'London programme' of administrative improvements. In addition to effective main and house drainage, Chadwick's programme called for an ambitious unified state administration of metropolitan paving, street cleansing, water supply and extramural interment.[44] Once the MCS had been established (and well stocked with Chadwick's supporters) the supersession of the existing paving boards and the establishment of a new street cleansing regime would follow. Chadwick's expulsion from the MCS in 1849 and the political clout of the water companies, however, made water and interment reform much more difficult to effect.[45] In the wake of his alienation from the MCS, Chadwick would be forced to advocate metropolitan water and interment reform from his position on the General Board of Health – an institution which had no jurisdiction over London. Vestry radical opposition to the substance of Chadwick's reform plans, and to GBH meddling in metropolitan affairs generally, revealed a movement motivated by entrepreneurial as well as democratic values and priorities

Chadwick himself admitted to applying identical principles to both extramural interment and water reform.[46] Each reform sought to promote the interests of the metropolitan poor by challenging the advantages that an

---

43 Toulmin Smith, *Centralisation or representation?*, pp. xi–xii.
44 See Finer, *Life of Chadwick*, 309–10.
45 Lewis, *Edwin Chadwick*, 216–37; Hamlin, *Social justice*, 309–10; Finer, *Life of Chadwick*, 355–76.
46 Chadwick to Delane, Oct. 1851, Chadwick papers, 608.

unregulated marketplace had given to a relatively small group of interested parties – the water company directors on the one hand and the shareholders of the joint stock cemeteries on the other. From 1849 Chadwick's push for utility regulation touched off a wave of radical protest. Prior metropolitan radical opposition to Whig administrative reform had hinged mainly on the preservation or extension of local self-government. Now, with the prospect of central state provision of metropolitan water and interment services, prominent vestry radicals began to articulate an entrepreneurial critique of centralisation. Like the issue of municipal corporation reform, Chadwick's proposed reforms jolted the vestry radicals out of their reactionary pose. Rather than merely defending the *status quo* against further intervention by the central state, as had been done in relation to church rates and reform of the poor law, vestry radicals began during the 1850s to elaborate a positive vision of how local self-government could be reconciled with and used to promote the most potent of all Victorian values: free enterprise.[47]

Interment reform

Once the decision had been made by Chadwick to initiate the 'London programme' from his position on the General Board of Health, interment reform became a priority. Action was conveniently fast-tracked by an existing set of investigations and recommendations concerning the reform of urban burial practices, giving the GBH a cut-and-dried scheme in accordance with which they could craft legislation.[48] Given the overcrowded and unsanitary state of parochial intramural burial grounds and the unconscionably high fees being charged by the existing private extramural burial grounds, the solution favoured by the GBH was to prohibit further burial within London, while simultaneously buying out the joint-stock cemeteries and creating a state monopoly on the provision of burial services in the metropolitan area.[49] The GBH found a precedent for this in the burial practices of a handful of

---

[47] This 'mature' entrepreneurialist position suggests that Searle was wrong to locate 'entrepreneurial politics' exclusively in northern towns: *Entrepreneurial politics*, 2–3.

[48] *Report on the practice of interments in towns*, PP, xii (1843). See also Lewis, *Edwin Chadwick*, 70.

[49] Finer, *Life of Chadwick*, 381–6. For an idea of how these arrangements affected families see P. Jalland, *Death in the Victorian family*, Oxford 1996. For colourful descriptions of the joint stock cemeteries see P. Coones, 'Kensal Green cemetery: London's first great extramural cemetery', *Transactions of the Ancient Monuments Society* iii (1987), 48–76, and N. B. Penny, 'The commercial garden necropolis of the early nineteenth-century and its critics', *Garden History* ii (1974), 61–76.

continental states, and eventually adopted a model based on the Parisian system.[50]

When the Metropolitan Interments Bill was proposed to the House of Commons on 15 April 1850 it was immediately met by a welter of criticism in London. This was underpinned by two related objections. Firstly, the scheme for a government monopoly was characterised as an 'un-English' and 'unconstitutional' assault on free enterprise. Secondly, the scheme was described as an exercise in Whig 'jobbery' and 'plunder'.[51] In the opinion of the *Patriot*, for instance, the bill was 'detestable in principle, anti-constitutionalist in spirit, fraudulent in its design, and combining the worst features of monopoly, jobbing, imposition and despotism'.[52] All but the very staunchest of the government's critics agreed that intramural sites were far too overcrowded and that new ones were needed outside London's built-up area.[53] It was the radical view, however, that these new sites should be entrusted to the management of the vestries and that the existing joint-stock companies should be allowed to continue to act as alternatives to parochial burial grounds. Both local self-government and free enterprise would in this way be preserved.

The view taken by George DeLacy Evans on the related fortunes of local self-government and freedom of trade was representative of the vestry radical stance. Speaking at a meeting of parochial representatives chaired by the Marylebone radical John Nicholay on 24 May 1850, Evans promised his audience that

> if the principle [of the government bill] were to prevent all intramural interments, he should support it; but he feared that there is another principle involved even more prominently than that, and that was to convert the government into a great undertaking company. In the discussion which would take place in parliament upon this subject he should evince his partiality for local self-government and local management in opposition to any Government interference with private enterprise.[54]

By clearly juxtaposing 'government interference with private enterprise' against 'local self-government and local management', Evans's comments

---

[50] Minutes of the General Board of Health, 19 Nov. 1849, Chadwick papers, 59.
[51] The Marylebone churchwarden J. A. Nicholay called the Whig bill 'one big job': *The Times*, 24 May 1850, 8. See also *The Times*, 14 June 1850, 5; *Hansard* 3rd ser. cxi. 1076–9, 11 June 1850; *Hansard* 3rd ser. cxi. 678–709, 3 June 1850; and *The Times*, 26 Sept. 1849, 4.
[52] *Patriot*, 3 June 1850, 349.
[53] See, for instance, the pamphlet entitled *Walker testimonial fund*, London 1850.
[54] *The Times*, 24 May 1850, 8.

hint at the increasingly entrepreneurial agenda entertained by many of the localists. Similar sentiments were later echoed at the same meeting by another speaker who claimed that if the government 'interferes in this matter, they might go the round of every trade, and they will find all of them to be an imposition to the consumer'.[55] Meetings held throughout the metropolis in late May and early June expanded on these claims. In the Lambeth vestry, for instance, Pearson and D'Eyncourt each took instructions to reject the Interments Bill on the grounds that it infringed upon free enterprise. 'It has been said and thought', the vestry members told Pearson,

> that the undertakers of the metropolis are the only parties that have been vociferous in denouncing the Bill – that is not so – and if it were, who can wonder at it? A large, respectable body of tradesmen, and their poorer dependents conceiving their means of living about to be snatched from them, naturally enough become excited and alarmed; and that being the case, who, we should like to know, can justly censure their opposition? The legitimate province of the legislature is, to make laws for the government of trade upon fair and equitable principles, and not to become traders themselves.[56]

As the vestry radicals had hoped, debate in the Commons, where the Marylebone vestry nominee Lord Dudley Coutts Stuart took the lead in prosecuting the case against the bill, reflected these concerns. While making it clear that he understood the necessity of terminating intramural interments, Stuart objected strenuously to almost every other feature of the bill, and especially to its restriction of free enterprise, which he called the bill's 'most objectionable provision'. Stuart's prominence in the debate had been marked very early on by his co-authorship of a petition opposing state interference with the burial industry.[57] The petition's other co-author, the joint stock cemetery owner Sir Richard Broun, assailed the government bill and its supporters in the MSA by mixing essentially commercial concerns with localist rhetoric, claiming, for instance, that the bill violated 'not only every sound commercial principle, but our dearest personal rights and natural affections ... of all systems, that of an army of CENTRAL FUNCTIONARIES for all sorts of local objects, is that which is least accordant with the precedents, and least congenial with the spirit, of Englishmen'.[58] While Broun himself led

---

[55] Ibid.

[56] *The Ratepayer, or the London Borough of Lambeth and Southwark Parochial, Literary, and Scientific Journal*, 1 June 1850, 6.

[57] *The Times*, 30 Apr. 1850, 8. *The Times* took quite a cynical view of Braun's relationship with Stuart. See the issue of 4 June 1850, 5.

[58] Braun, *Extramural interment*, 11.

an extra-parliamentary agitation accusing the government bill of promoting both centralisation and monopoly, Stuart made similar accusations within the Commons. 'It is not the business of Government to regulate trade', argued Stuart in an early debate on the proposed measure. Trade, he vehemently maintained, 'should be regulated on the usual principles of political economy, namely by those of demand and supply ... it is said that the undertakers are extortionate. Even if some of them are so, that is no reason why government should interfere with the whole trade'.[59]

Again, the board's interference with free enterprise was characterised as a symptom of the executive's overgrown power and the simultaneous decline of local self-determination. While the bill was in committee, Stuart drew on these links to justify his opposition to clause 27, which proposed a regulation of underkeeping. 'There is no sufficient ground', he argued, 'for abandoning the sound principles of free competition ... whether the undertakers were extortionists or not, is it right for Parliament to interfere with free competition? Why should not the people be let to protect themselves? It was by encouraging free competition that the public interest would be best promoted.' Of the proposed alternative of state provision of burials, meanwhile, Stuart foresaw artificially raised fees stemming from 'a system of favouritism and jobbing' and described this as 'an exceedingly oppressive arrangement'.[60] Only free competition could serve the public interest, and only the extension of local self-government could preserve free enterprise from the unwanted interference of the central government. For their part, the Whig architects of this 'centralising' legislation were awake to the popularity of radical arguments based on the preservation of free enterprise, and they made great efforts to counter these arguments with the claim that a centralised system would promote rather than stifle free competition.[61] However, this did not stop radicals from pressing their case that centralisation was inimical to both self-determination and the rights of commerce.

By the middle months of 1850 vestry radicalism had become so closely associated with the cry for 'free enterprise' as to become an object of parody in the pages of *Punch*. The magazine imagined the effect that recent vestry activism might have had on metropolitan hackney cab drivers, who were at the time being threatened with legislation for greater regulation of their trade. A fictitious cabbie therefore wrote to *Punch* 'arxing' Toulmin Smith

to speke hup for the Cabbies, wich that gent as made hout to evryboy's satisfacshun, as ow this ere country as allus ad lokal self-guvment till the wigs

---

[59] *Hansard* 3rd ser. cxi. 679, 3 June 1850.

[60] Ibid. 903, 7 June 1850.

[61] See, for instance, the *Quarterly Review* lxxxviii (1851), esp. p. 443.

come in, and now sentylisation is a goin to be our rewin, wich it's safe to be with us poor cabbies … and I say that the Cabbies as a rite to self-guvment, acos there's a grate many of us, and we nows more aboute fairs and distances, and such like, than MR. MAINE any day, and has a stronger ineterist in the same, wich sentrylisation can't ave.[62]

This appeal for the 'lokal self-guvment of us poor cabbies' captured perfectly the sense that the crusade for 'local self-government' had become as much an elaboration of the rights of free trade, as a defence of democratic self-determination.

The water question

In late May 1850, just as the radical furore over interment reform was reaching its peak, a report detailing the necessity for the reform of the water supply was published by the government.[63] The report proposed three principle reforms: that the Thames must be abandoned as a source of supply; that the existing water companies must be consolidated and placed under state supervision; and that any reformed water supply must be administered in conjunction with a unified system of drainage. As with the interment question, very few radicals disagreed with the government view that some measure of reform was needed, and most agreed with the government's assessment that the nine existing metropolitan water companies had been largely responsible for the poor quality of London's water supply.[64] Moreover, while a minority of radicals endorsed Taberner's plan to supply water from a network of parochially managed artesian wells, most agreed with the government that new sources at Hindhead and Farnham would be perfectly suitable.[65]

---

62 *Punch* xx (1850), 242. *Punch* was obviously suspicious of the 'catch-all' cry for local self-government. It is worth noting that the cabbie calls Toulmin Smith 'Toolman Smith', perhaps a reference to Smith's readiness to defend the rights of industry. It is also worth noting that Toulmin Smith had recently been retained by a London water company: Finer, *Life of Chadwick*, 410.

63 E. Chadwick, *Report on metropolitan water supply*, London 1850 (Chadwick papers 58).

64 On the neglect of the metropolitan water companies see A. Hardy, 'Water and the search for public health in London in the 18th and 19th centuries', *Medical History* xxviii (1984), 250–82; A. Mukhopadyay, *Politics of water supply: the case of Victorian London*, Calcutta 1981; D. Lipschutz, 'The water question in London, 1827–1831', *BHM* xlii (1968), 510–26; and W. Stern, 'J. Wright, pamphleteer on London water supply', *Guildhall Miscellany* i (1953), 31–4. For contemporary sources, see [W. O'Brien] 'The supply of water to the metropolis', *Edinburgh Review* xci (1949–50), 377–408, and [W. H. Wills] 'The troubled water question', *Household Words* i (1850), 49–52.

65 Memo (undated) 1851 and memo, 17 Nov. 1850, Chadwick papers, 59.

The consensus on the culpability of the water companies and the need for new sources of water did not, however, induce metropolitan radicals to support the government's plan for the amalgamation of the companies and their subjection to centralised state supervision. As on the questions of interments, the radical position was grounded firmly on entrepreneurial values, and particularly in an opposition to monopolies. Once legislation had been drafted by the government to reform the water supply, DeLacy Evans and Wakley each warned that it was merely creating a new 'monster monopoly' and a Whig patronage network in place of the existing water monopolies.[66] Rank-and file-parochial radicals echoed this view. Speaking on behalf of the parochial interest, the *Ratepayer* described the government water scheme as 'a perfect humbug, and an attempt to protect nine monopolies by consolidating them into one monopoly, thereby creating Whig patronage and power, in order, as much as possible, to retain within their grasp the whole interests of the metropolitan constituencies'.[67]

In the Commons, Benjamin Hall articulated this thesis throughout the debate on the government bill, which he consistently referred to as 'this monopolising measure'. Hall assured the Commons that his opposition to the measure stemmed primarily from its prohibition of competition. 'Instead of perpetuating the evils that at present exist', argued Hall in late April 1851, 'every inducement should be given to parties coming forward to abolish the monopolies which have existed so long, and have made vast returns to their shareholders at the expense of the community.'[68] In the course of later debates, Hall appealed to the example of gas provision, which had been subject to more extensive competition and which was characterised by a better product and consistently lower rates. Parliament's reluctance to introduce a similar level of competition into the metropolitan water supply, Hall reasoned, was due to the influence of the directors and shareholders of water companies – seventy of whom sat in the Commons.[69]

Hall's accusations were bolstered by the key role played by William Clay, MP for Tower Hamlets and chairman of the Grand Junction and Southwark and Vauxhall water companies, in defining the priorities of the government bill. Since becoming secretary to the board of control in Melbourne's second government, and receiving his baronetcy in 1841, Clay had been consistently loyal to successive Whig administrations. By 1850 his allegiance to the Russell government and his prior association with the Health of Towns Asso-

[66] *Hansard* 3rd ser. cxvii. 508–10, 5 June 1851.
[67] *Ratepayer*, 1 July 1851, 4.
[68] *Hansard* 3rd ser. cxvi. 328, 29 Apr. 1851.
[69] *Hansard* 3rd ser. cxvii. 471–2, 5 June 1851.

ciation had won him a large measure of influence over the government's plans for water reform.[70] Moreover, Clay's 1849 pamphlet *Remarks on the water supply of London* had impressed Chadwick, and had convinced him that Clay could be a formidable ally in the debate on the water supply. Chadwick had been particularly won over by Clay's insistence that the reformed water authority should be 'a direct emanation from the state, – not elective – nor subject in any way to parochial or local influence', and by his promise that he would help to fight the 'difficulties of overcoming the inevitable opposition of the City and the boroughs of Finsbury, Marylebone, and Westminster, and of the parochial bodies by which the members for those boroughs are guided'.[71] If Clay was quick to dismiss the opposition of the vestries, he gave much greater attention to the opposition of the existing water companies, and to the ways in which this opposition could be overcome. His suggestions concerning the compensation, and reorganisation, of water companies went some ways toward shaping the eventual government bill, which the Metropolitan Sanitary Association, Ebrington and even Chadwick himself eventually denounced as a water company directors bill.[72] The government's complete neglect of vestry criticisms, coupled with its over-attention to the demands of the water companies, intensified radical outrage over the bill's seeming protection and even extension of the principle of monopoly.

Although the debate over water supply gave prominent metropolitan radicals a platform from which denounce monopoly and promote competition, it also presented London's radical community with an excellent opportunity to articulate its own positive alternative to the often invoked spectre of Whig 'state centralisation'. Previous radical critiques of Whig 'centralising' policies had invoked the vague and fundamentally negative, or at least preservationist, concept of 'local self-government'. Now, in relation to reform of the water supply, metropolitan radicals began to articulate detailed plans for a municipal administration which reached beyond mere preservation of the existing vestry system. These plans differed in many respects from both the City-influenced vision of Toulmin Smith and the earlier, vestry-oriented, vision of Thomas Murphy.

Rather than focusing upon the parish as its fundamental administrative unit, the new radical plan proposed to divide London into seventeen districts, each containing roughly the same population as the St Marylebone parish.

---

[70] Clay had also been a strong advocate of Morpeth's successive health legislation. For his attitude on these reforms see William Clay to Chadwick, 28 Apr. 1848, Chadwick papers, 508.

[71] Clay to Chadwick, 23 July 1850, ibid.

[72] *The Times*, 21 June 1851, 8; *Hansard* 3rd ser. cxvi. 328–34, 29 Apr. 1851.

Each of these districts was to elect, through its ratepayers as organised in electoral wards, two representatives to sit on a central board or commission for
the whole of London.[73] The Lord Mayor and Common Council of the City
Corporation and the executive government would send a further four representatives each to this body, which would comprise a total of seventy-six
members. Representatives would be unpaid nominees of the ratepayers in
their respective districts, but would nominate from amongst themselves five
members and a secretary, who would be paid, as full-time officers of the
Commission or Board. The remit of this central board would cover both
water supply (by granting competitive contracts) and all drainage; it would
thereby render the MCS redundant.[74]

This solution to the London government problem had grown out of a
vague desire, first expressed at a Southwark parochial meeting, to obtain from
parliament 'powers to place the whole of the water service under the management of a board of parochial representatives appointed by the ratepayers of all
the metropolitan parishes'.[75] By the early months of 1850 this agenda had
been taken up by the Parochial Water Supply Association (also variously
known as the Metropolitan Parochial Supply Association, or the Association
of Parochial Representatives), an organisation the leadership of which
included the future first chairman of the Metropolitan Board of Works, John
Thwaites, and John Nicholay, churchwarden of the Marylebone vestry. By
this time the organisation had also won the support of a number of metropolitan MPs, including the Southwark duo, William Molesworth and Alderman
Humphery, both of whom helped it to gain an audience with Russell in
March at which the prime minister first learned of the parish-based scheme.[76]
As the plan evolved it acquired further adherents, including the old
Southwark opponent of the New Poor Law John Day, the soon-to-be-
metropolitan MPs Apsley Pellatt and Thomas Challis and even Joshua
Toulmin Smith.[77] By December 1850, when a second deputation waited
upon Russell, the municipal solution had gained the support of the major
Hobhouse vestries as well.[78] All the while, Chadwick remained dismissive of

---

[73] J. Toulmin Smith, *The Metropolis Local Management Act*, London 1855, 10–15; *Hansard*
3rd ser. cxix. 221–5, 6 Feb. 1852.

[74] *Hansard* 3rd ser. cxvii. 494–5, 5 June 1851.

[75] *The Times*, 11 Dec. 1849, 4.

[76] See *Illustrated London News*, 21 Feb. 1852, 154; *The Times*, 13 Feb. 1850, 8; 15 Mar.
1850, 7.

[77] *The Times*, 5 July 1851, 8.

[78] Smith, *Metropolis Local Management Act*, 5. According to the *Ratepayer* (1 Mar. 1851, 6)
the MSA lobbied Russell to reject the scheme proposed by this deputation. The Hackney
Parochial Association, meanwhile, also requested that East and West Hackney be divided
into wards: *Morning Advertiser*, 12 Jan. 1850, 3.

vestry agitation for a single municipal system, and he tried to convince Delane (whose paper was coming around to support the parochialists) that the agitation was actually not representative of wider metropolitan wishes concerning sanitation and local administration. 'I believe', Chadwick wrote to Delane that

> you will find that the proceeding is one of a very small agitation [consisting?] of very large parishes but by no means countenanced even in those parishes by the inhabitants at large. I have been informed of several parishes having been requested to join in the agitation but that they refused, often having fairly discussed the matter, and determined that however insufficient the present Commission might be they, the parishioners, were incompetent to judge either of the plans or of the [form?] ... what a new metropolitan municipality would be is shown by what the municipality of the City is now.[79]

The parochial plan for a London municipality composed of seventeen districts was finally proposed as a bill by Francis Mowatt, MP for Penryn and Falmouth and a Marylebone vestryman, in early February 1852. Mowatt's plan quickly gained endorsements from Hall, Evans, Wakley, Coutts Stuart, Williams and other radical MPs with strong vestry connections. Dudley Coutts Stuart, for instance, seconded Mowatt's motion and during the parliamentary debates on the government bill, Benjamin Hall himself referred to the 'municipal' solution as the only alternative to a system of free competition.[80] Chadwick himself was predictably dismissive of Mowatt's municipal alternative, but some of his Russellite allies took the threat much more seriously.[81] Ebrington, for one, echoed the MSA's criticisms of the government bill while simultaneously warning the House of the sanitary dangers inherent in giving ratepayers the power to initiate improvements. In addition, he claimed, echoing the objection first proposed by the 1837 *Report*, a London municipal government such as the one proposed by Mowatt could very easily become a rival to the national government and legislature. The fear of an overly powerful metropolitan municipal legislature had been a prominent feature of Whig thinking on the London government problem since the 1837 Municipal Corporations *Report* first alerted them to the potential dangers of a single metropolitan corporation. As Chadwick and the MSA had always

---

[79] Chadwick to Delane 27 Nov. 1850, Chadwick papers, 608.
[80] *Hansard* 3rd ser. cxvii. 476, 5 June 1851. There was a great deal of discussion of Mowatt's bill in the St Pancras vestry, where Stuart was a strong supporter: *Observer*, 4 Apr. 1852.
[81] 'Water supply central establishment and parochial establishments in the metropolis', Chadwick to Delane, 27 Nov. 1850, Chadwick papers, 608.

done, Ebrington suggested Paris, Vienna and Berlin as models of how London should be governed.[82] As it happened, London would soon forgo all of these models for a completely unique form of local government that incorporated many elements of the municipal solution to the water question.

The 1854 Royal Commission on the Corporation of London

Before the details of Mowatt's bill could be incorporated into Hall's Metropolis Local Management Act, however, one last royal commission would offer its own alternative solution to the London government problem. The commission was established on 22 June 1853 and led by the firmly anti-Chadwickian liberals Henry Labouchere, Sir John Patteson and George Cornwall Lewis. Although the commission made a raft of suggestions for reform of the City Corporation, it also had much to say about the broader London government problem.[83] Moreover the commission's conclusions differed in important respects from those put forward in the 1837 *Report*. Whereas that report had suggested that London's local government might be organised into a single municipality under the control of a crown-appointed commission, the 1854 *Report* took a thoroughly localist and corporate approach. In the first place, it argued, metropolitan London was far too large and contained far too many separate communities to be incorporated into a single municipality of any kind. 'London, taken in its full extent', the Commissioners found,

> is (as it has with literal truth been called) a province covered with houses; its diameter from north to south and from east to west is so great that the persons living at its furthest extremities have few interests in common; its area is so large that each inhabitant is in general acquainted only with his own quarter, and has no minute knowledge of other parts of town. Hence the two first conditions for municipal government, minute local knowledge and community of

---

[82] *Hansard* 3rd ser. cxix. 225–7, 6 Feb. 1852.

[83] Chief among these 32 recommendations were: (1) the consolidation of all previous City charters into one new one; (2) that the Lord Mayor be elected by the Common Council; (3) that Aldermen be elected by burgesses of each ward for 6 years; (4) that the Court of Aldermen be abolished; (5) that the number of wards be reduced; (6) that election for Common Hall be abolished; (7) that a number of the smaller courts be abolished: *Report of the commissioners appointed to inquire into the existing state of the corporation of the City of London, and to collect information respecting its constitution, order, and government*, London 1854, pp. xv–xxi.

interests, would be wanting, if the whole of London were, by an extension of the present boundaries of the City, placed under a single municipal corporation.[84]

Moreover, it was suggested, any extension of the City's Corporate boundaries to incorporate a larger metropolitan area 'would entirely alter the character of the Corporation of London, and would create a municipal body of unmanageable dimensions'.[85]

While the commissioners argued forcefully against extending the City Corporation to include the rest of the metropolis, they remained confident that the corporate administrative structure was still preferable to all other forms of local government. Consequently, the commission proposed that London would most profitably be governed through a network of semi-autonomous corporations. Ultimately, the authors of the 1854 *Report* seem to have been swayed by suggestions made by members of the London Municipal Reform Society that each of London's parliamentary boroughs should be made into autonomous corporations which would, in turn, send members to a central board.[86] In this respect the commission's suggestions found common ground with Mowatt's earlier plan. 'In the event of a division of the entire metropolis', wrote the Commissioners,

> such as we have ventured to indicate, being hereafter made by the authority of Parliament, we suggest the creation of a metropolitan board of works, to be composed of a very limited number of members deputed to it from the council of each metropolitan municipal body, including the Corporation of the City. We propose that the management of public works, in which the metropolis has a common interest, should be conducted by this body ... we propose further that the metropolitan board of works should be empowered to levy a rate upon the entire metropolis, for any improvement of general utility, within a certain poundage, to be fixed by Act of Parliament.[87]

This recommendation reflected a general dissatisfaction with the Russellite approach. By the time of the *Report*'s publication in 1854, the Chadwickian solution to the London government problem, and its attendant centralised health authorities, had lost favour and political protection. In early July Hall made a scathing attack both on Chadwick's lack of credentials as a sanitary reformer and the doctrinaire manner in which he was said to have presided

---

[84] Ibid, p. xiv.
[85] Ibid, p. xxxiv.
[86] Ibid, pp. xxvi, xxxv, and paragraphs 24–79, 865–8.
[87] Ibid, pp. xxxv–xxxvi.

over the GBH.[88] Chadwick was overwhelmed and defeated. His greatest critic, meanwhile, was on the cusp of power.

The creation of the Metropolitan Board of Works

When Benjamin Hall was appointed president of the reconstructed Board of Health on 6 August 1854 his trenchant and much publicised attack on Chadwick was still fresh in the public memory. Far from damaging his credibility (as it might have done since many of the accusations that he had made against Chadwick were unfounded and untrue) Hall's diatribe had only served to enhance his public profile and strengthen his position on the board. With the goodwill of London's parochial representatives, Hall jumped straight into work, claiming to Palmerston that the local authorities were 'falling into the scheme very willingly'.[89] Hall had been preceded as president by William Molesworth, who had himself been hostile to the board's close relationship with central government, and who, by refusing to work with Chadwick, had also hastened the 'Prussian Minister's' fall from power.[90] Although Molesworth had taken steps toward reforming the board's relationship with the metropolitan vestries, and while he had always been sympathetic to the vestry position on metropolitan local government, he had not been in a position, as president of the unreformed board, to bring widespread reform to London. London had then remained outside the board's proper jurisdiction: Molesworth's strict reading of this was yet another censure of the board's improper meddling in metropolitan matters during Chadwick's earlier term as secretary. Reconstruction, and Hall's strongly vestry-oriented agenda, altered the board's relationship with London. As a veritable nominee of the powerful St Marylebone vestry, the new president necessarily understood his appointment as an opportunity to finally settle the London government problem. He would do this by establishing an entirely new system of vestry-based metropolitan governance. By October Hall had already begun drafting a bill towards this end and had begun recruiting influential allies such as the Speaker of the House of Commons, Charles Shaw-Lefevre.[91]

Hall's bill would, of course, pass into law in August 1855 as the Metropolis Local Management Act, a measure that protected vestry autonomy and

[88] *Hansard* 3rd ser. cxxxiv. 1301–7, 6 July 1854.
[89] Benjamin Hall to Palmerston, 25 Aug. 1854, Palmerston papers, PP/GC/HA/5/.
[90] William Molesworth to George Hamilton Gordon, 4th earl of Aberdeen, 11 Mar. 1853, 4th earl of Aberdeen papers, BL, MS Add. 43200.
[91] Fraser, 'Benjamin Hall and the administration of London', 73.

influence while simultaneously providing for concerted metropolitan action through the creation of central Metropolitan Board of Works. It was important for radical advocates of local self-government that the new act also democratised and standardised London's local government. It did this by reforming all metropolitan vestries in accordance with the terms of the Hobhouse Select Vestries Act. Ratepayer self-determination was further strengthened by the measure's insistence that all powers that had previously been vested in unaccountable bodies such as paving and lighting boards under local acts would now be transferred back to the reformed vestries. Ratepayer democracy had finally become a reality. Yet the creation of the Metropolitan Board of Works meant that London's seventy-eight civil parishes were not completely autonomous democracies. The new board would be given a brief to carry out pan-metropolitan projects such as the reform of and improvements to streets or commons. Moreover, although this new 'super vestry' enjoyed limited rating powers, it was not a directly elected body. Rather, the board's forty-five members would be appointed by London's various organs of local government. London's six largest vestries would each appoint two members; sixteen slightly smaller vestries would appoint one member each; the remaining fifty-five vestries would be grouped into fourteen 'district boards', each of which would appoint one member; and the City Corporation appointed three members. Service on the board was unpaid, with the exception of the position of chairman, which came with a salary of between £1,500 and £2,000 per year.[92]

During the parliamentary debates on Hall's bill, Ebrington had been an outspoken critic. He had raised, for instance, the by now familiar concern that a metropolitan municipal body would pose a clear threat to the authority of both parliament and central government, while simultaneously criticising the bill's proposal to make Hobhouse's act compulsory. Ebrington feared the effect that this clause would have on the powers of metropolitan landlords. 'The whole power of deciding work effecting the property of the long lease-holders and landlords of the metropolis', he noted sensationally, 'is to be confined to the temporary ratepayers; so that the bill would create this anomaly, that London would be the sole place in England where the only persons excluded from the control of the expenditure would be those who had to defray it.'[93] Similar concerns were expressed by fellow Whig Henry Fitzroy, himself a large landowner in north London, who considered the ratepayers to be unfit to make important decisions concerning rates and

---

[92] *Hansard* 3rd ser. cxxxvii. 699–721, 16 Mar. 1855.
[93] Ibid. 3rd ser. cxxxvii. 726.

sewerage.[94] At the other end of the political spectrum, Joshua Toulmin Smith had his own reservations. Whereas Ebrington and Fitzroy criticised the bill for being too democratic, Smith argued that it was not democratic enough. The issue for him was not the indirect election or appointment of MBW members (as might have been expected from an arch localist) but rather the indirect election of district board members.

The district boards, which enjoyed the same powers as the larger or 'schedule A' vestries, were composed of members elected by representatives from the fifty-five smaller vestries rather than directly by the ratepayers of these vestries themselves. Approximately one third of all Londoners lived in parishes serviced by these smaller vestries and was therefore subject to indirectly elected local government as well as to a central administration that was twice removed from ratepayer accountability. This made Smith especially uneasy. 'The secondary method [of appointment or indirect election] is proper enough for appointment to the Metropolitan Board, which was, in fact, a standing conference of committees on special points', he noted shortly after Hall's bill became law, 'but it is totally inapplicable to the immediate and constant affairs to be dealt with by the district boards.'[95] Still, Smith granted, the district boards were only one disappointing feature of an otherwise sound measure, and even these might be made to work. 'Whatever its defects may be', he wrote, 'there is no doubt that very much may be done to overcome many omissions and imperfections in the Act ... it need only be added, that it is the first duty, and should be the constant effort, of each of these Bodies, to show itself conscious of the responsibilities, and thus worthy of the name, of "*the Local Authority*".'[96]

Despite Toulmin Smith's slight misgivings over the district boards, Hall's reform received strong endorsements from many of London's vestries and leading vestrymen. In the wake of the act's passage into law, the *Ratepayers' Journal* declared that 'Sir Benjamin Hall deserves the thanks of every good citizen for the attempt, the gigantic attempt for reforming that which was by many considered too great to be reformed ... he [Hall] combines in himself the courage to think with the courage to act.'[97] According to the *South London Advertiser*, meanwhile, vestries throughout London whole-heartedly endorsed the new act, which, along with Hobhouse's act, was described as a 'Magna Carta of parochial liberties ... Lambeth is to have a House of

---

[94] Ibid. 3rd ser. cxxxvii 722–3.
[95] Toulmin Smith, *Metropolis Local Management Act*, 38–9.
[96] Ibid. 39–40, 41.
[97] *The Ratepayers' Journal*, 2 Feb. 1856, 2–3.

Commons of its own ... every parish, on either side of the Thames, is to have, like Marylebone, its little Senate, and its great debates'.[98] The St Pancras radicals were especially pleased with Hall's bill, and not least for the way in which it would consolidate the parish's numerous paving boards.[99] Even Camberwell, which was to become part of a district board, supported the measure.[100] In St Marylebone, the leading vestry radical J. A. Nicholay paid special tribute to the measure, and the vestry joined him in describing it as a giant leap forward for the representative principle.[101] In fact, Nicholay was such an enthusiastic devotee of Hall's vision for metropolitan government reform that he even volunteered to be temporary chairman of the very first meeting of the MBW. Nicholay's replacement as chairman, John Thwaites, had been equally supportive of Hall's measure from within the Southwark vestry of St Saviours. As an elected member of the final Metropolitan Commission of Sewers, Thwaites had long represented vestry opinion and had long supported the principle of local self-government – commitment to which is attested by his prominent membership of the Parochial Water Supply Associations.[102] In Tower Hamlets, meanwhile, the ultra-radical vestry reformer William Newton wholeheartedly endorsed Hall's measure, not least for the fact that it would make the Hobhouse act compulsory and by doing so would save his own vestry from the Sturges Bourne restrictions. Newton had first turned to the parochial reform movement during the vestry water supply agitation, and after his 1852 Tower Hamlets election defeat he became a prominent member of the Mile End Old Town vestry. Like Nicholay and Thwaites, Newton translated his support and enthusiasm for Hall's measure into a leadership role on the MBW.

Many accounts of Hall's reform have insisted that it was heavily influenced by the findings of the 1854 commission.[103] While there is some truth in this view, an overemphasis on its role has obscured the perhaps greater influence which the vestry-driven water supply agitation of 1850–2 had had on Hall's thinking. According to Toulmin Smith, Hall's act was based almost entirely on the vestry plan laid before the Home Secretary George Grey in January 1851.[104] Although it is likely that Hall was assisted in drawing up his

---

98 *South London Advertiser*, 1 Sept. 1855.
99 See *Observer*, 10 Dec. 1854; 1 Apr. 1855.
100 W. H. Blanch, *The parish of Camberwell*, London 1875, repr. 1976, 99–100.
101 See *The Observer*, 29 Apr., 6 May, 24 June 1855.
102 *South London News*, 24 Oct. 1857; *Observer*, 23 Dec. 1855; J. Thwaites, *A sketch of the history and prospects of the metropolitan drainage question*, London 1855. For Thwaites's involvement in the push for the municipal plan see also *The Times*, 13 Feb., 15 Mar. 1850; 11 June 1851.
103 See especially Owen, *Government of Victorian London*, 32.
104 Toulmin Smith, *Metropolis Local Government Act*, 14–15.

bill by the 1854 commissioner Sir George Cornwall Lewis, that *Report*'s recommendations played only a secondary part in moulding is content.[105] In fact, Hall's bill rejected many of the key recommendations of the 1854 *Report*, while adopting many of the most important details of Mowatt's earlier bill and of the plan outlined by the Parochial Water Supply Association for the unification of water supply and drainage in the metropolis. Hall believed, for instance, that 'the greatest inconvenience would arise' from the 1854 *Report*'s suggestion that each parliamentary borough should be incorporated.[106] His alternative proposition, that smaller parishes be grouped together into districts of between 60,000 and 70,000 inhabitants, had much in common with the vestry plan. The bill's scheme for dividing each large parish and each district into wards also echoed earlier parochial suggestions rather than the recent recommendations of the commissioners.[107] In fact, the only significant recommendation of the *Report* adopted by Hall (the creation of a Metropolitan Board of Works), had also been suggested by Mowatt.

Hall prefaced the introduction of his bill to parliament by describing the mind-numbing heterogeneity of London's unreformed local administration. Qualifications and eligibility for vestry franchise varied widely from locale to locale, Hall argued, and the confusing tangle of administration merely hindered the execution of efficient and just government.[108] His measure sought to rationalise, standardise, democratise and unify London's local government in much the same way that the 1835 Municipal Corporations Act had endeavored to rationalise, standardise and democratise provincial local government. Ultimately, this was a bill that vestries could rally behind because it sprang from vestry concerns. David Owen's claim that Hall's solution represented a betrayal of the localist position and that his acceptance of the need for a central board was 'a bitter cup for Toulmin Smith and the anti-centralisation hosts',[109] simply does not hold up when Hall's act is considered in the context of vestry reaction to water reform, or, for that matter, in the light of Toulmin Smith's own admission that the MBW was necessary. Interpretations such as that offered by Owen misrepresent the vestry radicals as unrealistic supporters of 'localism at any cost'. In fact, all that they wanted was self-determination for ratepayers and a level playing field. These Hall's measure gave them.

---

105 See Fraser, 'Benjamin Hall and the administration of London', 75. For Hall's use of the *Report* see *Hansard* 3rd ser. cxxxvii. 716–20, 16 Mar. 1855.
106 *Hansard* 3rd ser. cxxxvii. 717, 16 Mar. 1855.
107 Toulmin Smith, *Metropolis Local Management Act*, 14.
108 *Hansard* 3rd ser. cxxxvii. 702–10, 16 Mar. 1855.
109 Owen, *Government of Victorian London*, 31.

Marylebone in 1854:
From Conflict to Compromise

Preceding chapters have emphasised the centrality of conflict to London's liberal political culture. It has been argued that discrete liberal subgroups, which subscribed to incompatible and in many ways antagonistic sets of political priorities, emerged within the reformed metropolitan constituencies during the mid-1830s and immediately began to compete with one another for political supremacy. This competition was intensified, or at the very least reinforced, by the cultural fault-lines which lay between these groups. Whereas the input of London's 'shopocracy' tied vestry radicalism to the related causes of government retrenchment and ratepayer self-determination, the cultural orientations of London's large professional community ensured a fairly substantial support base for the paternalist reform programme offered by Russellite Whiggery. Moreover, professionals by and large rejected market-driven and retrenchment-minded liberalism in favour of a bureaucracy of 'experts' which might protect London's poorest and most vulnerable from the self-interested parsimony of the ratepayers. London's paternally-minded social elites, of which there were many, joined the professionals in rejecting ratepayer democracy – many doing so out of the associated realisation that 'government by experts' would also protect the metropolitan landlords from the myopic parsimony of the ratepaying leaseholders and tenants. At the same time as London's professionals were hitching their star to Whiggery, the vestry camp was beginning to find its own parliamentary voice through an increasingly close association with populist 'titled radicals' such as Thomas Duncombe and Charles Tennyson D'Eyncourt. The speed with which many of London's socially Whiggish 'titled radicals' defected into the ultra-radical vestry camp during the mid- and late 1830s exacerbated the divisiveness of London's liberal political culture and eventually precipitated a polarisation of metropolitan liberalism during the 1840s and '50s.

While all of these alliances and oppositions suggest that liberalism was a heavily contested creed and culture within London, there none the less exist a number of curious incidents which seem to undermine the view that Whigs and radicals were continually at odds in the metropolitan context. In addition to the surprising ease with which Benjamin Hall's supposedly anti-ministerial Marylebone constituents accepted his appointment to a ministerial position in 1854, Lord Ebrington's simultaneous election as MP for Marylebone prompts difficult questions over whether the analysis of London liberalism presented above has favoured an overly or even artificially schematic interrelation at the expense of nuance, contradiction and complexity. Ebrington was, of course, an arch-Russellite (perhaps more 'Russellite' than Russell himself) while Marylebone was in 1854 still London's greatest bastion of localist radicalism. In fact, in 1855 *The Times* still felt confident enough to call the St Marylebone vestry 'that last sanctum of the principles of Anglo-Saxon Liberty'.[1] How is Ebrington's success to be interpreted if, as the conflict-centred interpretation maintains, Whigs and Marylebone localists advanced diametrically opposed approaches to liberalism? How, moreover, did the prominent vestry radical and scourge of Russellite Whiggery J. A. Nicholay come to play an important role in Ebrington's election committee? This chapter hopes to answer these questions by arguing that, while Ebrington's return certainly complicates the picture, it in no way undermines the wider schematic established in the preceding chapters. If anything, the events of December 1854 reinforce this schematic by explaining the important ways in which local politics were integrated into national politics in London and by illustrating the extent to which Ebrington's candidature brought issues such as 'centralisation', 'local self-government', 'aristocratic politics' and 'commercial freedom' to the fore. Ebrington's victory owed much more to expediency and local factionalism than to any sort of ideological change of heart.

Marylebone in 1854

In 1854 two entirely unexpected events conspired to shake Marylebone from a brief period of political complacency and to prepare the constituency for the final round in the London government debate. First, in August, Benjamin Hall was appointed president of the reconstructed Board of Health – a development which, while welcomed in some quarters, was by no means universally approved in the borough. Then, in November, Dudley Coutts Stuart died quite suddenly while visiting Stockholm. Although his death was universally mourned, it was also seized upon by some as an opportunity to

[1] *The Times*, 25 Jan. 1855, 6.

change Marylebone's political culture. Since 1852 Marylebone had been in the grip of a strange political inertia. In the wake of Russell's fall from power, and with Chadwick stripped of the robust ministerial support provided by the outgoing regime, the Marylebone radical agenda lost much of its urgency. At the same time, political contention within Marylebone's representative parishes had been stifled, and the leadership positions occupied by Hall and Stuart in the borough had been consolidated and then extended. At the general election of 1852, the first uncontested election in Marylebone's short history as a parliamentary borough, Hall and Stuart had been returned unopposed. Throughout 1853 and early 1854 Hall enhanced his personal profile by making a series of well-timed attacks on the dying Chadwickian regime at the General Board of Health. Stuart's advocacy of Polish independence, meanwhile, began to catch the current of anti-Russian popular feeling during the build up to hostilities in the Crimea.

Given Hall's sustained and often trenchant criticism of the mere existence of a General Board of Health, his appointment to the presidency of the, albeit reconstructed, board could have been disastrous for his radical credibility and his reputation as a man of principle. Historians have been tempted by this line of thinking, and a few have even gone so far as to suggest that Hall's new position necessarily compromised his commitment to 'local self-government'.[2] But while sections of the press questioned Hall's motives in accepting the position, his appointment was nearly universally acclaimed within the constituency's radical community. A mere six days after Hall was called on by Aberdeen, the St Marylebone vestrymen wrote to their MP to let him know that his acceptance of the office had 'given general satisfaction in the borough. Every person who takes an interest in the affairs of the parish approves of your doing so, and says that the government have paid the borough a compliment in having selected one of their members'. The radical J. A. Nicholay duly moved a vote of thanks in the vestry and referred to the appointment in glowing terms.[3] At a constituency meeting organised on 16 August to congratulate Hall, only a single Marylebone vestryman questioned the desirability of the appointment. After reminding his fellow vestrymen of former Marylebone MP Henry Bulwer's slavish devotion to the Melbourne administration as a placeman, the vestryman warned of similar developments

---

2   See, for instance, Finer, *Life of Chadwick*, 468–73.
3   M. Fraser, 'Sir Benjamin Hall in parliament, in the 1850s: part II', *National Library of Wales Journal* xv (1967), 116–17. The National and Constitutional Association, which brought *Leader* circle radicals such as P. A. Taylor together with vestry radicals such as J. A. Nicholay and John Day, endorsed Hall's appointment in the strongest terms: *Morning Advertiser*, 24 Feb. 1855, 5.

in Hall's politics, and consequently voiced a 'most decided objection to any man having one sort of politics [without?] a place and another sort of politics to keep a place'. Worse still, he reasoned, Hall 'would only be carrying out the Whig principle of centralisation' through his new place.[4] Retrench-ment-minded Marylebone radicals had always taken a strongly unfavourable view of government placemen, especially those whose offices enabled an enlarged central government. Of course, Marylebone's vestry power structure had expelled both William Horne and Henry Bulwer from the borough repre-sentation for precisely this reason. As solicitor-general, Horne had supported the government on both church rates and poor law reform, whereas Bulwer always seemed to represent the government first and Marylebone second. Yet, at the vestry meeting of 16 August, objections over ministerial ties were exceptional among the responses to Hall's appointment.

Radical support within Marylebone for Hall's appointment can be attrib-uted to two related factors. First, vestry radicals such as Nicholay and W. D. Cooper believed that Hall's appointment would help the cause of local self-government by placing one of its strongest advocates at the heart of the Aberdeen coalition. In the immediate wake of his appointment, Hall himself repeatedly reiterated his commitment to the principle of local self-government, and promised that this commitment would guide him to rede-fine the board's mission – not least through ensuring that the board would never again meddle in metropolitan affairs.[5] In respect of the board's rightful provenance (i.e. the provincial municipalities) Hall assured the St Pancras vestry that 'the duties of his office should ever be transacted with a view to the upholding of the principle of local self-government as contra-distinguished from that of centralisation'.[6] When confronted with the charge that the office itself was unavoidably an office of centralisation, no matter how strong Hall's personal commitment to local self-government, he responded that the object of the new board was to 'do away with centralisa-tion'.[7]

These justifications seem to have satisfied radical opinion in the borough. Nicholay's congratulatory speech in the St Marylebone vestry on 12 August, for instance, described Hall's appointment as 'a great compliment to that borough, and as a triumph for the principle of local self-government'.[8] Hall had turned a potential liability into a political asset by deploying the

4   *The Times*, 17 Aug. 1854, 8.
5   *Daily News*, 14 Aug. 1854.
6   *The Times*, 15 Aug. 1854, 5.
7   *Daily News*, 17 Aug. 1854.
8   *The Times*, 14 Aug. 1854, 10.

language of retrenchment and by promising to use the office to ensure that the present government honoured the principle of local self-government in its wider initiatives as well.

Beyond the specific issue of local self-government, Marylebone radicals were also comforted by the belief that Hall had not sought his appointment, and in fact only took it up after a great deal of pleading from the new government. In this scenario Hall could not be portrayed as in any way self-interested or place-seeking. Some supporters of the appointment went so far as to claim that Hall had dissuaded the government from calling on him. Dudley Stuart, for one, assured his constituents that Hall had not sought the appointment, but that it had been urged on him by Palmerston, who was at this time becoming quite a popular figure within metropolitan radical culture.[9] Hall repeatedly made the same point himself, claiming that 'so far from my ever having sought for office, I really, when applied to last Sunday week upon the subject, recommended a person whom I believe to be a fit person to fill the important post'.[10] The narrative of the government's persistent courting of Hall reinforced a radical interpretation of the appointment: it was a sign of the Aberdeen coalition's support for local self-government. Of course it also helped that the brand of liberalism promoted by the Aberdeen coalition, and by Palmerston in particular, was far more palatable to the Marylebone radicals than Russellite Whiggery had ever been. Hall cleverly exploited these natural sympathies and justified his actions, claiming that his appointment would 'democratise' cabinet decision-making by taking it away from the representatives of 'the miserable boroughs comprised in schedule A and schedule B' and placing it instead in the hands of MPs who represented the 'largest, the wealthiest, and the most important constituencies in the empire'.[11]

After the surprising ease with which Marylebone's vestry radicals had come to terms with Hall's appointment, Dudley Stuart's sudden death was a shock and a genuine setback to radical strength and momentum. Stuart's popularity within the constituency had grown as Britain had drifted into war with Russia and as popular anti-Russian feeling began to peak. While other Russophobes could be accused of opportunism, Stuart's long-term devotion to the cause of Polish independence was held up as evidence of both his true commitment to liberal principles and his powers of foresight.[12] It was even

---

[9] *Morning Chronicle*, 14 Aug. 1854.

[10] *Observer*, 20 Aug. 1854, 3; *The Times*, 15 Aug. 1854, 5.

[11] *The Times*, 17 Aug. 1854, 8.

[12] Stuart raised a great deal of money for both the Polish and Hungarian refugees by throwing fundraising balls. The most successful of the events raised nearly £1,500: D. C. Stuart to Cobden, 21 Oct. 1849, Cobden papers, MS Add. 43668, fo. 46. The Permanent

rumoured that Stuart was personally responsible for Palmerston's conversion to Russophobia.[13] At the same time, Stuart's close friendships with Prince Adam Csartoryski and Lajos Kossuth gave his public profile a 'romantic' lustre that Urquhart and other radical Russophobes lacked. Because of his personal associations, Stuart was often represented as a heroic figure, one of the great (though not persecuted) advocates of European freedom.

Moreover, Stuart's advocacy of the Polish and Hungarian nationalist movements won plaudits in Marylebone partly by way of association with the principle of local self-government. Like his friend Joshua Toulmin Smith, Stuart often drew links between the Hungarian and Polish movements for self-determination, on the one hand, and the English movement for government retrenchment and local self-government on the other. From his place on the central committee of the Hungarian Association Stuart argued that Hungarian freedom had been prevented by Hapsburg 'centralisation', just as Marylebone's own self-government had been compromised by Whiggish interference in local matters. Elsewhere, he maintained that the ancient Hungarian constitution was 'as similar to the constitution of this country as any mentioned by history', meaning that both nations were unaccustomed and unsuited to centralised forms of government.[14] Attitudes such as these were more than appreciated by Stuart's retrenchment-minded constituents, who moved upon his death that 'a more uncompromising, unflinching, and independent man never entered the House of Commons … he was not less the friend to suffering humanity wherever he found it, and the noble Lord, though frequently imposed upon, was never known to refuse assistance where he deemed it was deserved'.[15] The genuine affection that Marylebone's vestrymen seem to have felt for Stuart was on full display at the funeral procession through Hereford: eighteen leading vestry reformers were given privileged places next to Stuart's own family and the nationalist heroes of Poland and Hungary.

Council of the Poles in London greatly preferred the activities of Stuart and the LAFP to the Manchester School's 'absurd' doctrine of non-intervention: Permanent Council of the Poles in London, *The French empire and the Poles*, London 1853, 22.

[13] Stuart had long recognised Palmerston as an ally on Poland. As far back as 1841, for instance, Stuart lamented that 'the time approaches when, according to all probability, you will cease, at least for a time, to preside over the department of foreign affairs, and when those, who like me take an interest in Poland will no longer have a friend at the foreign office': Stuart to Palmerston, 13 Aug. 1841, Palmerston papers, GC/ST/142. Benjamin Hall took the same view, especially with respect to Hungary: ibid. GC/ST/149. For Stuart's influence over Palmerston see T. Kabdebo, 'Lord Dudley Stuart and the Hungarian refugees of 1849', *BIHR* xliv (1971), 258–69.

[14] *Hansard* 3rd ser. cvii.815, 21 July 1849.

[15] *The Times*, 22 Nov. 1854, 6.

With Stuart buried, the St Pancras radicals urged the borough's electors to find a replacement whose support for the 'present just war' would equal his.[16] The search began, appropriately enough, with an entreaty to the Russophobic diplomat Sir George Hamilton Seymour, though he quickly declined the offer. After this false start, the borough radicals turned their attentions to the retrenchment-minded war hero Sir Charles Napier, who had in fact represented the borough during the mid-1840s. By 1854 Napier had become known for his strongly anti-Russian views and his romantic and heroic reputation as a naval commander. Like Seymour, however, Napier found himself unable to stand for the borough, as he was still needed in the Baltic. Radical attentions then shifted to the ageing Charles Tennyson D'Eyncourt, who had recently been beaten in Lambeth and who now began to consider standing for the vacant metropolitan seat. Although D'Eyncourt was favoured by Nicholay and other prominent St Marylebone radicals he ultimately opted to devote the remaining years of his life to the Gothic 'restoration' of Bayorn Manor.[17] To the great frustration and disappointment of Marylebone's radical community, this series of false starts and rejections eventually left Hugh Fortescue (known, until 1859, as Viscount Ebrington) and the local pharmacist and Marylebone vestry member Jacob Bell as the only two remaining candidates. The *Observer*, the quasi-official organ of Marylebone localism during this period, thought that both candidates were inadequate, though for different reasons. Ebrington was described as a centraliser and an opponent of local self-government, 'a principle so much prized and cherished by the people of Marylebone, St. Pancras, and Paddington'. Bell, meanwhile, was thought to be 'not quite up to the mark of what a representative for Marylebone ought to be'.[18] Although he had extensive local connections, some felt that Bell was not quite grand enough or politically savvy enough to represent such a wealthy, extensive and important district. None the less, the *Observer* acknowledged that he was still generally considered to be preferable to Ebrington.[19]

Bell's advantages were obvious. To begin with, he enjoyed extensive local connections which amounted to a very useful ready-made election committee. In addition to being an established and influential member of the St Marylebone vestry, he owned a very successful Oxford Street pharmacy

16 Ibid.
17 *Observer*, 4, 11 Dec. 1854, 5; *The Times*, 2 Dec. 1854, 12.
18 Bell was understandably reluctant to mention his experience as MP for St Albans, as it had been stripped of its parliamentary representation due to his own alleged bribery during the 1852 election.
19 *Observer*, 11 Dec. 1854, 5.

which by the 1850s had become something of a local institution.[20] Bell's status as a substantial employer and ratepayer legitimised his influence in the vestry, which he referred to as 'the Marylebone parliament' and where he made all the right noises. Bell steadfastly defended the principles of retrenchment and strict economy, for instance, and pledged that, regardless of whether he was returned to parliament, he would continue in his capacity as a vestryman to 'endeavour to do what he could for the benefit of the borough – to protect their independence, to serve the poor, and to maintain their local self-government'. In the event that the principle of local self-government should ever come under attack in the House of Commons, Bell pledged to 'use all his influence, as he had hitherto done, to preserve it and to assist in carrying it out in an efficient manner'.[21] Bell also possessed something of a unique wildcard, 'celebrity endorsements' from Landseer and Frith who, while not local in a strict sense, were both close friends of his and who both campaigned on his behalf.[22]

Not all Bell's strengths were purely local, and his wider political ideology also yielded some advantages. As a Quaker he was a fierce critic of the church rates and a strong advocate of disestablishment. In a constituency such as Marylebone, which was renowned for its violently anti-Anglican politics, these views was very likely to win votes. Just as important, Bell was also a firm believer in commercial freedom, and in the course of his campaign he went out of his way to criticise the Public Houses Act as an unjust infringement on the rights of trade. His work on pharmaceutical reform, meanwhile, which was carried out with the aid of Thomas Wakley, honoured entrepreneurial principles while also promoting professional training and education. Bell sought to improve, rather than to regulate, the pharmaceutical trade and regarded Whig 'medical reformers' as naturally inimical to his plans. Where regulation was needed, Bell argued that self-regulation by chemists and druggists was preferable to any sort of government-imposed regulatory scheme. 'The "medical reformers"', Bell claimed,

> have not abandoned their design. They are only waiting for the opportunity to carry it into execution, and they are likely to persevere until an alteration of some kind is effected in the department under consideration. It being evident therefore that Chemists must and will be included in the scheme of 'reform', it remains for them to decide whether they will allow measures of this descrip-

---

[20] 'My dear Mr. Bell': letters from Dr. Jonathan Pereira to Jacob Bell, 1844–1853, ed. J. Burnby, C. P. Cloughly and M. P. Earles, London 1987.
[21] The Times, 21 Dec. 1854, 7.
[22] Bell commissioned Frith's painting Derby Day.

tion to be forced upon them by persons who are indifferent or opposed to their interest, or whether they will maintain their independence under such regulations as shall conduce to their own welfare.[23]

Unlike Bell, Ebrington had very few natural affinities with the Marylebone electorate, and he had no local connections whatsoever. Whereas Bell advocated church disestablishment, Ebrington was an outspoken supporter of the Anglican establishment; whereas Bell promoted commercial freedom, Ebrington called for the regulation of working hours and other state interference in trade. More important still, whereas Bell had for many years agitated as part of the St Marylebone vestry for state retrenchment and local self-government, Ebrington had done all within his power (as secretary of the MSA, MCS and the Central Poor Law Board – a golden triangle of centralisation) to deny the ratepayers. A more committed, consistent, outspoken and notorious believer in Chadwickian centralisation could hardly be found anywhere. Predictably, Ebrington's past as a 'central functionary' sat uneasily with many Marylebone electors and was frequently raised as grounds for his unsuitability as a candidate. During the very early stages of his campaign, at a meeting in Kentish Town convened to determine Ebrington's suitability as a candidate, speakers pointed out that, as secretary of the Poor Law Board, Ebrington had 'insulted the people of England'.[24]

For his part, Bell repeatedly attacked Ebrington on this point, and at the nomination reminded the Marylebone electors that 'if they should select as their representative the centralising noble lord ... they would place in jeopardy their liberties and their independence, and would be striking a nail into the coffin of their local self-government'.[25] Elsewhere, Bell referred to Ebrington as a 'red hot advocate of centralisation' and a 'Whig of the rank centralising school'.[26] One consequence of Ebrington's centralising prejudices, Bell maintained, was a disdain for the borough's representative vestries. He claimed that Ebrington 'looked upon the vestries of this borough, which are the only means of communication between the ratepayers and the government, as a set of vulgar fellows'.[27] Wherever possible, Bell contrasted Ebrington's advocacy of administrative centralisation with his own consistent support for local self-government. At an important meeting of electors held at the St Pancras vestry hall, for instance, Bell promised those in atten-

[23] J. Bell, *Observations addressed to the chemists and druggists of Great Britain on the Pharmaceutical Society*, London 1841, 3.
[24] *The Times*, 28 Nov. 1854, 6.
[25] *Daily News*, 19 Dec. 1854.
[26] *The Spectator*, 23 Dec. 1854, 1343; *Morning Advertiser*, 19 Dec. 1854, 6.
[27] *Morning Advertiser*, 19 Dec. 1854, 6.

dance that he 'stood before them as the staunch supporter of local self-government, and as one determined to maintain the right of the taxpayer to control the expenditure of their own funds, and manage their own affairs, and opposed to the principles of centralisation to the utmost'. Ebrington, meanwhile, was shouted down under cries of 'no centralisation' and 'no poor law commissioners'.[28] A week later, as the poll approached, Bell again reiterated that he would 'resist any infringement upon the rights of those who paid rates to have control over the expenditure of their own money'.[29] The fact that Ebrington's campaign was being managed by the Chadwickian Sir John Easthope further illustrated Ebrington's credentials as a centraliser.

While Bell carefully oriented his debates with Ebrington around the issue of 'local self-government', he also made political hay out of Ebrington's various other disadvantages. Ebrington's aristocratic social background, for instance, was seized upon by Bell, who cleverly cast himself as a fellow sufferer from aristocratic misrule. The fundamental question put to the electors by Bell was whether they would 'prefer as their representative one of themselves, one who, having been a tradesman himself, was more likely to sympathise with their interests than a noble lord who, belonging to the aristocracy had no such sympathy with them'.[30] Bell very clearly promoted himself as a member and an advocate of the productive classes (and therefore as a 'contributor' to society), whereas Ebrington was described as a classic aristocratic Whig placeman and therefore a drain on revenues and a cause of high taxes.[31] Ebrington's example, and particularly his career as a placemen, was held up by Bell as instructive of the great danger inherent in sending Lords to the House of Commons – namely, the aristocratic willingness (perhaps even need) to increase income tax and the legacy duties.[32] At times, Bell cleverly combined his anti-aristocratic theme with warnings about Ebrington's thirst for centralisation, thereby imparting a powerful synergy to his critique. Bell's nomination speech, for instance, contained a warning: 'to those who had a prejudice in favour of great Lords as their representatives, he might allude to the fable of the frogs who chose a stork to represent their interests. The stork was a strong advocate for centralisation, and as soon as he took office he began to centralise the frogs into his own stomach'.[33] While this tongue in cheek analogy was obscure in its origins, it was quite clear in its message. The

---

[28] Ibid. 12 Dec. 1854, 3. For further statements of Bell's commitment to local self-government see *The Times*, 19 Dec. 1854, 10.
[29] *Observer*, 17 Dec. 1854, 5.
[30] Ibid.
[31] *The Times*, 21 Dec. 1854, 7.
[32] *The Spectator*, 23 Dec. 1854, 1343.
[33] *The Times*, 19 Dec. 1854, 10.

aristocracy comprised a wholly separate estate and acted according to a unique set of interests that just happened to be diametrically opposed to the interests of the 'froggish multitude'.

Bell's two-pronged attack was perfectly suited to the prejudices of the Marylebone radicals – especially those in the vestries who naturally equated aristocratic wastefulness with bloated centralised government. S. R. Stockton, W. B. Billet, W. D. Cooper and other important radical members of the St Pancras vestry certainly found these arguments extremely compelling.[34] Yet, almost from the start of the contest, Nicholay, Thomas D'Iffanger, Jr, Edward Hodges and other influential radicals within the St Marylebone vestrymen (all fervent localists who would go on to occupy influential roles within the MBW) backed Ebrington. As if the opposition of Nicholay was not enough, by the time that the dust had settled Bell's natural constituency of dissenters had also defected into the camp of the uncompromisingly Anglican Ebrington. How had Ebrington won over (and how had Bell alienated) these two crucial groups?

In the first place, Bell's commitment to commercial freedom ultimately alienated many of his Nonconformist supporters. In 1854 the Public Houses Act (also called the 'Beer Act') was a hot topic in Marylebone, especially among the borough's licensed victuallers and publicans, who vigorously opposed government regulation of their trade.[35] In an effort to secure the support of these two pressure groups, Bell pledged to repeal the Beer Act, and described the measure in strong language as an unjust and unwarranted restriction on commercial freedom.[36] Ebrington's position, on the other hand, was much more ambiguous. When asked to pledge his support for repeal, Ebrington repeatedly replied that he would need to better acquaint himself with the issue.[37] Ultimately, Ebrington's moderation and Bell's aggressive opposition to the Beer Act was said to have pushed many dissenters out of the Bell camp. According to Bell, these defections comprised the 'only one circumstance connected to the election to which he could look back with regret', and indeed they seem to have been quite costly.[38] In the *Observer*'s view, these defections 'materially aided in turning the scale against Mr. Bell'.[39]

The defection of the dissenters was not Bell's only difficulty. Bell's ambig-

34 *Observer*, 17 Dec. 1854, 5; *Morning Advertiser*, 12 Dec. 1854, 3.
35 See *Observer*, 3 Sept. 1854, 2.
36 *Morning Advertiser*, 12 Dec. 1854, 3; *Observer*, 17 Dec. 1854, 5.
37 *Observer*, 11 Dec. 1854, 5.
38 *The Times*, 21 Dec. 1854, 7.
39 *Observer*, 24 Dec. 1854, 5.

uous position on the war confused potential supporters and antagonised aggressively patriotic radicals like Nicholay. While he was at pains to establish that he did not belong to the 'Peace Society' and was in no sense actively opposed to the war, Bell himself admitted that he 'could not adopt that war cry'.[40] When he sounded his commitment to the war, he was called a hypocrite and traitor to his principles and faith; when, on the other hand, his support for the war was only lukewarm, he was branded unpatriotic. Political expediency prevented Bell from openly opposing the war, but this only brought further criticism. 'What would the Czar say', wondered Ebrington's campaign chairman Sir John Easthope at a meeting held at the Literary Institute, 'of a man who would violate his religion, who would compromise his conscience, and act contrary to the principles of his sect, by doing that which they believed was the right and proper thing to be done in the present crisis of the affairs of this country.'[41] This put Bell in an exceedingly difficult position. Russophobia, which had long been a fundamental component of Marylebone radicalism, had generated a great deal of support for the war in the borough.

For his part, Ebrington rarely hesitated from contrasting Bell's inchoate position with his own unflagging commitment to what he felt was a 'just and necessary' war. His introductory address to the electors of Marylebone, for instance, was dominated by passages which justified prosecuting the war to the fullest possible extent. 'If, above all', Ebrington wrote, 'you feel with me that we ought to strain every nerve to succour effectively and at once, our struggling forces in the Crimea … I shall endeavour to merit your approbation, and testify my gratitude by a diligent attention to my public duties and a sedulous promotion of your local interests.'[42] By tying together Marylebone's local interests with what he called 'the purpose of checking the encroachments of despotism' Ebrington cleverly engaged with a powerful radical trope, and quite brazenly began to recast himself as a defender of local self-government. Ebrington also used his support for the war cleverly to undermine Bell's criticisms of aristocratic political leadership. At his nomination, he questioned Bell's claim that 'a lord could not sympathise with the people', and asked whether there had been 'any jealously at Alma or Inkerman, where lords and their comrades shed their blood side by side like water?'[43] Taking this line of reasoning a step further, Ebrington noted that none of Bell's Quaker forebears had made the ultimate sacrifice for English liberty and

40 *The Times*, 21 Dec. 1854, 7.
41 *Observer*, 11 Dec. 1854, 5; *The Spectator*, 23 Dec. 1854, 1343.
42 *The Times*, 8 Dec. 1854, 6.
43 *The Spectator*, 23 Dec. 1854, 1343; *Observer*, 11 Dec. 1854, 5.

greatness.[44] Perhaps, he hinted, an Anglican aristocrat had more in common with the electors of Marylebone than a shopocratic Quaker after all.

As such rhetoric suggests, Ebrington's social status was by no means a complete liability. Although narratives of 'old corruption' continued to inform radical thinking on 'big government' and taxation, Marylebone reformers had none the less made a habit of returning aristocratic figures to parliament. As one journalist put it, Marylebone had 'always hankered after the honour of being represented by a scion of the aristocracy'.[45] Hall and Stuart were each thoroughly aristocratic figures, yet each styled himself a defender of popular opinion and an enemy of 'old corruption'. When objections were first raised against Ebrington on account of his aristocratic orientations, reformers in Kentish Town responded by pointing out that the same objections had been raised against Dudley Stuart when he first presented himself to the borough, but he had proved himself to be a first rate representative. With this in mind, Ebrington went out of his way to advertise his close social connections to Lord Dudley Coutts Stuart in the hope that their relationship might remind the electors of Stuart's own aristocratic background.[46] Hall had also initially been suspect to the St Marylebone vestry, and had more recently been singled out by the journalist Edward Whitty as a prominent example of the political genus 'titled radical'. In Whitty's view, however, Hall's aristocratic social orientation actually intensified his radicalism.

Like Hall and Stuart before him, Ebrington presented his aristocratic social credentials as virtues rather than shortcomings. His campaign continually emphasised his 'independence' while simultaneously rejecting the idea that MPs should ever be mere delegates. 'If I cannot be returned as an independent Representative', Ebrington proclaimed in his introductory borough address, 'I will not be returned at all.'[47] The institution of pledging, meanwhile, was repeatedly berated by Ebrington as a practice which 'demoralises candidates more than [their] constituents and sacrifices the Member's to the Electors' independence, making him their delegate rather than their representative'.[48] In taking this line, Ebrington often implied that Bell's status as a man of business (particularly one with local private interests), and his will-

44 *Morning Advertiser*, 19 Dec. 1854, 6.
45 *Sunday Times*, 10 Dec. 1854.
46 *Morning Advertiser*, 19 Dec. 1854, 6.
47 *The Times*, 8 Dec. 1854, 6.
48 H. Fortescue, *Parliamentary reform: Lord Ebrington's address to the electors of Marylebone*, London 1859, 6–7. For Ebrington's views on pledging see also *The Times*, 19 Dec. 1854, 10, and 21 Dec. 1854, 7.

ingness to make pledges, compromised his ability to stand aloof from sectional interests within the borough. Ebrington's desire to see 'constituencies untempted and members incapable of corruption' also cleverly engaged with Bell's recent disqualification from the borough of St Albans, where he had been found guilty of corruption.[49] Only Ebrington's aristocratic independence could protect Marylebone from similar abuse. This strategy cleverly undermined the strength of Bell's 'local appeal' and made his status as a 'man of the people' a liability. Hence the doubts within the borough over whether Bell 'had what it takes' to represent it in parliament.

Whereas Ebrington tried to defuse the issue of aristocratic 'separateness' by elaborating its advantages, he dealt with Bell's charges of 'centralisation' through simple denial. From his very introduction to the borough, Ebrington quite remarkably presented himself to the electors as a 'promoter of good local self-government, and of that efficiency in local administration which is the only true economy'.[50] Despite his reputation as a leading Chadwickian, Ebrington repeatedly claimed to recognise the desirability of metropolitan local self-government and he even characterised himself as someone 'who was no centraliser – who loved local self-government, but who wished to see it economical and efficient, in order that it might be strong and respected – who had never designated the vestries "vulgar", but who thought that their parochial management might be improved'.[51] Seeing his best hope for election potentially undermined by Ebrington's 'conversion' to the cause of local self-government, Bell accused his opponent of disingenuousness. After reminding the electors of his own unfailing support for local self-government, Bell claimed that Ebrington was a clear advocate of centralisation and had 'raised the cry of local self-government as a stalking horse for the purpose of throwing dust in the eyes of the electors'.[52] The vestrymen of St Pancras seemed to endorse this view. At a speech at the St Pancras vestry hall Ebrington was practically laughed off stage for declaring himself a supporter of local self-government.[53]

Close examination of Ebrington's 'pamphlet advocating centralisation' (a work entitled *Representative self-government for the metropolis: a letter to Lord Palmerston* which had been published just months before the Marylebone election) more than justifies Bell's charges of disengenuousness. Far from being a public declaration of Ebrington's conversion to local self-

[49] *Morning Advertiser*, 19 Dec. 1854, 6.
[50] *The Times*, 8 Dec. 1854, 6.
[51] Ibid. 19 Dec. 1854, 10; *The Spectator*, 23 Dec. 1854, 1343.
[52] *Morning Chronicle*, 19 Dec. 1854.
[53] *The Times*, 12 Dec. 1854, 12.

government, the *Letter* was, in fact, an attempt to scare Palmerston away from Hall's municipal solution to the London government problem.[54] In it, Ebrington presented an alternative scheme, which would protect both metropolitan London and the imperial parliament from the dangers supposedly inherent in Hall's solution.[55] In a passage that anticipated his contribution to the parliamentary debate on Hall's Metropolis Local Management Bill, Ebrington warned specifically of the challenge that a metropolitan legislature might pose to the supremacy of the imperial parliament, and predicted that such a body would concern itself as much with questions of national politics as with issues of local importance.[56] While the *Letter* acknowledged that government executed entirely by commissions was neither popular nor practicable, it in no way endorsed the principle of local self-government.

To begin with, the *Letter* quite clearly claimed that local self-government was in no way inherently 'better' than centralised government – it was merely more popular. In fact, Ebrington was clear in his own view that crown-appointed commissions had proven to be both more efficient and more economical than representative assemblies in carrying out municipal improvements. Yet while commissions had been more efficient, they had also proven to be unpopular, and were therefore unacceptable. 'No system of government can be considered successful', Ebrington conceded, 'unless it works not only well, but is, on the whole, acceptable to the governed.'[57] Although Ebrington acknowledged the need for a popularly endorsed system, at no point in his *Letter* did he show any sympathy for ratepayer concerns over self-determination. To the contrary, Ebrington's view of the 'ratepayer position' was consistently unflattering and cynical. The vestries were to Ebrington's mind tools of *petit bourgeois* oppression over all below and above them. Indeed, the wholesale enfranchisement of the ratepayers had been in Ebrington's estimation the chief shortcoming of the Municipal Reform Act, under which

> too large a share of power has been given to the ratepaying class, with too little protection both to the large and unrepresented majority below, and to the small and equally defenceless minority of owners above them in the social scale; and ... much of the backwardness of our Municipal Corporations in promoting sanitary improvement is attributable to this.[58]

---

[54] The *Letter* was published some months before Ebrington was called upon to stand for Marylebone, and therefore should not be read as an attempt to woo the vestry radicals. In fact, more than one passage is openly critical of precisely these vestry groups.

[55] Fortescue, *Representative self-government*, 62.

[56] Ibid. 17–18.

[57] Ibid. 21.

[58] Ibid. 28.

Ebrington's *Letter* conveys the strong impression that only the self-interested parsimony of the 'shopocracy' stood in the way of a system of efficient and comprehensive government by commission.

Ebrington's complex solution to the London government problem sought to address ratepayer concerns by splitting the functions of local government between three semi-autonomous authorities or departments. The first of these would regulate works (including water and gas supply, sewerage, improvement of roads and the removal of nuisances among other things); a second would discharge what Ebrington called 'the government of persons and the administration of justice'; while a third would confine its activities to matters of interment, where the government would have a monopoly. The most interesting feature of Ebrington's scheme was the way in which the separate bodies were to be elected and organised. Ebrington felt the need to create separate constituencies with distinct electoral divisions and slightly different voting qualifications for each of the three departments. Only in this way might each department's independent identity and function be retained and each department's influence over wider political issues weakened. As part of this scheme, Ebrington advocated ratepayer democracy for the department in charge of the 'government of persons', but at the same time recommended that a certain proportion of this department's board members should be appointed by the imperial government. The metropolitan police, meanwhile, would be left entirely under government control. The department of 'works' was to be organised along even less democratic lines. Ebrington recognised the fundamentally different set of interests and priorities held by short-term occupier ratepayers and landlords. The 'real interest' of the former group, he claimed, was to keep rates low at the expense of efficiency (since the ratepayer had no long-term interest in the condition of his property), while the interest of the landlord was that 'the structural arrangements on and about his property should be as lasting and good as possible'.[59] With these conflicting sets of interests in mind, Ebrington suggested that one third of the department responsible for carrying out works should consist of 'representatives of the landlords, elected out of the landlord class independently of the ratepayers'.[60] In the same vein, Ebrington urged that each landlord should have a number of votes proportional to the value of his interests or property. This sounded suspiciously like a Sturges Bourne arrangement and, as rating would still be the central issue, it would prove unacceptable to Hobhouse vestry radicals. Ebrington's further suggestion, that a crown-appointed commission direct both the works and interments bodies until the private

[59] Ibid. 27.
[60] Ibid. 29.

cemeteries were shut down and the sewerage system reformed, severely undermined his claim to have been converted to the cause of local self-government.[61]

It is little wonder, given the arguments presented in his pamphlet, that Ebrington was widely thought to favour a return to a uniform Sturges Bourne system of local government. He, of course, denied this, but in doing so he also voiced his dissatisfaction with the principles of Hobhouse's act, which he felt required a 'revision'.[62] This view was nothing short of anathema to all good vestry radicals, and was compounded by the explicit criticism, made in Ebrington's *Letter*, of the role that Marylebone's two Hobhouse vestries had played in national politics. In addition to questioning the wisdom of the Hobhouse act, the *Letter* attacked the personal qualities of the vestry leadership. At one point the pamphlet claimed that the obsession of the St Marylebone vestry with national politics had resulted in severe mismanagement of the parish's local affairs.[63] Elsewhere it was claimed that the 'shopocrats' who ran Marylebone's two Hobhouse vestries only did so because in Marylebone 'most men know nothing even of their next door neighbours, and to this ignorance, I would remark, no small proportion of these governors are indebted for their official position'.[64] These insults alone should have ensured uniform vestry hostility to Ebrington's campaign. Instead, Ebrington received strong support from leading members of the St Marylebone vestry.

Despite the influence of the war and the Beer Act, factionalism within the vestry of St Marylebone, and between the vestries of St Marylebone and St Pancras, was almost certainly the single most important factor in Ebrington's electoral success. The Marylebone vestry radical movement had produced many of London's most important radical figureheads – from Thomas Murphy in the 1830s to John Nicholay in the 1850s. Yet within the borough itself, the vestry reform movement had never been completely united. The St Pancras vestrymen had always been slightly more radical than their counterparts in the wealthier St Marylebone, who often favoured relatively moderate liberal parliamentary candidates over ultras. On at least one occasion this conflict had divided the borough's liberal constituency sufficiently to precipitate the return of a Tory, Lord Teignmouth, for one of Marylebone's seats. At the same time the St Marylebone vestry itself was by no means a unified body, and as various parochial factions continually vied for supremacy, dissension within the vestry was often intense. By 1840 the Barlow Street committee of

---

[61] Ibid. 34, 60.
[62] *Sunday Times*, 17 Dec. 1854, 4.
[63] Fortescue, *Representative self-government*, 18.
[64] Ibid. 31.

St Marylebone had become an entrenched local oligarchy,[65] and over the following decade its stranglehold over both the business of the vestry and the nature and direction of the wider Marylebone reform movement generated a great deal of discontent among excluded borough radicals. A similar development had taken place in Westminster during the 1820s, when ultra-radical Rotundaists had been alienated by the way in which Francis Place and his Westminster Reform Committee had directed the metropolitan radical movement.

In 1849 a new group, calling itself the Ratepayer's Protection Association, emerged within the parish and challenged the supremacy of the Barlow Street committee. Under Joseph Hume's guidance the RPA (also known within the borough as the 'Alligators') claimed that the committee had lost sight of its mission to extend local economy and had become too interested in national political issues. The RPA styled itself as a politically non-partisan alliance of Tories, Whigs and radicals interested more in the management of local rates than in the nature of national politics. This strategy was successful, but almost immediately after achieving local prominence, the RPA itself became the target of yet another insurgent parochial faction.[66] In May 1852 a group calling itself the Ratepayers' Association (and known generally within the parish as the 'Orientals') won a majority of seats in the vestry by promising to restore 'decency and order' to parochial proceedings.[67] By the time that Ebrington and Bell stood against each other in the 1854 Marylebone by-election, the Orientals had come under heavy attack from an avowedly liberal group of parochial reformers known as the 'Independents', many of whom had been prominent Alligators in 1852. Although the 'Independents' advertised themselves as 'the popular party' vis-à-vis the Orientals, each faction seems to have contained both radicals and conservatives.[68]

In 1854 Jacob Bell was himself a leading member of both the St Marylebone vestry and the 'Orientals' faction. When, in late 1854, the 'Orientals' came under fire for nepotism, jobbery and an irresponsible rating scheme, Bell's electoral fortunes also took a turn for the worse. The insurgent 'Independent' faction, which was led by an influential clique of Oxford Street tradesmen that included John Nicholay, Clement George and Richard Mitchell, but which also included the prominent local radicals Thomas

---

[65] See especially Brooke, *Democrats of Marylebone*, 31–43.

[66] *Observer*, 11 Apr. 1852, 2.

[67] Ibid. 29 Feb. 1852, 2. Although the Orientals came to being regarded within the parish as a High Church Tory faction, they professed to being both non-partisan and non-sectarian: *Observer*, 7 Mar. 1852, 2; 18 Apr. 1852, 2; 16 May 1852, 3.

[68] *Ratepayer's Journal*, 29 Dec. 1855, 1.

D'Iffanger Jr, Edward Hodges and Charles Freeth (each former members of the RPA), initially gave its endorsement to the radical candidate (and former Lambeth MP) Charles Tennyson D'Eyncourt.[69] When it became clear that neither D'Eyncourt nor Napier would be able to contest the borough, the Independent faction was faced with no other alternative than to support Ebrington. In his public declaration of support for Ebrington, the borough king-maker Nicholay admitted that while 'the political views of Lord Ebrington fall short of my own', he had been enticed to support Ebrington out of his strong opposition to Bell.[70] Like Nicholay, each important member of the 'Independent' faction also belonged to Ebrington's central election committee, from conservatives like Clement George to radicals like Edward Hodges. Many of Bell's most energetic supporters, meanwhile, were leading members of the Orientals. During his campaign Bell himself made sure to repeatedly denounce the political influence of the 'Oxford Street clique' within both the vestry and the borough.[71]

Given the extreme hostility that Nicholay and his fellow 'Independents' felt towards administrative centralisation, and given Ebrington's strong antipathy to local self-government, there is no other way to account for 'Independent' support for Ebrington than to see it as a function of his paro-chial struggle against Bell and the Ratepayer's Association.[72] This was certainly the way in which the St Pancras vestryman, prominent anti-centraliser and Bell supporter William Ross understood the borough's patterns of candidate allegiance in 1854. Early in the campaign Ross had expressed his view that 'opposition to Mr. Bell had originated in parochial differences. Now, in St Pancras', Ross went on, 'although there are two parties, bitterly opposed to each other parochially, in this instance they have cordially united together in support of Mr. Bell as the "local self-government"

---

[69] *Observer*, 11 Dec. 1854, 5.

[70] *The Times*, 16 Dec. 1854, 5.

[71] George Poland, Thomas Henry Filmer and Thomas D'Iffanger, Sr, who were among the most prominent members of the RA, were also members of Bell's election committee. Compare Bell's committee list (*The Times*, 16 Dec. 1854, 4) with RA membership (*Rate-payer's Journal*, 29 Dec. 1855, 2; *Observer*, 18 Apr. 1852, 2). For Bell's thoughts on the Oxford Street clique see *Observer*, 17 Dec. 1854, 5, and *Morning Advertiser*, 19 Dec. 1854, 6, where the Oxford Street clique's support for Ebrington was attributed to their status as local aristocracy.

[72] Nicholay, D'Iffanger, and Hodges were each important members of the MBW. In fact, in 1857, D'Iffanger was described by the *Elector* newspaper (which was an organ of the MBW) as 'the foe of government centralisation, and a friend of the representation of people in all matters affecting their interests. He has made himself obnoxious to those, who, for many years, were interested in Marylebone, in the heavy taxation of the people, by coming out as champion and protector of the ratepayers' (26 Aug. 1857, 1).

and really liberal candidate, and I urge the parochial parties in Marylebone to follow our example.'[73] It was no coincidence that Ross made his claim in response to Edward Hodges's motion that Bell was unfit to represent the borough.

Ross's claim that St Pancras was united in its support for Bell highlights another important issue. The two St Pancras parties, known as the Pinks and the Blues, had been in conflict with one another since the early 1830s, when the Blues had come out in opposition to the Hobhouse act and the Pinks had come out in strong favour of it. During the 1830s the Pinks had been led by the influential demagogue Thomas Murphy, whose influence within the parish gradually marginalised the more moderate Blues. Over the course of the following decade, in response to their decreasing profile, the Blues themselves became increasingly more radical, until at some point during the early 1840s the political differences between the Blues and their parochial rivals became negligible. This convergence effectively ended factional struggle for control of the vestry, and the parish parties shortly thereafter became united in their joint advocacy of decentralised government and by their radical outlook in general. By 1854, with the Pinks comfortably in control of parish affairs, and in the absence of pronounced ideological dispute, the vestry was able to unite in support of Jacob Bell.[74] At the same time, not all Bell's St Pancras supporters were extreme radicals. The moderate free trader and St Pancras churchwarden Thomas Henry Farrer, for instance, who was every inch the establishment figure, was appointed chairman of Bell's election committee and played an important part in rallying parish support for his candidate. From the council of the St Pancras Administrative Reform Association, Farrer joined ultra-radical Pinks such as Thomas Ross, S. R. Stockton, and W. D. Cooper (each of whom was a member of Bell's central election committee) in advocating a thorough streamlining of the administrative apparatus of government.[75]

Although almost the entire St Pancras vestry was united in support for Bell, Ebrington was none the less able to attract small pockets of support. Conservatives such as the senior churchwarden John Flather proved particularly drawn to Ebrington's campaign. In fact it was claimed that many borough conservatives voted for Ebrington in the belief that his return would ultimately frustrate the radical and liberal vestry cliques.[76] Provided that this

---

[73] *Observer*, 11 Dec. 1854, 5.
[74] Ebrington was said to have 'very ugly quarrels to settle with the vestry of St. Pancras': ibid.
[75] Ibid. 13 May 1855, 6.
[76] Ibid. 24 Dec. 1854, 5.

was true, local conservatives showed foresight, for Ebrington's strongly
Russellite outlook frustrated the likes of Nicholay and D'Iffanger throughout
Ebrington's time as borough representative. By 1857 vestry hostility to
Ebrington was exceptionally pronounced, and even D'Iffanger had grown so
disillusioned with his behaviour that he announced his willingness to support
a rival candidate.[77] On the rare occasions when Ebrington appeared at vestry
meetings, he generally proved unreceptive of vestry advice and entreaty. In
fact, Ebrington often openly defied vestry wishes on important issues. As
Hall's Metropolis Local Management Bill made its way through parliament,
for instance, Ebrington ignored the strong support given to it by both
Marylebone representative vestries, and attempted to undermine both the
bill and its author at various stages. Exasperated vestry liberals were eventually forced to pass a vote of censure on Ebrington's obstructionism, and some
even claimed that Ebrington sought to wreck the bill with 'the most obnoxious Chadwickian principles'. Others called Ebrington a 'tool and lover of the
Poor Law Chadwickian principle' and insinuated that his true aim was to
re-establish the Sturges Bourne Act across the metropolis.[78] In the face of
these criticisms, Ebrington refused to apologise and even took his argument
directly to the vestries.[79] He justified his defiant attitude towards the vestries
through an invocation of his independence and a defence of an MP's duty to
privilege national issues over local ones. As he had done during the election,
Ebrington also repeated his belief in the desirability of paternal, aristocratic
leadership and judgement.

In 1854 war, dissent and vestry factionalism combined temporarily to
undermine the normal order of Marylebone politics and to neutralise Bell's
appeal. In fact, in this context, many of Bell's greatest 'advantages' turned out
to be his greatest weaknesses. Had this unusual constellation of events and
issues not converged, Bell would almost certainly have won the borough.
Moreover, had Tennyson D'Eyncourt, Napier or any other marginally suitable radical stood for the borough, Ebrington would most likely not have had
the support of the Oxford Street clique. Bell's campaign strategy, and
Ebrington's hardly credible reaction to this strategy, reinforced the importance of issues such as centralisation and ratepayer self-determination in
metropolitan politics. Ironically, Ebrington's ultimate return is an even better

---

[77] *Ratepayer's Journal*, 28 Mar. 1854, 195. Nicholay and Hodges remained supportive
however.
[78] *Observer*, 10 June 1855, 3. Of course, Ebrington's objections to Hall's measure rested on
its confiscation of landlord influence.
[79] H. Fortescue, *To the representative vestries of Marylebone, St. Pancras, and Paddington*,
London 1857.

indicator that vestries and vestry factions exerted a great deal of power when it came to parliamentary elections. This influence is especially evident in the role played by Nicholay and his Oxford Street clique. In the wake of Ebrington's return, the *Ratepayer's Journal* asked 'who have the electors to thank for such a disgraceful state of things?' The answer was unequivocal. 'Is it not patent to the whole world', the *Journal* asked,

> that those men who, whilst holding out professions that they were the friends of local self-government, did all they could to destroy it, by inviting that notorious centraliser and enemy to the right of the ratepayers to manage their own affairs, Lord Ebrington, who have been the cause of the existing evil? We say it is. We say it is those disciples of Old Nic, the Oxford Street Clique ... these are the individuals who dare talk of 'dictation'.[80]

Insofar as the influence of the Oxford Street clique and the Independent faction secured Ebrington's return, the election illustrated the location of power within both the St Marylebone vestry and the borough itself. The input of Thomas Murphy and fellow St Pancras ultra-radicals had once played a significant part in the construction of Marylebone's political culture. By the early 1850s, however, moderation and liberalism had replaced extremism, and was in fact beginning to pave the way for acceptance of the Palmerstonian approach. Marylebone was not alone in its appreciation of Palmerston.

---

[80] *Ratepayer's Journal*, 28 Mar. 1857, 192.

Conclusion

From the later 1840s radical and liberal critics of Russell's government found in Lord Palmerston a handy foil to the unpopular prime minister. Although Palmerston served as foreign secretary throughout Russell's first administration, he was no Russellite and certainly no ministerial stooge. He was, as Russell grudgingly conceded, the only truly 'popular' minister within the government. From 1848 Russell understood that his increasingly weak ministry could not survive Palmerston's defection, and he consequently often indulged Palmerston's borderline insubordination.[1] During the 1850s Palmerston's growing reputation among liberals and radicals proceeded from an admiration of his foreign policy, and from an appreciation of Palmerston's qualities as a statesman and leader. Whereas Russell's support for the Hungarian, Italian and Polish independence movements was equivocal at best, Palmerston was a committed and outspoken champion of continental liberties.[2] These differences of perspective and priority on European issues were thrown into pronounced relief from 1850, when a series of public disagreements brought the prime minister and his foreign secretary into direct confrontation. Russell's final estrangement from Palmerston began in September, with Palmerston's provocative handling of the Haynau affair. Tellingly, this only enhanced Palmerston's popularity, while further damaging Russell's.[3]

In the wake of the Haynau affair, tensions between Russell and Palmerston again escalated when Palmerston was ordered by Russell not to meet with Kossouth. Although Palmerston complied, he none the less received, and endorsed, a deputation from Finsbury radicals (including Wakley, George

---

[1] See, for instance, D. Southgate, 'The most English minister …': the policies and politics of Palmerston, London 1966, 285.
[2] It is somewhat unfair to make the comparison, as Russell agreed in principle with much of what Palmerston did, but was hamstrung by diplomatic decorum and the necessity of keeping on good terms with Queen Victoria, who abhorred Palmerston's policy: Russell to Palmerston, 17 Dec. 1851, in S. Walpole, The life of Lord John Russell, New York 1889, ii. 139–40.
[3] Palmerston described Haynau as 'a great moral criminal' and called his visit to England 'a wanton assault on the people of this country'. See Southgate, Most English minister, 284.

Rogers, the Muswell Hill circle radical William Shaen, and the former anti-centralisation union co-chairman Charles Elt) which referred to the Russian and Austrian emperors as 'odious and detestable assassins' and which offered congratulations on Palmerston's anti-Russian policy.[4] Defenders of Palmerston's actions were quick to emerge. In parliament, Ralph Bernal Osborne defended Palmerston against critics of his Hungarian policy, and urged Liberals to join him in this defence and support.[5] Palmerston's sacking in 1851 over his support for Napoleon III's *coup d'etat* advertised even more starkly the great differences between his priorities and those promoted by Russell. The metropolitan radical journal *Reynolds Weekly* interpreted his dismissal as an opportunistic move by a cabinet fundamentally at odds with its foreign secretary. In verse, the journal wrote

> small Lord John has been and gone
> and turn'd adrift Lord Palmerston
> amongst the lot the only don
> who didn't take care of number one;
> out spoke Home Secretary Grey,
> I wish old Palmy were away,
> aye, turn him out they all did say,
> for he's the people's darling.[6]

Strangely, for someone who had endorsed the cessation of representative government in France, Palmerston became something of a martyr to the cause of European liberalism. Although his popularity declined elsewhere, he retained much of his support in Marylebone, where radicals considered asking him to replace the ailing D. C. Stuart as the borough's parliamentary representative.[7] Mazzini, meanwhile, confessed to W. H. Ashurt's youngest daughter his belief that Palmerston's dismissal would 'ensure certain hardships to our poor exiles who have had in him a protector'.[8]

There can be little doubt that much of Palmerston's popularity in the metropolitan boroughs was due to London's 'ultra-patriotism' during and in the run-up to the Crimean war.[9] Francis Newman, for one, went so far as to

---

[4] Palmerston claimed to be 'extremely flattered and highly gratified' by the deputation: *The Times*, 19 Nov. 1851, 8.

[5] See *Hansard* 3rd ser. cvi.786–93, 21 July, 1849. In the course of his speech, Osborne condemned all forms of 'paternal government', which he described as the source of Hungary's 'misery'.

[6] This is quoted in K. Martin, *The triumph of Lord Palmerston*, London 1924, 70–1.

[7] The coup was by no means unpopular in Marylebone. At the height of the crisis over Louis Napoleon's policy toward Italy in 1859, the Marylebone radicals met to reaffirm their support for the 1851 coup: *Reynold's Newspaper*, 15 May 1859, 6.

[8] Guiseppe Mazzini to Emilie Ashurst, 12 Jan. 1852, *Mazzini's letters*, i. 207.

[9] This is the explanation given by Antony Taylor in his 'Modes of political expression

claim that wartime jingoism disguised Palmerston's complete lack of domestic principles. 'It seems to me', wrote Newman shortly after the end of the war, 'that Mr. Disraeli has acutely exposed Lord Palmerston's policy – vis, having <u>no</u> domestic principles <u>whatever</u> on which he can attach supporters to himself, he is necessitated to knock up a "British flag" interest, and keep us in hot water somewhere.'[10] Yet Palmerston's metropolitan popularity was not solely due to his 'British flag' foreign policy. Miles Taylor has rightly pointed out that the brand of patriotism promoted by Palmerston drew heavily on eighteenth-century 'constitutionalist' discourses. Liberal support for Palmerston therefore extended well beyond foreign policy and into the realm of domestic reform.[11] Palmerston's attitude toward administrative reform was especially attractive to metropolitan radicals. Whereas Russell's zeal for administrative centralisation was seemingly boundless, Palmerston's Canningite priorities gave him a healthy distrust of government and a desire to effect further state retrenchment. Palmerston's opposition to Austrian and Russian 'tyranny' echoed the arguments made by Toulmin Smith, Newman, Linton and others – arguments which equated retrenchment with liberty, and centralisation with despotism, arguments which often used international events as metaphors for the supposed degradation of English local self-government.

Such parallels were particularly important to metropolitan radicals. Linton and Holyoake, both of whom drew such parallels themselves, enthusiastically endorsed Palmerston's reading of the European situation. Moreover, Palmerston's ideological commitment to decentralisation was carried into effect as policy during his time at the Home Office. According to Thomas Frost, Palmerston's commitment to domestic retrenchment and his agenda for the 'reinstatement' of local self-government made him the 'idol of the shopkeepers'.[12] Vestry radicals such as R. T. Webb and John Nicholay became even more convinced of Palmerston's commitment to these ideals when Sir Benjamin Hall was appointed to the presidency of the Board of Health in 1854.[13] Throughout 1854 and 1855, first in his capacity as home secretary and then as prime minister, Palmerston worked closely with Hall to

and working-class radicalism: the London and Manchester examples', unpubl. PhD diss. Manchester 1990.

[10] Newman to Holyoake, 2 Apr. 1857, Holyoake papers, GJHCC/913.

[11] Taylor, *Decline of British radicalism*, 150.

[12] T. Frost, *Forty years recollections, literary and political*, London 1880, 272.

[13] The metropolitan vestry radicals were not alone in seeing Hall's appointment as a reaffirmation of Palmerston's retrenching priorities. The Permanent Under-Secretary for Home Affairs, Waddington, rightly understood Hall's appointment as a 'censure' upon the Chadwickian priorities of the Board: Palmerston papers, HA/F/5/5.

craft a bill for the reform of metropolitan local government. The resulting Metropolis Local Management Bill relied heavily on the reform recommendations of the City Corporation, and signalled the final failure of Russell's paternalist solution. In the course of supporting the bill during its passage through the Commons, Palmerston congratulated Hall on his defence of the principle of local self-government, which he 'found most congenial with the feelings of the people of this country'.[14] Hall later repaid the compliment by declaring to the St Marylebone vestry that Palmerston was responsible for making the 'representative principle' the main feature of the realignment of metropolitan local government. 'It was certainly a step in that direction which had never been taken by any Secretary of State before and [it] showed the liberal and enlightened views of the noble viscount at the present moment at the head of the Home department.'[15]

By 1855 Hall had long promoted Palmerston as an alternative to Russell as party leader. Hall's friend and colleague John Williams felt that there was an 'easy understanding' between the two men, and Henry Fitzroy thought that Hall's personal influence on Palmerston 'could be instrumental in effecting a reconciliation of the Cabinet and Lord Palmerston' in December 1853.[16] Although Hall enjoyed a particularly close relationship with Palmerston, his support for 'Lord Cupid' was by no means unusual among metropolitan MPs. Palmerston had long enjoyed the strong support of leading anti-Russellite metropolitan radicals such as Thomas Duncombe, Dudley Coutts Stuart, Charles Tennyson D'Eyncourt, Thomas Wakley and Ralph Bernal Osborne. In the immediate aftermath of the Don Pacifico incident, these and other metropolitan MPs hosted a dinner in honour of Palmerston at the Reform Club during which Palmerston was suggested as a replacement for Russell at the head of a new-look Liberal party. Miles Taylor has rightly noted that those who attended the dinner had been

> amongst the most vocal critics of Russell's sluggish leadership inside and outside parliament since 1847 ... the long-term expectation which these MPs had of Palmerston was not that he should play the part of Britannia in Europe, but, as Lord Clarendon later observed, that of Lord Durham in parliament – an aristocratic reformer lending his weight to the people's party.[17]

14 *Hansard* 3rd ser.cxxxvii.727, 19 Mar. 1855.
15 *The Times*, 17 July 1854, 9. It is telling that Palmerston took advice from the St James vestryman, ex-GBH member, and virulent anti-Chadwickian John Leslie on the restructuring of metropolitan local government: Palmerston papers, HA/F/7, 8.
16 Fraser, 'Sir Benjamin Hall in parliament in the 1850s, part II', 113, 117.
17 Taylor, *Decline of British radicalism*, 153. Lord Durham had long been popular with the vestry radicals. In 1837 the vestry radical newspaper the *Marylebone Journal and Metro-*

Only a few short years later, the Southwark radical MP William Molesworth heartily congratulated Palmerston upon his accession to the premiership and advised him to 'avoid appearing to re-establish ... the old Whig government'.[18]

Support for Palmerston among metropolitan MPs (and metropolitan constituencies, for that matter) remained strong well into the late 1850s, as the results of the 1857 general election suggest. In Finsbury, Duncombe, who had formerly looked to Lord Durham as a liberal leader, was unstinting in his support for Palmerston, who, he believed, had 'introduced a more liberal system of government'.[19] Throughout his 1857 campaign, Duncombe castigated parliamentary critics of Palmerston's Chinese policy and defended him against charges of 'Toryism'.[20] Palmerston was given similar support in Southwark, where the veteran metropolitan campaigner and committed Palmerstonian Charles Napier routed his anti-Palmerston opponent Apsley Pellat. In Tower Hamlets the *Leader* circle radical G. J. Holyoake joined forces with A. S. Ayrton to sing Palmerston's praises and force out the old Russellite William Clay. Ayrton in particular declared that 'the great services rendered by Lord Palmerston to the nation, during the crisis of the Russian war, place him in the highest rank of public men, entitle him to every honour which he can receive, and deserve to be remembered with gratitude by the country'. Ayrton combined this support with advocacy of further domestic retrenchment. 'Local government', he claimed, 'is directly responsible to the people, secures to them an efficient control, and a ready means of redress, not always obtainable from central officers of the state.'[21] Hall, meanwhile, praised Palmerston's leadership qualities throughout his campaign and promised his Marylebone constituents that Palmerston would introduce in the

---

politan Register of News, Politics, and Literature, for instance, called for 'a ministry of undoubted liberal views and acknowledged enlightened tendencies, which shall have a man such as Lord Durham at its head' (22 Apr. 1837, 1). Duncombe also spoke of Durham's popularity in London: Duncombe to Durham [n.d. 1834], Earl Durham papers, D.P.13, box 3.

18 Molesworth to Palmerston, 22 Feb. 1855, Palmerston papers, GC/MO/3/1.

19 This is quoted in E. D. Steele, *Palmerston and liberalism, 1855–1865*, Cambridge 1991, 77. For Duncombe's admiration for Palmerston as a statesman see his *Life and correspondence*, i. 196–8.

20 *Leader*, 4 Apr. 1857, 319; *The Times*, 31 Mar. 1857, 7.

21 Election poster for Ayrton (1857), Bishopsgate Institute, Holyoake collection, GJHCC/905. For Holyoake's support for Palmerston see his pamphlet 'To the electors of the Tower Hamlets', ibid., in which Holyoake claims that 'the spectacle of Lord Palmerston, a Tory Premier, defending Sir John Bowring, a man of the people, has very deservedly won the admiration of the country'. See also G. J. Holyoake, *Sixty years of an agitator's life*, London 1906, i. 227–8.

course of the coming session a further measure of parliamentary reform.[22] Nicholay and other Marylebone radicals supplemented Hall's Palmerstonian campaigning by holding a series of meetings intended to demonstrate their own support for, and appreciation of, Palmerston's leadership qualities. Eventually, the St Marylebone vestry collectively declared its opinion that 'Lord Palmerston's Government is entitled to the confidence of the country.'[23] In 1857 each metropolitan candidate professing support for Palmerston was returned.

Much of Palmerston's reputation as an alternative liberal leader thus proceeded from his rivalry with Lord John Russell. Palmerston's Tory past and Canningite priorities were well known, and he was therefore popularly understood to represent an alternative political heritage to Russell's Foxite Whiggery. He was identified by both the Finsbury Chartist Thomas Cooper and G. J. Holyoake, for instance, as a sort of 'republican Tory'. Historians have disagreed over the strength of Russell's personal commitment to centralisation and over the extent to which the growth of the executive was uniquely 'Whiggish'. Whereas Peter Mandler and David Roberts have presented centralisation as a central feature of Russell's paternalism, others, such as John Prest, have championed the view that Russell and Peel were equally fond of the growth of government.[24] Regardless of Russell's personal commitment to centralisation, it is indisputable that the early Victorians themselves (and especially early Victorian radicals) tended to identify administrative centralisation and government growth as defining features of Russellite Whiggery. Whereas accusations of 'Whig centralisation' were prevalent throughout the early Victorian period, 'Tory centralisation' was unheard of. For Disraeli, 'centralisation' and the 'degradation' of organs and institutions of local government were fundamental to what he called the 'spirit of Whiggism'. 'Local institutions', he observed, 'supported by a landed

---

[22] *The Times*, 17 Mar. 1857, 5.

[23] *People's Paper*, 21 Mar. 1857, 7; *The Ratepayers' Journal and Local Management Gazette*, 192.

[24] See, particularly, J. Prest, *Liberty and locality: parliament, permissive legislation, and ratepayers democracies in the nineteenth century*, Oxford 1990. Interestingly, David Roberts has argued that Palmerston's true sympathies lay with the metropolitan commission of sewers, and in fact Ebrington interpreted Palmerston's appointment at the Home Office as a triumph for the Chadwickians. In May 1853 Ebrington confessed to wishing that 'we had him [Palmerston] at the head of the board of works instead of Molesworth': Hugh Fortescue, Viscount Ebrington, to Chadwick, 15 May 1853, Chadwick papers, 755. Palmerston was, in other words, every inch the paternalist, yet he was popularly perceived as a champion of 'local rights'. See F. W. Roberts 'Lord Palmerston at the Home Office', *Historian* xxi (1959), 63–81; Brundage, *England's Prussian minister*, 152–3; *Hansard* 3rd ser. cxxv.967–1005, 2 May 1853.

gentry, check them [the Whigs]; hence their love of centralisation and their hatred of unpaid magistrates.' Disraeli even went so far as to claim that without their 'favourite scheme of centralisation … the Whigs can never long maintain themselves in power'.[25] Unlike his colleagues, Palmerston was rarely portrayed as an out-and-out Whig, and was almost never portrayed as a 'centraliser'.

At the same time, unlike Russell, Palmerston had no personal, estate or family interests in the reorganisation of London's local government. This arguably freed him from a number of the constraints under which Russell had laboured. 'Centralisers' such as Russell and Grosvenor had immediate, vested interests in maximising the rights and powers of metropolitan landlords, through mechanisms such as plural and proxy vestry franchises, in order to ensure the long-term integrity and respectability of their metropolitan estates. Estate interests almost certainly played some role in motivating Russell, Fitzroy and Grosvenor, among other politically active metropolitan landlords, to oppose Wakley's 1836 scheme for imposing Hobhouse's Select Vestries Act throughout the metropolis, and to suggest that the new MBW would trample the rights of metropolitan landlords. Moreover, the duke of Bedford's estate interests in Bloomsbury seem to have prompted Whitbread's 1807 bill to introduce plural and proxy voting into the St Giles vestry. Indeed, during the 1830s Bedford, who served as churchwarden in St Giles, was personally involved in parish politics. Lord John Russell, meanwhile, also found time to maintain a high profile in the St George, Bloomsbury, vestry, and in fact in 1830 even attempted to use his political clout to restrict the vestry franchise to occupiers of premises rated at £30 or above.[26] Hobhouse, who at the time was working with Place on his 1831 legislation, criticised the bill in the House and the Southwark MP Robert Wilson believed that the bill 'was of so aristocratic and unjust a nature to the poorer ratepayers, that he trusted the House would not sanction it'.[27]

It is worth noting that London's vestry radical movement was most pronounced within parishes dominated by great aristocratic estates. Many of these estates belonged to Whig families. This relationship had much to do with the social character of the estates, and in particular their greater concentrations of middle-class residents. The Grosvenor estate in Belgravia, for

---

[25] Disraeli, *Whigs and Whiggism*, 331, 354.
[26] See Hobhouse to Burdett, 18 Nov. 1820, Burdett papers, MS Eng. Letters, d. 96, fos 7–8, and *St. Giles-in-the-Fields, and St. George Bloomsbury: substance of the proceedings at two public meetings of the above parishes*, London 1820.
[27] *Hansard* 3rd ser. xxiii.1125–7, 1 Apr. 1830; *St. Giles-in-the-Fields and St. George, Bloomsbury, vestry bill: explanation of the objects of the bill*, London 1830.

instance, was more or less co-terminous with the St George, Hanover Square, vestry, a predominantly middle-class Hobhouse vestry presided over by the arch-localist and virulent anti-Chadwickian John Leslie. Those other hotbeds of vestry radicalism, St Marylebone and St George, Bloomsbury, were likewise located on large Whig estates and populated by middle-class residents. When the debate over the 'London government problem' is considered in terms of metropolitan estate interests, some conventional assumptions about the disinterested, benevolent and moralistic nature of Victorian philanthropy (and therefore the Russellite public health schemes) and the parsimonious character of vestry localism become slightly less credible. Although the 'shopocrats' who populated the vestries have been criticised for taking a narrow, petty and self-interested position at the expense of the welfare of the urban poor, the behaviour of the 'centralisers' and philanthropists can be described as equally self-interested.

London's Whig landlords had not always been the object of radical ire. Indeed, prior to the parliamentary reform of 1832, the metropolitan political culture had been thoroughly Whiggish and conflict between the radicals of the Westminster Committee and the Whigs of Holland House had been infrequent. In fact, the unreformed parliamentary representation of Westminster was happily shared between the two groups and metropolitan radical representatives such as Burdett, Hobhouse and Wilson were rarely openly critical of their Whig counterparts. Instead, common effort was made to oppose Toryism. From 1834 the dynamics of this relationship became less co-operative and more antagonistic. Duncombe's caustic assessment of his fellow metropolitan MPs is illustrative of this. 'Some metropolitan members', he observed,

> turned their popularity to profitable account. They advocated the interests of the People and looked to their own. Government secured their support by advancing them to dignities or employments, or permitting them to exercise extensive patronage. Very edifying was the change of some of these fortunate individuals from the loudest democratic sentiments to a quiet adoption of those of the aristocracy – from the principles of extreme liberalism to those more in accordance with a position of the government.[28]

The reasons for this reorientation, and the nature of this antagonism, have been the focus of this book. One important, perhaps even decisive, cause of reorientation was Whiggery's elevation to a creed of government rather than opposition. It had been easy enough to find common cause in reaction and

---

[28] Duncombe, *Life and correspondence*, ii. 119.

opposition to Tory policy, but accepting a common positive legislative agenda proved far more difficult. The second, and perhaps more decisive, cause was the increasing incompatibility of Whig and radical views on local self-government. Largely because of this, by 1855 Whiggery had become a spent force in the metropolitan boroughs. Those Whigs who did survive, such as Ebrington in Marylebone and Grosvenor in Middlesex, did so only by repudiating their previous beliefs. Robert Grosvenor made a particularly striking about-face. Although he continued to refuse the abolition of the church rates, he none the less endorsed the vestry's right to set these rates, and even went so far as to acknowledge in 1861 that 'our parochial system is one of the oldest and best established of the component parts of that system of local government, of which we are so justly proud, and from which we have obtained such wonderful results'.[29] He had come a long way from condemning, via his position on the Metropolitan Sanitary Association, the vestries as instruments of narrow and parsimonious middle-class interests. The triumph of vestry radicalism, and Palmerstonian liberalism, was complete; Whiggery's metropolitan eclipse was total.

[29] Grosvenor, *The only compromise possible*, 6.

Bibliography

Unpublished primary sources

Chester-le-Street, Lambton Park Archives
1st earl of Durham papers

Durham University, Archives and Special Collections
2nd Earl Grey papers

London, Bishopsgate Institute
G. J. Holyoake papers
George Howell papers

London, British Library
4th earl of Aberdeen papers
Charles Babbage papers
Baron Broughton papers
Richard Cobden papers
William Ewart Gladstone papers
Robert Grant papers
Holland House papers
Leigh Hunt papers
2nd earl of Liverpool papers
William Lovett papers
Francis Newman – Joshua Toulmin Smith correspondence
Sir Robert Peel papers
Francis Place papers

London, Lambeth Archives, Minet Library
Charles Tennyson D'Eyncourt papers

London, Public Record Office
Poor Law Commission papers
Lord John Russell papers

London, University College Special Collections
Sir Edwin Chadwick papers
Francis Newman papers
Papers of the Society for the Diffussion of Useful Knowledge

London, Westminster Archives
Vestry minute books: St James; St George, Hanover Square; St Marylebone

Manchester, John Rylands University Library
Edward Davies Davenport papers
George Thompson papers

Manchester, National Co-Operative Archive
G. J. Holyoake papers

Muncaster Castle, Cumbria
Muncaster papers

Newcastle-upon-Tyne, Tyne and Wear Archives Services
Joseph Cowen papers

Newport, Gwent Record Office
Sir Benjamin Hall papers

Oxford, Bodleian Library
Henry Wentworth Acland papers
Francis Burdett-Coutts papers
4th earl of Clarendon papers
Benjamin Disraeli papers
Lord Robert Grosvenor journal and papers
Stephen Lushington papers
Toynbee family papers

Southampton, University of Southampton Archives
3rd Viscount Palmerston (Broadlands) papers
1st duke of Wellington papers

Published primary sources

Official publications (in chronological order)

Reports of the select committee appointed to inquire into the general operation and effect of the laws and usages under which select and other vestries are constituted in England and Wales, PP, 1830
Municipal corporations in England and Wales: first report from the Royal Commission on Municipal Corporations, PP, xxiii (1935)
Municipal corporations in England and Wales: London and Southwark, London companies, PP, xxv (1837)
Report on the prevalence of certain physical causes of fever in the metropolis, which might be removed with proper sanitary measures, PP, xxviii (1837–8)

Fourth annual report of the poor law commissioners, London 1838

Fifth annual report of the poor law commissioners, London 1839

Sanitary condition of the labouring population, PP, xxvi (1842)

Sanitary condition of the labouring poor: supplementary report: interment in towns, PP, xii (1842)

Report on the practice of interments in towns, PP, xii (1843)

First report of the commissioners appointed to inquire whether any and what special means may be requisite for the improvement of the health of the metropolis, PP, xxxii (1847–8).

Report from the select committee on church rates together with the proceedings of the committee, minutes of evidence, appendix and index, PP, ix (1851)

Report of the commissioners appointed to inquire into the existing state of the corporation of the City of London, PP, xxvi (1854)

Hansard's *Parliamentary debates*, 3rd series

Newspapers and periodicals

The Ballot

The Beehive

The Charter

Clapham Gazette and Local Advertiser

Cobbett's Weekly Political Register

Daily News

East London Observer

Eclectic Review

The Elector

English Chartist Circular

The Examiner

Hackney Magazine and Parish Reformer

Illustrated London News

Lambeth Gazette and South London Advertiser

The Lancet

Leader

The London Dispatch; and People's Political and Social Reformer

London Mercury

Marylebone Journal and Metropolitan Register of News, Politics, and Literature

Morning Advertiser

Morning Chronicle

Morning Herald

Municipal Corporation Reformer

Municipal and Poor Law Gazette and Local Functionary

The New Vestryman

Nonconformist

North London Examiner and Weekly Advertiser

The Observer

The Operative

Parochial Chronicle

Parochial Expositor; or Anti-Church Rate Payers Gazette

Parochial Gazette

The Patriot
People's Journal
People's Paper
Poor Man's Guardian
Punch
Quarterly Review
Ratepayer and Borough Chronicle: The Tower Hamlets Reporter
Ratepayer, or the London Borough of Lambeth and Southwark Parochial, Literary, and
    Scientific Journal
Ratepayers' Journal and Local Management Gazette
Reasoner
The Reformer, a Daily Evening Newspaper
Reynolds' Newspaper
Reynolds' Political Instructor
Reynolds' Weekly News
The Rimes
Shoreditch Advertiser
South London Advertiser
South London News and Surrey County Advertiser
South Place Magazine
The Spectator
Sunday Times
The Times
Tower Hamlets Magazine; or the Public and Domestic Miscellany of Politics, Litera-
    ture and Commerce
True Sun
True Vestryman and Borough of Marylebone Gazette
The Vestryman and Metropolitan Parochial Gazette
Weekly True Sun
West London Guardian and General Advertiser
West London Observer

Contemporary books and articles

Anderson, C., An account of the alterations, reductions, exposures, etc. effected by
    the United Parishioners Society of St. George the Martyr, Southwark, London
    1833
Anon., Another lay minstrel, dedicated to Sir Francis Burdett, London 1810
Anon., Sir frantic, the reformer; or, the humors of the Crown and Anchor, London
    1809
Anon., To the electors of Westminster, London 1819
Ashurst, W. H., Corporation register, London 1832
Austin, H., Metropolitan improvements, London 1842
An authentic narrative of the events of the Westminster election which commenced on
    Saturday, February 13 and closed on Wednesday, March 3 1819, London 1819
Bell, J., Observations addressed to the chemists and druggists of Great Britain on behalf
    of the Pharmaceutical Society, London 1841

Bisset, R., *The Spectator: a new edition in eight volumes; with illustrative notes, to which are prefixed the lives of the authors*, London 1794

Blanch, W. H., *The parish of Camberwell*, London 1875, repr. 1976

Braun, R., *Extramural interment and the Metropolitan Sanitary Association*, London 1852

Britton, J., *The original picture of London enlarged and improved being a correct guide for the stranger as well as the inhabitant of the metropolis of the British empire together with a description of the environs*, London 1827

Brooke, J. W., *The democrats of Marylebone*, London 1839

Brougham, H., *Life and times of Henry Brougham*, London 1871

Burdett, F., *Memoirs of the life of Francis Burdett*, London 1810

Chadwick, E., *Report on metropolitan water supply*, London 1850

—— *Report on the sanitary condition of the labouring population of Great Britain*, ed. M. W. Finn, Edinburgh 1965

Challis, T., *Government majorities: letter to the right honorable Lord John Russell M.P. on the new ministerial device for the subversion of local self-government*, London 1851

—— *To the electors of Finsbury*, London 1852

Charter of incorporation of the Metropolitan Association for the Improvement of the Dwellings of the Industrious Classes, London 1845

—— *Supplemental charter*, London 1850.

The church establishment considered in relation to the state and the community, London 1837

Church Rate Abolition Society, *Address of the committee to the people of Great Britain and Ireland*, London 1836

Clay, W., *Remarks on the water supply of London*, London 1849

—— *Speech of William Clay on moving the second reading of the church rate abolition bill*, London 1856

Cochrane, C., *An address to the business-like men of Westminster on their present candidates*, London 1847

Collet, C. D., *History of taxes on knowledge: their origin and repeal*, London 1899

Conway, M. D., *Autobiography: memories and experiences*, London 1904

Copy of the poll for the election of two knights of the shire to serve in parliament for the county of Middlesex, London 1803

Corner, G. R., *A concise account of the local government of the borough of Southwark, and observations upon the expediency of uniting the same more perfectly with the City of London or of obtaining a separate municipal corporation*, London 1836

Courtauld, S., *At a meeting of the friends of civil and religious liberty*, London 1840

—— *The Braintree church-rate case: report of the proceedings on the occasion of the presentation of a testimonial to Samuel Courtauld*, London 1857

Creevey papers, ed. H. Maxwell, London 1909

Day, J., *A few practical observations on the New Poor Law*, London 1838

The D'Eyncourt testimonial, London 1853

Disraeli, B., *Whigs and Whiggism*, London 1913

Dod, C., *Dod's parliamentary companion*, London 1833–68

Doyle, J., *A fine old gentleman, one of the olden time*, London 1837

Duncombe, T. H., *The life and correspondence of T. S. Duncombe, late MP for Finsbury*, London 1868

Egan, P., *Life in London; or the day and night scenes of Jerry Hawthorne, esq and his* elegant friend Corinthian Tom, accompanied by Bob Logic, the Oxonian, in their rambles and sprees through the metropolis, London 1821

Evans, G. DeLacy, *A letter to the electors of Westminster*, London 1833

Firth, J., *Municipal London*, London 1876

Fortescue, H., *Metropolitan sewers bill*, London 1851

—— *Representative self-government for the metropolis: a letter to Viscount Palmerston*, London 1854

—— *To the representative vestries of Marylebone, St. Pancras, and Paddington*, London 1857

—— *Parliamentary reform: Lord Ebrington's address to the electors of Marylebone*, London 1859

Frost, T., *Forty years recollections, literary and political*, London 1880

A full report of the speeches of Sir Francis Burdett at the late election, London 1804

Grant, J., *The great metropolis*, London 1838

Greville, C. C. F., *Greville's England: selections from the diaries of Charles Greville, 1818–1860*, ed. C. Hibbert, London 1981

Greville memoirs, 1814–1860, ed. L. Strachey and C. Fulford, London 1938

Grosvenor, R., *The only compromise possible in regard to church rate*, London 1861

—— *The laity and church reform*, London 1886

Hall, B., *A letter to his grace the archbishop of Canterbury on the state of the Church*, London 1850

—— *Church abuses, a letter to the Rev. E. Phillips*, London 1852

Hawes, B., 'Address to the electors of Lambeth' (London 1832), in Hill, *Electoral history of Lambeth*, 17–18

HTA, *Abstract of the proceedings of the public meeting held at Exeter Hall, 11 December, 1844*, London 1844

—— *Report of the Health of London Association, on the sanitary condition of the metropolis*, London 1847

—— *Address of the committee … to the bishop of London*, London 1848

—— *Practical suggestions as to the measures proper to adopt in anticipation of the cholera*, London 1848

—— *Report of the sub-committee on the state of towns*, London 1848

—— *The sanitary condition of the City of London*, London 1848

Hickson, W. E., 'City administration', *Westminster Review* xliii (1845), 553–79

—— 'The Corporation of London and sanitary improvement', *Westminster Review* xlix (1848), 421–40

Hill, G. (ed.), *The electoral history of Lambeth since its enfranchisement in 1832 with portraits and memoirs of its representatives during 46 years*, London 1879

Hobhouse, J. C., *Recollections of a long life*, New York 1910

The Holland House diaries, 1831–1840, ed. Abraham Kriegel, London 1977

Holyoake, G. J., *The polity and resources of freethinking*, London 1848

—— *Secularism distinguished from Unitarianism*, London 1855

—— *History of co-operation*, London 1879

—— *Sixty years of an agitator's life*, London 1906

An inhabitant of Southwark, *Statements of the inhabitants of Bridge Ward Without*, London 1836

A letter to the radicals of the United Kingdom, describing the position of the radicals of Marylebone, London 1838

Letters to 'the Times' on the attacks made by sir B.H. ... on the water works companies of London, London 1855

Linton, W. J., *Bob Thin, or the poor house fugitive*, London 1845

—— *James Watson: a memoir*, London 1879

—— *Memories*, London 1895

Literary Association of the Friends of Poland, *Address of the association ... to the people of Great Britain and Ireland*, London 1846

—— *Address of the Literary Association ... to the Poles*, London 1850

Living picture of London, for 1828, and stranger's guide through the streets of the metropolis, London 1828

The local government of the metropolis; a sketch, London 1836

London radicalism, 1830–1843: selections from the papers of Francis Place, ed. D. J. Rowe, London 1970

LWMA, *The rotten House of Commons*, London 1837

Lushington, C., *Dilemmas of a churchman, arising from the discordant doctrine and political practices of the establishment*, London 1838

Marshall, L. J., *Substance of a speech delivered by Lawrence J. Marshall, Esq. at a parish meeting at Hackney, on the 28th February, 1833 for the repeal of the house and window tax*, London 1833

Martin, G., *A brief statement of the effect of the judgments given in the Braintree case on the law of church rates*, Exeter 1854

Mayhew, H., *London labour and the London poor*, London 1884

Mazzini, G., *Mazzini's letters to an English family*, London 1920

Meliora, or, better times to come: being contributions of many men touching the present state and prospects of society, London 1849

Memoir and letters of Francis W. Newman, ed. I. G. Sieveking, London 1909

Metropolitan Anti-Corn Law Association, *Observations on a pamphlet relating to the corn laws*, London 1840

—— *Resolutions of the Metropolitan Anti-Corn Law Association, passed 18th of August, 1842; address of the Metropolitan Anti-Corn Law Association to their fellow citizens*, London 1842

Metropolitan Association for the Improvement of the Dwellings of the Industrious Classes, *Charter of incorporation of the Metropolitan Association for the Improvement of the Dwellings of the Industrious Classes*, London 1845

—— *Supplemental charter of the Metropolitan Association for the Improvement of the Dwellings of the Industrious Classes*, London 1850

Metropolitan Association for Promoting the Relief of Destitution and for Improving the Condition of the Poor, by Means of Parochial and District Visiting, *First annual report*, London 1844

Metropolitan Parliamentary Reform Association, *Address to the people of Great Britain*, London 1842

MSA, *First report of the commissioners*, London 1847

—— *Public health a public question: first report of the Metropolitan Sanitary Association on the sanitary condition of the metropolis*, London 1850

—— *Public agency or trading companies*, London 1851

—— *Memorandum ... on the pending metropolis water bills*, London 1852

Metropolitan Working Class Association for the Improvement of the Public Health, *First address*, London 1845

—— *On the ventilation of rooms*, London 1847

—— *Water supply: especially for the working classes*, London 1847

'Mister Duncombe and Mr. Fraser', *Fraser's Magazine* x (Sept. 1834), 494–5

Murphy, T., *A letter to the radicals of the United Kingdom, describing the position of the radicals of Marylebone*, London 1838

Murray, J. F., *Physiology of London life*, London 1844

'My Dear Mr. Bell': letters from Dr. Jonathan Pereira to Jacob Bell, 1844–1853, ed. J. Burnby, C. P. Cloughly and M. P. Earles, London 1987

NPA, *Report of the National Philanthropic Association (instituted March, 1842) for the promotion of social and sanitary improvements and the employment of the poor*, London 1847

—— *Sanitary progress: being the fifth report of the NPA*, London 1850

NPU, *A test for candidates*, London 1831

National Reform Association, *National reform tracts*, London 1850

Newman, F. W., *An appeal to the middle-classes on the urgent necessity of numerous radical reforms, financial and organic*, London 1848

—— 'Austria and Hungary', *Prospective Review* v (Nov. 1849), 369–408

—— *Lectures on political economy*, London 1851

—— 'The tendencies of England', *Westminster Review* ii (July 1852), 110–28

—— 'The administrative example of the United States', *Westminster Review* vii (Apr. 1855), 492–516

[O'Brien, W.], 'The supply of water to the metropolis', *Edinburgh Review* xci (1949–50), 377–408

Osborne, R. B., *Speech … on Mr. Hume's motion for reform of parliament*, London 1848

Palgrave, F., *Observations on the principles to be adopted in the establishment of new municipal corporations*, London 1832

—— *The rise and progress of the English commonwealth: the Saxon period*, London 1832

Pearson, C., *Mr. Charles Pearson's first letter to the electors of Lambeth*, London 1847

People's International League, *Address*, London 1847

—— *Report of public meeting … to explain the principle objects of the people's international league*, London 1847

Percy, S. and R. Percy, *The Percy history and interesting memorial on the rise, progress, and present state of all the capitals of Europe*, London 1823

Permanent Council of the Poles in London, *The French empire and the Poles*, London 1853

Place, F., *A letter to the electors of Westminster*, London 1832

—— *The peers and the people, municipal reform, corn laws, and taxes on knowledge*, London 1835

Portman, E. B., *Substance of a speech to the electors of the borough of Marylebone*, London 1832

Report of the proceedings during the late contested election for the county of Middlesex, London 1803

Report on the sanitary condition of the labouring population of Great Britain, ed. M. W. Flinn, Edinburgh 1965

Richardson, J., *Recollections, political, literary, dramatic, and miscellaneous, of the last half century*, London 1856

Rogers, G., *To the inhabitant householders of the united parishes of St. Giles in the Fields and St. George Bloomsbury*, London 1828

—— *A letter to T. Wakley ... being an answer to calumny, and a statement of reasons for not having supported Wakley at the recent Finsbury election*, London 1837

Romilly, S., *Memoirs of the life of Sir Samuel Romilly, written by himself; with a selection from his correspondence*, London 1840

Rules and regulations of the society called the United Parishioners of St. George-the-Martyr, Southwark, established 13 January, 1831, London 1833

Russell, J., *An essay on the history of the English government and constitution*, London 1823

St Giles-in-the-Fields and St George, Bloomsbury joint vestry, *Refutation of the charges against the select vestry*, London 1829

St Giles-in-the-Fields, and St George Bloomsbury: substance of the proceedings at two public meetings of the above parishes, London 1820

St Giles-in-the-Fields and St George, Bloomsbury, vestry bill: explanation of the objects of the bill, London 1830

St Giles-in-the-Fields, and St George Bloomsbury, Householder's Parochial Union, *An address to the members explaining the reasons for the expulsion of G. Rogers*, London 1837

Sanford, J. L. and M. Townsend, *The great governing families of England*, London 1865

Smith, T. S., *Results of sanitary improvement*, London 1854

Society of the Friends of Italy, *Address of the Society of the Friends of Italy*, London 1851

Speeches and letters of Sir Francis Burdett, bart. MP: or on his behalf, during the late contest for the representation of the city of Westminster in parliament, London 1837

Thompson, G., *Address to the electors of Tower Hamlets*, London 1847

Thwaites, J., *A sketch of the history and prospects of the metropolitan drainage question*, London 1855

Toulmin Smith, J., *Centralisation or representation? The laws relating to public health*, London 1848

—— *Government by commissions illegal and pernicious*, London 1849

—— *Parallels between the constitution and constitutional history of England and Hungary*, London 1849

—— *What is the corporation of London and who are the freemen?*, London 1850

—— *Local self-government as opposed to centralisation: characteristics of each; and its practical tendencies, as effecting social, moral, and political welfare and progress*, London 1851

—— *The metropolis and its municipal administration*, London 1852

—— *The parish: its obligations and powers*, London 1854

—— *The Metropolis Local Management Act*, London 1855

Toynbee, G. (ed.), *Reminiscences and letters of Joseph and Arnold Toynbee*, London n.d.

Toynbee, J., *The breath of life and the breath of death and a people without a country*, London 1866

The triumphal entry of Henry Hunt, esq. into London, London 1818

United Parishes of Westminster, *Facts (founded upon parliamentary returns) illustrative of the great inequity of the taxes on houses and windows, shewing how unjustly and oppressively they bear upon the middle and industrious classes*, London 1834

Vassall, E., *Elizabeth, Lady Holland to her son, 1821–1845*, ed. G. S. H. Fox-Strangeways, 6th earl of Ilchester, London 1946

Vassall-Fox, H., *Memoirs of the Whig party in my time*, London 1854

Venturi, Madame, *Mr. Morris's 80th birthday party*, London 1904

Walker testimonial fund, London 1850

Walpole, S., *The life of Lord John Russell*, New York 1889

Ward, F. O., 'Sanitary consolidation: centralisation and local self–government', *Quarterly Review* lxxxviii (1851), 435–92

Watson, J. and H. Hetherington, *Socialism set to rest by the* Weekly Dispatch, London 1840

Westminster election: a correct report of the meeting, 1 June 1818, London 1818

Whitty, E., *The governing classes of Great Britain: political portraits*, London 1854

—— *Friends of bohemia: or phases of London life*, London 1857

Williams, W., *An address to the electors and non-electors of the United Kingdom on the defective state of the representative system, and the consequent unequal and oppressive taxation and prodigal expenditure of public money*, London 1849

Williamson, V. A., G. W. S. Lyttleton and S. L. Simeon, *Memorials of Brooks's from the foundation of the club, 1764, to the close of the nineteenth century*, London 1907

[Wills, W. H.], 'The troubled water question', *Household Words* i (1850), 49–52

Wyndham, H., *Correspondence of Sarah Spencer, Lady Lyttelton*, London 1912

Secondary sources

Adburgham, A., *A radical aristocrat: the Rt. Hon. Sir William Molesworth*, Padstow 1990

Anderson, O., *A liberal state at war: English politics and economics during the Crimean war*, London 1967

—— 'The political uses of history in mid nineteenth-century England', *P&P* xxxvi (1967), 87–105

—— 'The administrative reform association', in Patricia Hollis (ed.), *Pressure from without in early-Victorian England*, London 1974, 262–88

Arnold, D. (ed.), *Re-presenting the metropolis: architecture, urban experience, and social life in London, 1800–1840*, Aldershot 2000

Aspinall, A., 'English party organisation in the early nineteenth century', *EHR* lxi (1926), 389–411

Bagenal, P. H., *The life of Ralph Bernal Osborne, MP*, London 1984

Bailey, P. (ed.), *The Oxford book of London*, Oxford 1995

Baron, X. (ed.), *London, 1066–1914: literary sources and documents*, Robertsbridge 1997

Baylen, J. and N. Grossman, *Biographical dictionary of modern radicals*, Hassocks 1981

Beales, D., 'Parliamentary parties and the "independent" member, 1810–1860', in R. Robson (ed.), *Ideas and institutions of Victorian Britain: essays in honour of George Kitson Clark*, London 1966, 1–19

Belchem, J., 'Henry Hunt and the evolution of the mass platform', *EHR* xciii (1978), 739–73

—— *Orator Hunt: Henry Hunt and English working-class radicalism*, Oxford 1988

—— and J. Epstein, 'The nineteenth-century gentleman leader revisited', *Social History* xxii (1997), 174–92

Biagini, E., *Liberty, retrenchment, and reform: popular liberalism in the age of Gladstone, 1860–1880*, Cambridge 1992

Blanch, W. H., *The parish of Camberwell*, London 1976

Bloom, E. and L. Bloom (eds), *Addison and Steele: the critical heritage*, London 1980

Bostetter, M., 'The journalism of Thomas Wakley', in J. Wiener (ed.), *Innovators and preachers: the role of the editor in Victorian England*, London 1985, 275–92

Brent, R., *Liberal Anglican politics: Whiggery, religion, and reform, 1830–1841*, Oxford 1987

—— 'The Whigs and Protestant dissent in the decade of reform: the case of church rates, 1833–1841', *EHR* ci (1987), 887–910

Briggs, A., 'The local background of Chartism', in A. Briggs (ed.), *Chartist studies*, New York 1959

—— *Victorian cities*, Harmondsworth 1963

Brock, M., *The Great Reform Act*, London 1973

Brundage, A. *The making of the new poor law: the politics of inquiry, enactment, and implementation, 1832–1839*, London 1978

—— *England's 'Prussian minister': Edwin Chadwick and the politics of government growth, 1832–1854*, University Park, PA 1988

Buckley, J. K., *Joseph Parkes of Birmingham*, London 1926

Burney, I., *Bodies of evidence: medicine and the politics of the English inquest, 1830–1926*, Baltimore 2000

Burns, A. and J. Innes (eds), *Rethinking the age of reform: Britain, 1780–1850*, Cambridge 2003

Burrow, J. W., *Whigs and liberals: continuity and change in English political thought*, Oxford 1988

Cannadine, D., *Lords and landlords: the aristocracy and the towns, 1774–1967*, Leicester 1980

—— *Pleasures of the past*, London 1990

—— and D. Reader (eds), *Exploring the urban past: essays in urban history by H. J. Dyos*, Cambridge 1982

Chase, M., *Chartism: a new history*, Manchester 2007

Claeys, G., 'Mazzini, Kossuth, and British radicalism, 1848–1854', *JBS* xxviii (1989), 225–61

Claus, P., 'Languages of citizenship in the City of London, 1848–1867', *LJ* xxiv (1999), 23–37

Clifton, G., *Professionalism, patronage and public service in Victorian London: the staff of the Metropolitan Board of Works, 1856–1889*, London 1992

Clive, J., *Scotch reviewers: the Edinburgh Review, 1802–1815*, London 1957

Clockie, H. M. and J. W. Robinson, *Royal commissions of inquiry*, Stanford 1937

Collini, S., D. Winch and J. Burrow (eds), *That noble science of politics: a study in nineteenth-century intellectual history*, Cambridge 1983

Conacher, J. B., *The Aberdeen coalition, 1852–1855*, Cambridge 1968

Conway, S., 'Bentham and the nineteenth-century revolution in government', in

R. Bellamy (ed.), *Victorian liberalism: nineteenth-century political thought and practice*, London 1990, 71–90

Coones, P., 'Kensal Green cemetery: London's first great extramural cemetery', *Transactions of the Ancient Monuments Society* iii (1987), 48-76

Corfield, P., *Power and the professions on Britain, 1700–1850*, London 1995

—— E. Green and C. Harvey, 'Westminster man: Charles James Fox and his electorate, 1780–1806', *PH* xx (2001), 157–87

Cowherd, R., *The politics of English dissent*, London 1959

Crossick, G., *An artisan elite in Victorian society: Kentish London, 1840–1880*, London 1978

Dart, G., 'Flash style: Pierce Egan and literary London, 1820–1828', *HWJ* li (2001), 181–205

Davis, J., *Reforming London: the 'London government problem', 1855–1900*, Oxford 1988

—— 'Modern London, 1850–1939', review article, *LJ* xx (1995), 56–90

—— 'Central government and the towns', in M. Daunton (ed.), *The Cambridge urban history of Britain*, iii, Cambridge 2000, 261–86

Davis, R. W., 'The Whigs and the idea of electoral deference: some further thoughts on the Great Reform Act', *Durham University Journal* lxvii (1974–5), 71–91

Desmond, A., *The politics of evolution: morphology, medicine, and reform in radical London*, Chicago 1989

Dickinson, H. T., *Liberty and property: political ideology in eighteenth-century Britain*, London 1977

Digby, A., *Pauper palaces*, London 1978

Dinwiddy, J. R., 'Charles James Fox and the people', *History* lv (1970), 342–59

—— *Radicalism and reform in Britain, 1780–1850*, London 1992

—— 'Sir Francis Burdett and Burdettite radicalism', in Dinwiddy, *Radicalism and reform*, 109–24

Driver, F., *Power and pauperism*, Cambridge 1993

Dunbabin, J. P. D., 'British local government reform: the nineteenth century and after', *EHR* xcii (1977), 777–805

Dyos, H. J., 'Greater and greater London: metropolis and provinces in the nineteenth and twentieth centuries', in Cannadine and Reader, *Exploring the urban past*, 37–55

—— *Victorian suburb: a study of the growth of Camberwell*, Leicester 1961

Earle, P., *The making of the English middle-class: business, society, and family in London, 1660–1730*, London 1989

Edsall, N., *The anti–poor law movement, 1834–1844*, Manchester 1971

—— 'A failed movement: the Parliamentary and Financial Reform Association, 1848–1854', *BIHR* xlix (1976), 108–31

Ellens, J. P., 'Lord John Russell and the church rate conflict: the struggle for a broad Church, 1834–1868', *JBS* xxvi (1987), 232–57

Epstein, J., *The lion of freedom: Fergus O'Connor and the Chartist movement*, London 1982

Epstein Nord, D., *Walking the Victorian streets: women, representation, and the city*, London 1995

Evans, D., *The life and work of William Williams*, London 1939

Fagan, L., *The Reform Club, 1836–1886: its founders and architect*, London 1887

Fawcett, M. G., *Life of the Rt. Hon. Sir William Molesworth*, London 1901

Feldman, D. and G. Stedman Jones (eds), *Metropolis London: histories and representations since 1800*, London 1989

Finer, S. E., *The life and times of Sir Edwin Chadwick*, London 1952

Finlayson, G., 'The municipal corporation commission and report, 1833–35', *BIHR* xxxvi (1963), 36–52

—— 'The politics of municipal reform, 1835', *EHR* lxxxi (1966), 673–92

Finn, M., '"A vent which has conveyed our principles": English radical patriotism in the aftermath of 1848', *JMH* lxiv (1992), 637–59

—— *After Chartism: class and nation in English radical politics, 1848–1874*, Cambridge 1993

Foster, J., *Class struggle and the industrial revolution*, London 1974

Fraser, D., *Urban politics in Victorian England: the structure of politics in Victorian cities*, Leicester 1976

—— *Power and authority in the Victorian city*, Oxford 1979

Fraser, M., 'Sir Benjamin Hall and the administration of London', *Transactions of the Honourable Society of Cymmrodorion* (1963), 70–81

—— 'Benjamin Hall, MP for Marylebone, 1837–1839', *National Library of Wales Journal* xiii (1964), 313–28

—— 'Sir Benjamin Hall in parliament in the 1850s, part ii', *National Library of Wales Journal* xv (1967), 72–88

Garside, P. L., 'London and the home counties', in F. M. L. Thompson (ed.), *Cambridge social history of Britain, 1750–1950*, I: *Regions and communities*, Cambridge 1993, 471–540

Gash, N., *Politics in the age of Peel: a study in the technique of parliamentary representation, 1830–1850*, New York 1953

—— *Reaction and reconstruction in English politics, 1832–1852*, Oxford 1965

Gatrell, V. A. C., 'Incorporation and the pursuit of liberal hegemony in Manchester, 1790–1839', in D. Fraser (ed.), *Municipal reform in the industrial city*, Leicester 1982, 15–60

Girouard, M., *The return to Camelot: chivalry and the English gentleman*, New Haven 1981

Goldman, L., 'The Social Science Association, 1857–1886: a context for mid-Victorian liberalism', *EHR* c (1986), 95–134

—— *Science, reform and politics in Victorian Britain: the Social Science Association, 1857–1886*, Cambridge 2002

Goodway, D., *London Chartism, 1838–1848*, Cambridge 1982

Green, D., *From artisans to paupers: economic change and poverty in London, 1790–1870*, Aldershot 1995

Greenleaf, W. H., 'Toulmin Smith and the British political tradition', *Public Administration* liii (1975), 25–44

Grugel, L. E., *George Jacob Holyoake: a study in the evolution of a Victorian radical*, Philadelphia 1976

Halevy, E., *The growth of philosophic radicalism*, trans. M. Morris, London 1952

Hamburger, J., *Macaulay and the Whig tradition*, Chicago 1976

Hamlin, C., 'Chadwick and the engineers, 1842–1854: systems and anti-systems in the pipe and brick sewer war', *Technology and Culture* xxxiii (1992), 680–709

—— Public health and social justice in the age of Chadwick, 1800–1854, Cambridge 1998

Hammond, B., James Stansfeld: a Victorian champion of sex equality, London 1932

Hardy, A., 'Water and the search for public health in London in the 18th and 19th centuries', Medical History xxviii (1984), 250–82

—— 'Public health and the expert: London medical officers of health, 1856–1900', in R. M. McCloud (ed.), Specialists, administrators, and professionals, 1860–1919, Cambridge 1988, 128–44

—— 'Parish pump to private pipes: London's water supply in the nineteenth-century', Medical History, supplement xi (1991), 76–93

Harling, P., The waning of Old Corruption: the politics of economical reform in Britain, 1779–1846, Oxford 1996

—— and P. Mandler, 'From "fiscal-military" state to laissez-faire state, 1760–1850', JBS xxxii (1993), 44–70

Helmreich, A. L., 'Re-forming London: George Cruikshank and the Victorian age', in D. Mancoff and D. J. Trela (eds), Victorian urban settings: essays on the nineteenth-century city and its contexts, New York 1996, 157–78

Hilton, B., The age of atonement: the influence of Evangelicalism on social and economic thought, 1795–1865, Oxford 1988

—— 'The politics of anatomy and the anatomy of politics, 1825–1850', in S. Collini, R. Whitamore and M. Young (eds), History, religion, and culture: British intellectual culture, 1750–1950, Cambridge 2000, 179–97

Himmelfarb, G., The idea of poverty: England in the early industrial age, London 1985

Hobhouse, H., Thomas Cubitt: master builder, London 1971

Hobsbawm, E. J., Primitive rebels, London 1959

Hone, J. A., For the cause of truth: radicalism in London, 1796–1820, Oxford 1980

Hostettler, J., Thomas Wakley: an improbable radical, Chichester 1993

Howe, A., The cotton masters, 1830–1860, Oxford 1984

Humphreys, A., 'G. W. M. Reynolds: popular literature and popular politics', Victorian Periodicals Review xvi (1983), 79–89

Huch, R., Joseph Hume: the people's M.P., Philadelphia 1985

Jalland, P., Death in the Victorian family, Oxford 1996

Jenkins, T. A., Gladstone, Whiggery, and the Liberal party, 1874–1886, Oxford 1988

Jennings, W. I., 'The municipal revolution', in H. Laski (ed.) A century of municipal progress: 1835–1935, London 1935, 55–65

Johnson, D., Southwark and the City, Oxford 1969

Johnson, R., 'Educating the educators: "experts" and the state, 1833–9', in A. P. Donajgrodzki (ed.), Social control in nineteenth-century Britain, London 1977, 77–107

Jones, G. Stedman, Outcast London: a study in the relationship between classes in Victorian society, London 1984

Joyce, M., My friend H: John Cam Hobhouse, Baron Broughton of Broughton de Gyfford, London 1948

Joyce, P., Visions of the people: industrial England and the question of class, 1840–1914, Cambridge 1991

Kabdebo, T., 'Lord Dudley Stuart and the Hungarian refugees of 1849', BIHR xliv (1971), 258–69

Keith-Lucas, B., *The English local government franchise*, Oxford 1952

Kelly, P., 'Radicalism and public opinion in the general election of 1784', *BIHR* xlv (1972), 73–88

Kingsford, P. W., 'Radical dandy: Thomas Slingsby Duncombe, 1796–1861', *History Today* xiv (1964), 399–407

Kitchel, A. D., *George Lewes and George Elliot: a review of records*, New York 1933

Knott, J., *Popular opposition to the 1834 poor law*, London 1986

Koss, S., *The rise and fall of the political press in Britain*, London 1990

Large, D., 'London in the year of revolutions, 1848', in Stevenson, *London in the age of reform*, 117–211

Laski, H. (ed.), *A century of municipal progress: 1835–1935*, London 1935

Lejuene, A., *White's: the first three hundred years*, London 1993

Lewis, D., *Lighten their darkness: the Evangelical mission to working-class London, 1828–1860*, London 1986

Lewis, R. A., *Edwin Chadwick and the public health movement, 1832–1854*, London 1952

Lipschutz, D., 'The water question in London, 1827–1831', *BHM* xlii (1968), 510–26

LoPatin, N., *Political unions, popular politics, and the Great Reform Act of 1832*, Basingstoke 1999

Lubenow, W., *The politics of government growth: early Victorian attitudes towards state intervention, 1833–1848*, Newton Abbot 1971

McCalman, I., *Radical underworld: prophets, revolutionaries, and pornographers in London, 1795–1840*, Oxford 1993

Maccoby, S., *English radicalism, 1832–52*, London 1935

Machin, G. I. T., 'The Maynooth Grant, the dissenters, and disestablishment, 1845–1847', *EHR* lxxxii (1967), 61–85

—— *Politics and the Churches in Great Britain, 1832–1868*, Oxford 1977

McLeod, H., *Class and religion in the late-Victorian city*, London 1974

Main, J. M., 'Radical Westminster, 1807–1820', *Historical Studies: Australia and New Zealand* xii (1966), 186–204

Mandler, P., *Aristocratic government in the age of reform: Whigs and liberals, 1830–1852*, Oxford 1990

Manning, B. L., *The Protestant dissenting deputies*, Cambridge 1952

Martin, K., *The triumph of Lord Palmerston*, London 1924

Massingham, H. and P. Massingham (eds), *The London anthology*, London 1950

Mazumdar, P., 'Anatomical physiology and the reform of medical education: London, 1825–1835', *BHM* lvii (1983), 230–46

Miall, A., *The life of Edward Miall*, London 1884

Midwinter, E. C., *Social administration in Lancashire, 1830–1860: poor law, public health, and police*, Manchester 1969

Miles, D., *Francis Place, 1771–1853: the life of a remarkable radical*, Brighton 1988

Mitchell, A., *The Whigs in opposition*, Oxford 1967

Mitchell, L., *Holland House*, London 1980

—— *The Whig world, 1760–1837*, London 2005

Morris, R. J., *Class, sect, and party: the making of the British middle-class: Leeds, 1820–1850*, Manchester 1990

—— and R. Trainor (eds), *Urban governance: Britain and beyond since 1750*, Aldershot 2000

Mukhopadyay, A., *Politics of water supply: the case of Victorian London*, Calcutta 1981

Munford, W. A., *William Ewart, MP, 1789–1869: portrait of a radical*, London 1960

Nead, L., *Victorian Babylon: people, steets, and images in nineteenth-century London*, London 2000

Nesbitt, G. L., *Benthamite reviewing: the first twelve years of the* Westminster Review, *1824–1836*, New York 1934

Neville, R., *London clubs: their histories and treasures*, London 1911

Newbould, I., 'Whiggery and the dilemma of reform: liberals, radicals, and the Melbourne administration, 1835–9', *BIHR* liii (1980), 229–41

—— 'The Whigs, the Church, and education, 1839', *JBS* xxvi (1987), 332–46

Olien, D. D., *Morpeth: a Victorian public career*, Washington, DC 1983

Olson, D., *Town planning in London: the eighteenth and nineteenth centuries*, New Haven 1964

—— *The growth of Victorian London*, London 1976

Owen, D., *English philanthropy, 1660–1960*, London 1965

—— *The government of Victorian London*, London 1982

Parry, J. P., *The rise and fall of liberal government in Victorian England*, New Haven 1993

—— 'Past and future in the later career of Lord John Russell', in T. C. W. Blanning and David Cannadine (eds), *History and biography*, Cambridge 1996, 142–72

Patterson, M. W., *Sir Francis Burdett and his times, 1770–1844*, London 1931

Pelling, M., *Cholera, fever, and English medicine*, London 1978

Penny, N. B., 'The commercial garden necropolis of the early nineteenth-century and its critics', *Garden History* ii (1974), 61–7

Perkin, H., *The origins of modern English society*, London 1969

Peterson, M., Jeanne *The medical profession in mid-Victorian London*, London 1978

Phillips, J. A. and C. Wetherall, 'Parliamentary parties and municipal politics: 1835 and the party system', *PH* xiii (1994), 48–85

Pickering, P., 'And your petitioners, &c.: Chartist petitioning in popular politics, 1838–1848', *EHR* cxvi (2001), 368–88.

Pocock, J. G. A., *The Machiavellian moment: Florentine political thought and the Atlantic republican tradition*, Princeton 1975

Port, H. M., 'West End palaces: the aristocratic town house in London, 1730–1830', *LJ* xx (1995–6), 17–46

Potts, A., 'Picturing the modern metropolis: images of London in the nineteenth century', *HWJ* xxvi (1988), 28–56

Prest, J., *Lord John Russell*, London 1972

—— *Liberty and locality: parliament, permissive legislation, and ratepayers democracies in the nineteenth century*, Oxford 1990

Prothero, I., 'The London Working Men's Association and the "people's charter"', *P&P* xxxviii (1967), 169–74

—— 'Chartism in London', *P&P* xliv (1969), 76–105

—— *Artisans and politics in the early nineteenth century: John Gast and his times*, London 1979

Quinault, R., 'Lord Randolph Churchill and Tory democracy, 1880–1885', *HJ* xxii (1979), 141–65

Rasmussen, S. E., *London: the unique city*, Cambridge, MA 1982

Read, D., *The English provinces, 1760–1960: a study in influence*, London 1964

Redlich, J., *The history of local government in England*, London 1958

Rendell, J., *The pursuit of pleasure: gender, space, and architecture in Regency London*, London 2002

Robbins, W., *The Newman brothers: an essay in comparative intellectual biography*, London 1966

Roberts, F. D., 'Lord Palmerston at the Home Office', *Historian* xxi (1958), 63–81

—— 'Jeremy Bentham and the Victorian administrative state', *VS* ii (1959), 193–210

—— *The Victorian origins of the British welfare state*, New Haven 1961

—— *The social conscience of the early-Victorians*, Stanford 2002

Robson, W. A., *The government and mismanagement of London*, London 1939

Roebuck, J., *Urban development in nineteenth-century London: Lambeth, Battersea, and Wandsworth, 1838–1855*, London 1979

Rose, M. E., 'The anti-poor law movement in the north of England', *Northern History* i (1966), 70–91

—— 'The anti-poor law agitation', in T. J. Ward (ed.), *Popular movements, 1830–1851*, London 1970, 78–94

Rowe, D. J., 'The London Working Man's Association and the "people's charter"', *P&P* xxxvi (1967), 169–74

—— 'The failure of London Chartism', *HJ* xi (1968), 472–87

—— 'Class and political radicalism in London, 1831–2', *HJ* xiii (1970), 31–47

Royle, E., *Victorian infidels: the origins of the British secularist movement, 1791–1866*, Manchester 1974

Rude, G., *Wilkes and liberty: a social study, 1763–1774*, Oxford 1962

Salmon, P., 'Local politics and partisanship: the electoral impact of municipal reform, 1835', *PH* xix (2000), 357–76

—— *Electoral reform at work: local politics and national parties, 1832–1841*, Woodbridge 2002

Sanders, L., *The Holland House circle*, London 1909

Schwarz, L., *London in the age of industrialization: entrepreneurs, labour force, and living conditions, 1700–1850*, Cambridge 1992

Searle, G. R., *Entrepreneurial politics in mid-Victorian Britain*, London 1993

Shaen, M. J., *William Shaen: a brief sketch*, London 1912

Shattock, J., *Politics and reviewers: The* Edinburgh *and the* Quarterly *in the early Victorian age*, London 1989

Sheppard, F., *Local government in Saint Marylebone, 1688–1835*, London 1958

—— *The infernal wen: London, 1790–1870*, London 1971

—— 'London and the nation in the nineteenth-century', *TRHS* xxxv (1985), 51–74

Shute, N., *London villages*, New York 1977

Sitwell, F., 'The Fox club', in Ziegler and Seward, *Brooks's*, 112–18

Smith, E. A., *Lord Grey, 1784–1845*, Oxford 1990

Smith, F. B., *Radical artisan: William James Linton, 1812–1897*, Manchester 1973

Smith, R. J., *The gothic bequest: medieval institutions in British thought, 1688–1863*, Cambridge 1987

Southgate, D., *The passing of the Whigs, 1832–1886*, London 1962

—— 'The most English minister ...': the policies and politics of Palmerston, London 1966

Spence, P., The birth of romantic radicalism: war, popular politics and English reformism, 1800–1815, Aldershot 1996

Spiers, E., Radical general: Sir George DeLacy Evans, 1787–1870, Manchester 1983

Sprigge, S. S., The life and times of Thomas Wakley, London 1899

Spring, D., The English landed estate in the nineteenth-century: its administration, Baltimore 1963

Steele, E. D., Palmerston and liberalism, 1855–1865, Cambridge 1991

Stern, W., 'J. Wright, pamphleteer on London water supply', Guildhall Miscellany i (1953), 31–4

Stevenson, J. (ed.), London in the age of reform, Oxford 1977

Sutherland, G. (ed.), Studies in the growth of nineteenth-century government, London 1972

Sykes, C. S., Private palaces: life in the great London houses, London 1985

Tanner, A., 'The casual poor and the City of London poor law union, 1837–1869', HJ xlii (1999), 183–206

Taylor, A., '"Commons stealers", "land grabbers", and "jerry builders": space, popular radicalism, and the politics of public access in London, 1848–1880', International Review of Social History xl (1995), 383–407

Taylor, M., The decline of British radicalism, 1847–1860, Oxford 1995

—— 'Rethinking the Chartists: searching for synthesis in the historiography of Chartism', HJ xxxix (1996), 479–95

—— Ernest Jones, Chartism, and the romance of politics, Oxford 2003

Tholfsen, T., Working-class radicalism in mid-Victorian England, New York 1976

Thomas, W., The philosophic radicals: nine studies in theory and practice, 1817–1841, Oxford 1979

Thompson, D. M., The Chartists: popular politics in the industrial revolution, London 1984

Thompson, E. P., The making of the English working-class, London 1980

Thompson, F. M. L., Hampstead: building of a borough, 1650–1964, London 1974

—— 'Moving frontiers and the fortunes of the aristocratic town house, 1830–1930', LJ xx (1995–6), 67–78

Thompson, P., Socialists, Liberals, and Labour: the struggle for London, 1885–1914, London 1967

Thorold, P., The London rich: the creation of a great city, from 1666 to the present, London 1999

Toase, C., Bibliography of British newspapers, London 1982–

Vernon, J., Politics and the people: a study in English political culture, 1815–1867, Cambridge 1993

Waddams, S. M., Law, politics, and the Church of England: the career of Stephen Lushington, 1782–1873, Cambridge 1992

Wallas, G., Life of Francis Place, 1771–1854, London 1918

Walpole, S., Life of Lord John Russell, New York 1889

Waters, C., British socialists and the politics of popular culture, 1884–1914, Manchester 1990

Webb, R. K., Harriet Martineau: a radical Victorian, London 1960

—— 'Flying missionaries: Unitarian journalism in Victorian Britain', in J. M. W. Bean (ed.), *The political culture of modern Britain*, London 1987, 11–31

—— 'The Gaskills as Unitarians', in Joanne Shattock (ed.), *Dickens and other Victorians*, Basingstoke 1988

—— 'John Bowring and Unitarianism', *Utilitas* iv (1992), 43–79

Webb, S., *The English local government franchise from the revolution to the Municipal Corporations Act: the parish and county*, London 1924

—— and B. Webb, *English local government from the revolution to the Municipal Corporations Act*, London 1963

Weinstein, B., '"Local self-government is true socialism": Joshua Toulmin Smith, the state, and character formation', *EHR* cxxiii, (2008), 1193–228

Wiener, J., *The war of the unstamped: the movement to repeal the British newspaper tax, 1830–1836*, London 1969

—— *Radicalism and freethought in nineteenth-century Britain: the life of Richard Carlile*, Westport, CN 1983

—— *Innovators and preachers: the role of the editor in Victorian England*, Westport, CN 1985

Williams, N., *The life and letters of Admiral Sir Charles Napier, K.C.B.*, London 1917

Winter, J., 'The "agitator of the metropolis": Charles Cochrane and early-Victorian street reform', *LJ* xiv (1989), 29–42

—— *London's teeming streets: 1830–1914*, London 1993

Young, G. M., *Portrait of an age: Victorian England*, London 1977

Young, K. and P. Garside (eds.), *Metropolitan London: politics and urban change, 1837–1981*, London 1982

Zegger, R., *John Cam Hobhouse: a political life, 1819–1852*, Columbia, MO 1973

Ziegler, P., 'Brooks's and the Reform Club', in Ziegler and Seward, *Brooks's: a social history*, London 1991

—— and D. Seward (eds), *Brooks's: a social history*, London 1991

Unpublished theses

Baer, M. B., 'The politics of London, 1852–1868', PhD, Iowa 1976

Hazleton-Swales, M. J., 'The Grosvenors and the development of Belgravia and Pimlico in the nineteenth century', PhD, London 1981

Hodlin, C., 'The political career of Sir Francis Burdett', DPhil., Oxford 1989

Pflaum, A. M., 'The parliamentary career of Thomas S. Duncombe, 1836–1861', PhD, Minnesota 1975

Pinkus, R. L. B., 'The conceptual development of metropolitan London, 1800–1855', PhD, New York at Buffalo 1976

Prochaska, A. M. S., 'Westminster radicalism, 1807–1832', DPhil, Oxford 1974

Saxton, W. E., 'The political importance of the "Westminster committee" of the early nineteenth-century, with special reference to the years 1807–1822', PhD, Edinburgh 1967

Taylor, A., 'Modes of political expression and working-class radicalism: the London and Manchester examples', PhD, Manchester 1992

Index

Addison, Joseph, 11, 12, 13, 24
Althorp, John Charles Spencer, Lord, *see* Spencer, John Charles
Anderson, Charles, 50, 67, 71
Anti-Centralisation Union, 94, 168
anti-church rate associations, *see* Church Rate Abolition Society; church rates; Lambeth Anti-Church Rate Association; Stepney Anti-Church Rate and Parochial Reform Society
Ashurst, William: and the church rates, 104, 109; and co-operation, 93; and the 'Muswell Hill brigade', 90, 91
Association of Parochial Representatives, 136
Austin, Henry, 79–80, 82, 125
Ayrton, Acton Smee, 171

Babbage, Charles, 39
Barber Beaumont, John Thomas, 17–18
Barlow Street committee: composition of, 49; and 1854 Marylebone election, 161–2; nomination of representatives, 49–50, 70; and opposition to the window tax, 112
Bedford, John Russell, 6th duke of, *see* Russell, John
Bedford estate, 16, 17, 18, 121, 173
Bell, Jacob: and composition of election committee, 163 n. 71; and opposition to Ebrington, 158; political philosophy of, 152–6; relationship to Marylebone parochial factions, 162–5; and St Marylebone vestry, 151
Bethnal Green, 73, 76
Bickersteth, Henry, 34
Billet, W. B., 155

Birmingham, 6, 116
'Blues' faction (St Pancras), 164–5
Board of Health, *see* General Board of Health
Braintree, 109–10
Briggs, Asa, 6
Bright, John, 56
Brooke, James Williamson, 49, 65
Brooks's Club: and memorialisation of C. J. Fox, 24, 26; and metropolitan MPs, 58; and Whiggery, 15, 22–3
Brougham, William, 30, 40, 41
Broun, Sir Richard, 131
Bulwer, Sir Henry, 147–8
Burdett, Sir Francis: and country ideology, 28–31, 49; and the Foxite legacy, 25, 29–31, 174; and metropolitan radical leadership, 7, 11, 27, 32–4; and 'titled radicalism', 56, 57, 58; and Toryism, 9, 62 n. 96
Butler, Charles Salisbury, 91
Byng, George, 24, 25, 32, 42

Carlton Club, 22
Carpenter, William, 52, 100, 110
Cartwright, John, 26, 31–2, 60
Central Anti-Poor Law Association, 67
Chadwick, Edwin: and the Board of Health, 81; and the 1834 poor law, 64; and the Health of the Metropolis Commission, 124–9; and the HOTA, 76–8; and metropolitan water supply, 135–7; and the *Report on the sanitary condition of the labouring population of Great Britain*, 72–5
Challis, Thomas, 91, 92, 136
Church Rate Abolition Society, 103, 106

general election, 39, 40, 41, 43; and opposition to the church rate, 107–8, 109, 111; and support for Lord Palmerston, 171; and volunteerism, 85, 86; and Whig electoral success, 2, 3, 54, 55, 71, 72; and William Clay, 134; and William Newton, 143
Toynbee, Joseph, 81–2
True Sun, 51, 102, 107, 113

United Parishioners Society, 50, 67

Vassell-Fox, Henry, 3rd Baron Holland, 15, 16, 18, 19, 21, 23, 36, 34, 71
volunteerism, 85–90

Wakley, Thomas: and the 1832 Finsbury election, 39; and the extension of the 1831 Select Vestries Act, 120, 121, 173; on the Health of the Metropolis Commission, 124; and metropolitan radical networks, 50, 51, 52, 53 n. 62; and metropolitan water provision, 134, 137; and opposition to the 1834 poor law, 67, 68; relationship to Jacob Bell, 152; relationship to T. S. Duncombe, 60; and support for Lord Palmerston, 167, 170; and the window tax, 115
Walter, John, 71
Ward, F. O., 123
water supply, 117, 133–8
Webb, R. T., 169
West London Democratic Association, 51
Westminster, Richard Grosvenor, 2nd marquis of, *see* Grosvenor, Richard
Westminster (borough of): and Charles James Fox, 23, 24, 25; and the 1831 Select Vestries Act, 50; and the 1833 by-election, 42, 43, 44, 45, 46; and the 1841 general

election, 71, 72; and J. T. Leader, 57; and metropolitan water provision, 135; and opposition to the 1834 poor law, 66, 68; and the unreformed metropolitan radical culture, 27–36; and volunteerism, 85, 87; and Whig landlordship, 17, 18, 174; and William Molesworth, 63; and the window tax, 98, 114
Westminster Reform Committee: and the 1833 Westminster by-election, 44, 45; and Sir Francis Burdett, 28–34; and John Cam Hobhouse, 98; and the Marylebone parochial associations, 162; and Thomas DeVear, 49; and the Westminster Reform Society, 87; and Whiggery, 27, 34, 35–6, 174
Westminster Sanitary Committee, 78
Whalley, Samuel, 30, 42, 49, 50, 55, 67, 84, 85
Whiggery: cosmopolitanism of, 11–15, 20–3; criticism of, 62–9, 84–97, 128–38; and legacy of Charles James Fox, 23–6; metropolitan electoral fortunes of, 39–43, 62–8, 71–2, 145–66; and metropolitan landlordship, 15–20; and professional culture, 79–83, 123–8; and titled radicalism, 58–9
Whig-Radicalism, 62–8
Whitbread, S. C., 18, 173
Whitechapel, 72
White's Club, 22
Whitty, Edward, 56, 157
Wilkes, John, 33
Williams, John, 170
Wilson, Sir Robert, 173, 174
Wilson, Samuel, 112
Wilson, William, 49
window tax, 45, 88, 98, 112–14
Wood, Benjamin, 71
Wood, Charles, 114, 125–6

Young, G. M., 6